Life in the Middle

T0355352

Life in the Middle

*Marginalized Moderate Senators in
the Era of Polarization*

NEILAN S. CHATURVEDI

OXFORD
UNIVERSITY PRESS

OXFORD
UNIVERSITY PRESS

Oxford University Press is a department of the University of Oxford. It furthers
the University's objective of excellence in research, scholarship, and education
by publishing worldwide. Oxford is a registered trade mark of Oxford University
Press in the UK and certain other countries.

Published in the United States of America by Oxford University Press
198 Madison Avenue, New York, NY 10016, United States of America.

Library of Congress Control Number: 2021015040

ISBN 978–0–19–759973–0 (pbk.)
ISBN 978–0–19–759972–3 (hbk.)

DOI: 10.1093/oso/9780197599723.001.0001

1 3 5 7 9 8 6 4 2

Paperback printed by LSC Communications, United States of America
Hardback printed by Bridgeport National Bindery, Inc., United States of America

Dedicated to my parents, Shilpa and Shrikant, my wife Vanessa, and to all the fallen moderates.

Contents

Acknowledgments

It has taken nearly ten years to get to this point, and I have several people to thank for getting this project here. This project was born out of an oral final exam with Matt Beckmann after one of his graduate seminars in American politics at UC Irvine. Though he may regret it now, that final exam led to my dissertation, this book, and his mentorship and friendship. Without Matt's insights, advice, and encouragement, this project could not have gotten off the ground. I am incredibly thankful for Matt's undying support. At UC Irvine, I was also lucky to have Marty Wattenberg as a mentor. Marty has read at least two or three different versions of each chapter and was kind enough to comment on them each time I came to him for help. Marty's sage advice and pragmatism helped me get through harsh reviews, article rejections, and (at least in my opinion) unfair criticisms. I am grateful to have Marty as a friend and mentor. I am also thankful for the helpful advice of Bernie Grofman, who pushed me to keep working on this project, even when I felt like I should give up. Louis DeSipio and Carole Uhlaner were always willing to hear an idea and offer direction on research ideas. Ben Bishin at UC Riverside was always a ready sounding board and guided me in the right direction.

At Seattle University, Erik Olsen and Rose Ernst offered feedback on early drafts of chapters. Peter Grieser and Katherine Baumgartner were two of the best undergraduate research assistants anyone could have and were crucial for finishing several chapters. Connie Anthony and Dan Dombrowski were incredibly supportive of my work and found ways to work with my schedule to write.

At Cal Poly Pomona, Jill Hargis was always supportive of finding me funding opportunities and time in my teaching schedule to complete this manuscript—and was a kind voice whenever I didn't get those funding opportunities. Dave Speak, Renford Reese, and Robert Nyenhuis were always kind to share their own publishing experiences. They were often willing to offer a sympathetic ear when I needed to air out my frustrations with my project. Mario Guerrero was a great sounding board to all my ideas (some half-baked), offering sage advice and wisdom beyond his years. As chair, he has been instrumental in finding me time in my teaching schedule to nail down the final aspects of this manuscript.

Many colleagues have helped me with this project. Peter Miller has read drafts, sent me articles, helped get access to people in DC, and offered feedback on my aforementioned half-baked ideas. I'm not sure this project would have been done without his support. Jennifer Garcia listened to early iterations of this project and helped steer it in the right direction. Early on, I told Kris Coulter that I didn't think I was smart enough to write this book; I'm lucky that she disagreed and pushed me to continue onward. Tom Le's great advice and willingness to respond to even the most inane messages helped get this project to the finish line.

I am also incredibly grateful to the six senators who spoke to me and provided huge insight into the inner workings of Senate politics. Thank you, Mark Pryor, Mary Landrieu, Norm Coleman, Lincoln Chafee, Byron Dorgan, and Mark Begich.

Several institutions helped fund this project, and I am grateful to them. At UC Irvine, the Center for the Study of Democracy helped fund two summers' worth of research. The Dirksen Center's Congressional Research Grant allowed me to conduct in-depth interviews with legislative directors that support this book to get to some of the behind-the-scenes politics that are difficult to capture. Angela Chnapko and Oxford University Press have been fantastic to work with, and I appreciate Angela's sage advice throughout the entire process.

Outside of academia, I am lucky to have supportive friends, even if they don't always understand why I'm so frustrated. To that end, Markus Micheaels, Patrick Satkunananthan, Leiren Marcelino, and Karan Singh were always willing to hear about my book project, even when what I had to say was far from their interests.

Finally, I'm not sure whether to thank or apologize to my family. My parents, Shilpa and Shrikant, insist they don't have a political bone in their body and hate to discuss politics, and don't have the slightest clue what I'm writing about. It is an impressive lie that people somehow believe—if it weren't for my mom making me watch a Clinton rally with her in 1992 or my dad leaving me the newspaper every morning to read so we could discuss the current events when he got home from work, I wouldn't be where I am today. Over the last ten years, they've had to hear me gripe and watch me grow ever more frustrated with myself as I toiled to complete this book. Throughout it all, they supported me in every way possible. If only everyone could have parents like them. Thank you, and I love you.

To my long-suffering wife Vanessa, who takes such an interest in what I do (despite being a medical professional by training) that all of my colleagues know who she is, thank you. You read things I send you to see if they make any sense, you listen to me talk about Joe Manchin more than any man ever should, and through it all, you are kind and supportive. I love you so much.

1

Introduction

The Conflicted Moderate

Amid the largest economic recession since the Great Depression, voters replaced outgoing Republican president George W. Bush and scores of other Republicans in Congress with Democrat Barack Obama and his fellow Democrats. Expectations for the successful passage of the president's agenda were at an all-time high, often drawing comparisons to Franklin Delano Roosevelt. Without the sixty votes needed to overcome filibusters, keen observers of Washington politics argued that power would rest not with the Democratic leadership, but with the handful of centrists. Obama and the Democratic leadership would have to rely on moderate Republican senators whose votes were needed to overcome a filibuster threat. Former representative Charlie Bass, head of the centrist Republican Main Street Partnership, was quoted as saying, "[Senators Susan Collins R-ME and Olympia Snowe R-ME] are going to be very critical players in the Senate, they will be in a position to police legislation." Senator Collins agreed with this assessment saying, "Democrats clearly will be reaching out to moderate Republicans, so it should strengthen the role that I play."[1]

In fact, both Collins and Snowe did play a vital role on Obama's first major policy proposal, the American Recovery and Reinvestment Act of 2009, a measure that injected millions of dollars into the economy to stimulate growth. The bill's goals were to save between 900,000 and 2.3 million jobs while boosting economic growth, though many criticized its $787 billion price tag.[2] Every congressional Republican apart from Collins and Snowe opposed the bill, citing its enormous size and its potential to impact the federal budget negatively. Still, Collins and Snowe delivered the fifty-ninth and sixtieth votes to end debate on the bill and usher it to its passage.[3]

While Senators Collins and Snowe appeared integral to the policy negotiations, their actual effect on the bill is less clear. Even though Collins's efforts to limit the bill's size were successful (she did lower the bill's spending by $100 million), Republican leaders still questioned their motives for voting

Life in the Middle. Neilan S. Chaturvedi, Oxford University Press. © Oxford University Press 2021.
DOI: 10.1093/oso/9780197599723.003.0001

for the bill. Senator Lindsey Graham commented on the Senate bill saying that the compromise that Collins helped engineer ended up having a higher price tag than the Democrat-controlled House's version; something that was against Collins's stated goals on the issue.[4] Media outlets claimed that it was not the compromise that won over Collins and Snowe but instead a need to please Maine's voters who had voted overwhelmingly for Obama in 2008.[5] Senate Minority Leader Mitch McConnell seemed to echo this sentiment by saying, "I think it is safe to say that Republicans in the Northeast are not the same as Republicans in the Deep South."[6] Even as these two senators helped pass salient legislation, party loyalists and leaders alike quickly brought the bill as well as their motivations for voting for the bill under scrutiny. Indeed, the framing of the issue seemed to suggest that Collins and Snowe did not necessarily get their preferred outcome, but instead voted for the bill to appease anxious Maine voters who supported Obama.

It is striking that Snowe, reacting to this partisan rancor, decided to retire instead of running for another term shortly after this debate. Representative Jim Cooper (D-TN) went so far as to proclaim, "We don't have a Congress anymore, we have a parliament."[7] Indeed this is the case—moderates are not the mighty conciliators that bring both parties together to pass legislation. Instead, they are looked upon as disloyal party members who betray the principles that their party represents.

This example is hardly an isolated case. For example, Republican senator Lincoln Chafee was once widely regarded as one of the most moderate senators of the early 2000 era. Heralded as a traditional "New England moderate," Chafee seemed to play rogue to the president's agenda, voting against the military action in Iraq, and both of the Bush tax cuts. Even Bush's pick for the position of ambassador to the United Nations could not escape Chafee's rancor. Upon finding out that Bush had nominated John Bolton for the position, Chafee said, "I remember when the Secretary of State called and said the president is going to appoint John Bolton, just leaving Rhode Island to come down, the whole way to Washington, I felt some kind of dread."[8]

Despite describing the dread that Chafee felt, the moderate senator voted in favor of Bolton's nomination, ultimately sealing Bolton's destiny as the US ambassador to the United Nations. This hemming and hawing behind the nomination but eventually acquiescing to the president is what life as a moderate is in the modern US Senate. Representing the liberal state of Rhode Island, Chafee was indeed a moderate in the aggregate—if the only definition of being a moderate is occasionally opposing (or in this case only temporarily opposing) one's party. But in reality, to preserve his conservative base while also maintaining support in a liberal state, Chafee balanced his political positions by appealing to different constituencies on different issues. For example, Chafee was pro-choice, supported embryonic stem cell research, opposed charter schools, supported gay rights, and voted against both Bush tax cut proposals. However, he also supported both NAFTA and CAFTA, co-sponsored the Class Action Fairness Act (which expands federal jurisdiction over class-action lawsuits), supported bankruptcy reform, and the USA PATRIOT Act. None of these significant policy positions is ideologically moderate—instead, they appeal to the poles of each party.

Another moderate, Chafee's partisan counterpart Democratic senator John Breaux, represented the relatively conservative state of Louisiana. Like Chafee, Breaux rarely championed "moderate" positions on legislation and instead chose either the conservative or liberal position. For example, Breaux favored NAFTA, tighter bankruptcy laws, abolishing the estate tax, and was pro-life. Still, Breaux did support tax relief for college education expenses and stricter gun control.

More recently, Senator Joe Manchin III, a Democrat from West Virginia, has increasingly earned the ire of liberals nationally by being the only Democrat who voted for President Donald Trump's controversial attorney general nominee, Jeff Sessions, and treasury secretary nominee, Steve Mnuchin. He was also only one of two Democrats who voted for EPA administrator nominee Scott Pruitt. While Manchin likely would make the argument that he was offering a conciliatory tone for the Senate, Manchin was voting for nominees whom mainstream Democrats viewed as extreme. Indeed, even Collins voted against Pruitt, suggesting that the pick was not a pick meant to suit ideological moderates. Instead of trying to represent the ideological center, Manchin was reaching out to his state's conservatives to demonstrate that he was capable of representing them as well. After all, his state voted for President Trump over Hillary Clinton by a 68.7–26.5 percent margin.

Senate centrists like Chafee and Breaux are often thought of as pivotal players in the legislative process who can move legislative proposals to their ideologically ideal location since they are often the final votes needed for passage. However, most moderate lawmakers do not take the role of the dealmaker. Instead, senators like Chafee and Breaux vote in ways that will maintain their weak electoral coalitions of voters from both ideological poles. That is to say, instead of exerting power and influence over the lawmaking process, moderate senators would rather avoid any attention to dodge the consequences of supporting legislation that may disturb their uneasy alliances.

For decades, political science scholarship has relied on the prevailing wisdom that the Senate, the world's most deliberative body, relied on a small number of moderates to help push the agenda. Indeed, with increased polarization, the conventional wisdom would dictate that the two sides would require powerbrokers in the middle to assist in reaching a compromise. All too often, we see centrists like Snowe, Collins, Chafee, Breaux, and Manchin get steamrolled on their ideological preferences. Even emerging scholarship on presidential lobbying practices demonstrates that presidents selectively lobby senators. One of the most successful presidents on domestic policy, Lyndon Johnson, used "The Treatment," or his strategy of persuasion where he mixed his physically intimidating stature with his affable nature to badger and flatter and threaten (See Beschloss 1998), to influence legislators to vote with him on crucial legislation. Beckmann et al. (2017) find that even Johnson, perhaps one of the most skilled legislative experts of the Senate, strategically lobbied members of each party's leadership far more than moderate, potentially pivotal, senators.

In the following chapters, I argue that unlike their ideologically pure counterparts that are elected from states that share their ideological identity, many of the so-called centrists are much more politically conflicted than they are "moderate." That is, while we expect moderates to behave in a way in which their preferences lie in the ideological center (i.e., they prefer policies that are not too liberal or not too conservative), the thudding reality is that in the era of polarization, they are elected from one of two constituencies: (1) states that have a partisan lean to one party but have enough "swing voters" to vote in a moderate from the opposite party; or (2) swing states in which there are an equal (or near equal) number of partisans from each side. Because of this, moderate senators cannot afford to be conciliators on major policy proposals, as it would affect their fragile coalitions adversely. What follows is a test of competing theories of lawmaking in the US Senate, with the goal of answering a fundamental question about power in the chamber; are moderates able to capitalize on their potentially pivotal positions in the Senate? Along the way, I will examine publicly available data from the congressional record on the effectiveness of legislators in the Senate, along with unique interview data from staffers on the Hill. In the remainder of the chapter, I examine in greater detail the rise of polarization and the impact it has had on constituency makeup for moderates in the Senate.

What It Means to Be a "Moderate Senator"

At the heart of this study is the question of what it means to be a "moderate." Intuitively, a moderate is anyone who sits in the ideological center between the liberal pole and conservative pole. Indeed, many moderates remain to be legislators that have preferences that lie in the middle, where they are not too liberal, or not too conservative. As I will discuss later in Chapter 4, many of the moderates studied in this book take positions that clearly fit this definition. Still, all too often, moderates are unable or perhaps unwilling, to push legislation to their ideal point of preference. Instead, they end up taking positions from the left and the right, as we see in the aforementioned examples earlier in the chapter. What makes it difficult to navigate the ideological center in the modern, polarized era? That is, why are moderates often running scared rather than pushing their own moderate agenda?

One possible explanation is the electoral argument that voters have sorted themselves better into consistent Democratic and Republican voters. Fiorina (2006) argues that voters are increasingly voting per their ideology; liberals consistently vote for Democrats while conservatives consistently vote for Republicans. Much of this sorting is a result of the transformation of conservative Southern Democrats to conservative Southern Republicans (McDonald and Grofman 1999; Theriault 2003; 2008). This political sorting among constituents is perhaps most clearly demonstrated through election results where voters are less likely to split their vote for one party for one office and another party for another office (Theriault 2008).

In addition to this political sorting, there is an increasing trend of geographical sorting as well. Many scholars have found that there is greater homogeneity with regard to socioeconomic status and racial identity within American neighborhoods, both of which correlate with voting choices (Gimpel and Schuknecht 2004; Oppenheimer 2005). In addition to these demographics, Americans also seem to choose to surround themselves with people who share similar education levels as well (Gimpel and Schuknecht 2003). That is to say, Americans now live in increasingly ideologically homogeneous areas in which liberals live around other liberals and conservatives live around other conservatives.[9]

All of this points to one simple fact: Democrats are increasingly representing the poor and lower middle class along with racial and ethnic minority groups, while Republicans are increasingly representing wealthy white voters (Stonecash et al. 2003; Grossmann and Hopkins 2016).[10] While this point certainly holds true in the US House (see, e.g., Bishop 2004), it is a plausible explanation for why polarization exists in the Senate, as political and geographical sorting is likely to occur at the state level if it happens at the district level. More important, it helps explain why moderates are in the precarious position. With fewer crossover voters, moderate senators must walk an ideological tightrope more than ever. This situation has created a number of states in which the there is an equal balance of Democrats and Republicans (or, at least, a very close ratio of the two). These states are commonly referred to as "swing states" for their capacity to "swing" from one party to another in presidential elections.

Another complication for a moderate senator is a competitive primary election. In 2010, Blanche Lincoln, a moderate Democrat from Arkansas, faced a tight general election challenge from state representative John Boozman, but before she could even face him, she had to first defeat a primary challenge from the left in liberal Lieutenant Governor Bill Halter.[11] Having a liberal base that was upset with the positions she had taken but an equally galvanized conservative opposition, Lincoln was marked for an electoral loss early in the campaign cycle. While it is difficult to say that she may have survived without the primary challenge, it certainly complicated things quite a bit. Tied very closely to the constituent sorting hypothesis, the extreme party activist hypothesis has its roots in electoral politics. The argument here is that party activists have moved to their respective poles to such a degree that legislators are now forced to cast ideological votes to avoid a primary challenge. As Richard Fenno (1978) finds in his book *Homestyle*, legislators need to focus on responding to two constituencies—a primary constituency made up of the legislator's party's base voters and a general election constituency that is more moderate. If a legislator gets a credible challenge from the extremes of her party, then the legislator must work to reestablish herself within the primary constituency before considering the greater electoral constituency.

Of course, if political and geographic sorting is occurring, it is only natural that the primary constituency will become even more ideological as the parties become more homogeneous in the electorate. But further research demonstrates that party activists or members of the political parties that have participated in at least three political activities have become even more ideologically extreme (Fiorina 2006; Layman and Carsey 2002). This move to the ideological extremes is also seen in delegates who attend the parties' national conventions (Herrera and Shafer 2004). Indeed, as I discuss further in Chapter 2, this situation creates "partisan-lean" states, in which states are generally conservative or liberal, but have a large enough constituency of ideologically moderate voters, as well as a strong ideological base to elect candidates of the opposing ideology.

Of course, anecdotal evidence from the 2012 primary election largely corroborates the storyline of primary challengers killing party members by being more ideologically extreme. Senator Richard Lugar (R-IN) was defeated in his primary by a more conservative challenger. Lugar, a party stalwart, was taking flack for voting for Obama's stimulus and the bailouts. As he struggled to demonstrate conservative credentials, his opponent, Richard Mourdock, capitalized and eventually won the primary contest (Good 2012). Indeed, Mourdock eventually lost the seat to Democrat Joe Donnelly in the general election due to his extreme positions. As such, moderates are less ideologically centered than they are cross-pressured from two ideological ends.

Senators beholden to their electoral constituencies should come as no surprise. In David Mayhew's (1973) assessment of Congress, the case is made that members of Congress are foremost concerned with reelection. While Mayhew avoids claiming that reelection is their only goal, he does assert that to pursue other goals, members of Congress must achieve reelection. As a result, the electoral connection argument claims that legislators focus on three activities: advertising, credit claiming, or position taking. That is, they advertise who they are to their constituency, claim credit for bills they passed that were especially helpful to their district, and use roll call votes and speeches to take positions that are popular with their constituents. Essentially, the argument states the congressional agenda depends less on what the party wants and more on what will help members of Congress in their reelection campaign.

Also, Fenno (1978) in his book describing the activities of eighteen members of Congress finds that legislators spend much of their time in their home districts cultivating trust with various constituencies. Jacobson (2004) concurs with much of this, finding that legislators spend a great deal of time attempting to represent their constituents to retain their seats in upcoming elections.

All of this research suggests that voters can have a significant impact on how legislators behave in Congress. That is, constituencies have policy demands that they ask of their representatives, and their representatives respond accordingly. Wahlke (1971) first explained this as the demand input model of representation in which constituents express their policy demands and preferences and representatives, in turn, represent these interests in the legislature. Scholars have debated, however, whether this occurs. Many studies have found that elected officials are responsive to constituency demands (Bartels 1991; Bianco 1994; Erikson 1978; Jackson and King 1989; Page et al. 1984, among many others). On the other hand, just as many studies found little to no evidence of representation (Bernstein 1989; Cohen and Noll 1991; Fiorina 1974; Kau and Rubin 1979; Poole and Rosenthal 1997, among many others). Still, others find that responsiveness is mixed and depends mainly on the salience of the issue (Achen 1978; Bond 1983; Hero and Tolbert 1995).

While many defer to the more theoretical model of the median voter theorem, suggesting that the representative need only satisfy a hypothetical median voter in the district (Downs 1957; Black 1958), Bishin (2008) argues that it is not necessarily the median opinion, or even majority opinion that the legislator needs to concern herself with. Instead, it is the most active subconstituency's opinion that the legislator should represent, as it is this constituency that can be activated to either reelect or vote out the representative based on her performance (Bishin 2008).

So, then, what does this scholarship demonstrate about moderates and their role in the lawmaking game—are they pivotal or weak? Sitting in the middle, after all, puts them in the unique position of being potentially pivotal in many areas of policy. As such, if they are pivotal, they should exert power as the necessary vote(s) to pass legislation. Then, if they are seeking reelection, they should boast about their accomplishments about being the most powerful senators on whom everyone relies to pass legislation, as Mayhew's electoral connection theory proposes—unless of course, their constituency would look down on such behavior.

Instead, it seems there may be key differences in the constituencies that senators represent that make being the powerbroker between two parties the less desired position. To understand this further, Table 1.1 lists the ten most moderate senators from the 113th Congress, according to the DW-Nominate Scores.

Table 1.1. Top Ten Most Moderate Senators in the 116th Congress (Based on DW-NOMINATE)

Senator (Party)	State	DW-NOMINATE Score	State's Presidential Vote Choice (2020)	State's Presidential Vote Choice (2016)	State's Presidential Vote Choice (2012)
Joe Manchin III	West Virginia	-.056	Trump	Trump	Romney
Doug Jones	Alabama	-.088	Trump	Trump	Romney
Krysten Sinema	Arizona	-.102	Biden	Trump	Romney
Susan Collins	Maine	.115	Biden*	Clinton*	Obama
Angus King	Maine	-.158	Biden*	Clinton*	Obama
Tom Carper	Delaware	-.176	Biden	Clinton	Obama
Mark Kelly	Arizona	-.187	Biden	Trump	Romney
Mark Warner	Virginia	-.202	Biden	Clinton	Obama
Lisa Murkowski	Alaska	.212	Trump	Trump	Romney
Jon Tester	Montana	-.215	Trump	Trump	Romney

*Maine allocates it's electoral votes by congressional district, as a result, in 2016 and 2020, Trump won electoral votes in Maine.

Source: voteview.com

Of these ten senators, five of them come from states in which the opposing party's presidential candidate has consistently won the state's electoral votes. Of the five remaining senators, two, Krysten Sinema (D-AZ) and Mark Kelly (D-AZ), come from states that have been newly designated as "swing states," in which the voters are nearly evenly divided regarding partisanship and ideology. Angus King, the only independent in the group, has chosen to caucus with the Democrats, a smart decision given the (mostly) liberal bent of his state. All of this is to say that of the ten most moderate senators in the current Congress, eight of them represent constituencies that are anything but moderate. Because of this, these senators must strike a balance between each ideological bent so as not to upset their core to invite a more ideological challenger, but also to not upset their general constituency and risk losing to a member of the opposing party.[12]

This is the crux of this book. To win reelection, these senators must modify their legislative behavior. Instead of being conciliators, they must work to avoid having this reputation, as it would anger both sides of their weak electoral coalition. Instead of taking the lead on legislation, centrists should instead avoid the spotlight and take a back seat in the legislative process.

Senate Polarization and Lawmaking

In the past, normative political theorists have argued that political parties, when in power, should rule using well-defined platforms that are distinct from the minority party, and should rule as a cohesive unit to enact the reforms from their platform (Schattschneider 1942; American Political Science Association 1950). E. E. Schattschneider describes the responsible party as a party that governs cohesively, giving little chance for moderates to arise. This argument leaves little room for bipartisanship and implies that winning "coalitions" are the majority party and that moderates who would seek to vote against the party would be removed, reprimanded, or nonexistent.

This theory, of course, is a normative theory of lawmaking and does not reflect how the legislative process works in the United States. In reality, the empirical congressional literature finds that many bills pass through bipartisan coalitions due to moderate members of Congress voting with members across the partisan aisle. In fact, Mayhew (1991) finds that bipartisan coalitions pass most salient legislation. Indeed, at one time moderates may have been much more essential to coalition building. Yet with the growing trends around partisan sorting discussed in the previous section, increases in polarization have changed the nature of lawmaking.

In his revision, even Mayhew (2005) amended his assessment of bipartisan coalitions, conceding that polarization had increased in the years since the first edition of his book. As mentioned earlier in the chapter, instead of running for reelection, many moderates are deciding to retire. From the 112th Congress, Democratic Senator Ben Nelson and Republican Senator Olympia Snowe decided to retire rather than run for reelection in what many expected to be challenging races. In addition to voluntary departures, moderates are also being defeated electorally at an alarming rate as well. For example, far right conservative Republican Josh Hawley defeated Democratic Senator Claire McCaskill from Missouri and has been a reliably conservative vote and Trump ally since his 2018 election.

While Cleland was defeated using a controversial attack tactic, Lincoln Chafee, the Republican Senator from Rhode Island, was defeated using a much more straightforward argument: despite the fact that Chafee is a political moderate, electing him would elect a Republican majority. His Democratic opponent Sheldon Whitehouse has since become a reliable vote for the Democrats (Chafee 2008).

The anecdotal evidence seems to suggest that the US Senate has lost most of its moderates and is becoming more and more polarized. Indeed, this evidence is buttressed by systematic empirical evidence as well. Using Keith Poole and Howard Rosenthal's DW-NOMINATE scores, which estimate the spatial location in policy spaces of members of Congress using roll call votes, we see that the US Senate is losing its moderates. Take, for example, the 88th Congress and the 111th Congress—two Congresses in which each Senate had a (relatively) large Democratic majority and a Democratic president (Lyndon Johnson and Barack Obama, respectively). The 88th Congress had 65 Democrats and 35 Republicans, while the 111th Congress was made up of 56 Democrats, 2 Independents who caucused with the Democrats, and 41 Republicans.[13] Each Senate passed landmark legislation—the 88th Congress passed the Civil Rights Act and the Clean Air Act, while the 111th Congress passed the Affordable Care Act and the American Recovery and Reinvestment Act (among many others). However, while Lyndon Johnson was able to move his agenda with at least some bipartisan support, Obama pushed his legislation through with mostly partisan votes. At face value, this is a remarkable feat considering that Johnson had fewer Republicans to negotiate with than Obama. Poole and Rosenthal's ideology measures seem to explain why.

Figures 1.1 and 1.2 demonstrate the ideological makeup of these two Senates. In the 88th Congress, Johnson had more Republicans to negotiate with, many of whom were more liberal than their Democratic counterparts. Obama had few moderate Republicans to work with, and most of them were too ideologically distant from his position to persuade.

Congressional scholarship has mostly agreed with this assessment. Many scholars have demonstrated that few if any centrist legislators remain in today's highly polarized legislature (Bond, Fleisher, and Stonecash 2009; Mayhew 2005; McCarty, Poole, and Rosenthal 2006; Sinclair 2006; Theriault 2006; 2008).[14] Given that moderate senators are disappearing at an alarming rate, this should theoretically empower the remaining few moderates, as there are fewer "deal brokers" to negotiate with.

Indeed, the US Senate is known for empowering individual senators and has been described as having undemocratic principles that employ anti-majoritarian rule (Dahl 2001). Unlike the House of Representatives, which typically employs simple majority rule in which the majority party's power can be centralized, the Senate offers the minority party the ability to block legislation using the filibuster, or the ability to debate a bill to its death—a

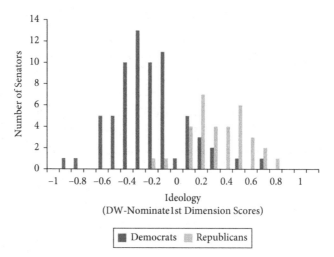

Figure 1.1. Ideological Distribution for the 88th Congress—Senate Only (1963–1965)

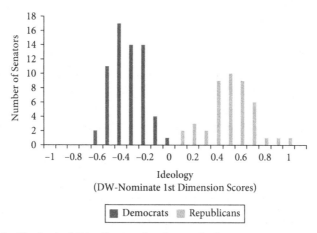

Figure 1.2. Ideological Distribution for the 111th Congress—Senate Only (2009–2011)

move that can be defeated only by a supermajority of sixty senators. That is, unlike the House, the majority party leadership has a much more difficult time setting a strong agenda as the rules of the debate cannot be limited in the Senate (Sinclair 2007).

Scholars, however, have debated the power of the filibuster, as Wawro and Schickler (2006) argue that the majority party needs only to convince moderates from the opposing party to end the debate to push their legislation through. Drawing from rational choice, voting models have long demonstrated that while votes may be distributed equally, only a specific number of voters will prevail in deciding the outcome (Downs 1957; Black 1958). Black's (1958) median voter theory argues that when a voting body is ordered on a one-dimensional issue space and the preferences of the voting members are single-peaked, the equilibrium outcome corresponds to the median voter's preferences. Krehbiel (1996; 1998) and Brady and Volden (1998) extend this logic by incorporating the Senate's supermajoritarian rules of the filibuster to build the pivotal politics theory of lawmaking.

The Pivotal Politics Theory of US lawmaking takes a collective choice approach to legislating. It assumes that policymaking occurs on a one-dimensional space where liberal ideas are located on the left, moderate in the middle, and conservative ideas on the right. On the continuum, there is an exogenous status quo point, which describes the current position on any given issue (Krehbiel 1996).

The players in this game are lawmakers and the president. Each has their single-peaked preference where the further a policy moves from the player's ideal point, the lower their utility they receive from the outcome. That is, a player always prefers policies that are closer rather than further away. In each issue model, pivotal players, or players whose support is crucial to the legislative process, exist. The president is one of these essential players, as he possesses constitutional powers to veto a bill. In the House of Representatives, the median voter acts as the pivotal player to pass legislation, and the 290th representative serves as the pivotal player to override a president's veto in that chamber. In the Senate, the median voter is the pivotal player to pass legislation, while the sixtieth senator is the pivotal player to overcome a filibuster (Krehbiel 1996). Figure 1.3 demonstrates the pivotal politics model when the president is liberal, and the status quo is conservative.

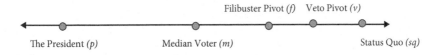

Figure 1.3. The Pivotal Politics Model

In this example, both Congress and the president prefer a more liberal alternative to the status quo. However, while the president favors a policy position that is very liberal, the filibuster pivot can threaten to vote with the minority and filibuster the president's proposal. Similarly, if the median voter is not satisfied, she can vote against the proposal as well, blocking any movement away from the status quo. The theory presumes that each senator can be placed on this one-dimensional ideological spectrum ranking each senator ideologically from 1 to 100 (in this case, most liberal to most conservative). In theory, this puts the senators that sit anywhere between the fiftieth and sixtieth location in a strong position. Indeed, this makes the senators that sit in the middle of the chamber potentially pivotal to every vote.

Beckmann (2009) finds that there is indeed some empirical evidence to support that those senators who sit at the aforementioned pivotal positions are as influential as the theory suggests. Specifically, he finds that presidents do strategically lobby pivotal players to pass their legislative agenda. To pass legislation, then, senators who sit in the middle of the chamber become potentially pivotal, as party leaders and the president rely on a handful of votes to pass their agenda. This finding is especially true considering the era of elite polarization in which moderates should possess even more power, as there are fewer and fewer moderates to negotiate with to assist in the passage of legislation.

Still, all too often we see cases like Collins who frequently get rolled. Indeed, few moderates can control the debate as much of the legislative legwork falls on party leaders. It may be the case that as polarization becomes more of the norm, the Senate is evolving into a version of the legislative game that is played in the House of Representatives. Scholarship studying the House of Representatives finds that the power of parties is much stronger and relevant to the legislative game. Aldrich (1995) argues that political parties solve the collective action problem of lawmaking. He says that even as congressional elections have evolved from wars between mass political machines to battles between issues-based candidates, "parties are designed as attempts to solve problems that current institutional arrangements do not solve and that politicians have to believe they cannot solve" (Aldrich 1995, 22). Rohde (1991) finds that the realignment of the political parties, in which Democrats gained control in the North while Republicans gained control in the South, only served to compound the effect that parties have on solving the collective action problem by creating two parties that are more homogeneous in their preferences. To be precise, scholars cite the signing of the Civil Rights Act in 1964 and the subsequent exodus of Southern voters from the Democratic Party to the Republican Party as one of the leading contributors to this increased homogeneity (McDonald and Grofman 1999; Theriault 2003; 2008).

Party effects are especially true in the House of Representatives, where the cartelization of the legislative process hands the power to solve the collective action problem to the majority party's leader (Cox and McCubbins 1993; 2004). Through its ability to set and change rules, the majority party primarily serves as a "cartel" in which it solves the dilemmas of governing by passing legislation that satisfies the "majority of the majority" (Cox and McCubbins 1993; 2004). Specifically, the majority party amends the rules of procedure to allow for the passage of the party's preferred bills and preventing gridlock by preventing defections to the minority.

Why are the power dynamics changing in the Senate? Or, to put it another way, why did President Obama have to rely solely on his Democratic caucus in the Senate while President Johnson was able to negotiate with Republicans? The answer lies in the evolving definition of the ideological moderate.

The Senate in the Age of Polarization

While there is a breadth of literature explaining the implications of polarization on the House of Representatives (i.e., the cartelization of the legislative process, Cox and McCubbins 2005), there is an emerging literature that explains how polarization has impacted the US Senate as well. For example, Binder and Smith (1997) find that legislative holds and filibusters have increasingly become commonplace in the Senate. Even more than the use of these procedures is the increased use of threatening to filibuster (Binder 2004).

Legislative holds, secretive as they are, have made it easy for individual senators to hold up legislation, while filibusters or even threats of a filibuster have made it easy for the minority party to hold up legislation. All of this has forced senators, who are traditionally much less beholden to their party, to rely on party leaders to push floor rules that can assist in the advancement of legislation. This is especially seen in the increased use of unanimous consent agreements, which have been used to limit the floor activity of senators trying to block legislation (Theriault 2008).

Frances Lee (2009) offers an even more nuanced explanation for polarization in the Senate—it is beneficial to legislators when seeking reelection. In her work, Lee finds that ideological disagreement is not the only explanation behind polarization in Congress. She finds that on issues that have no precise ideological bent, members of Congress continue to attack each other's proposals based on their partisanship. This allows lawmakers to rally around their own party's initiatives and works as a collective group to increase the salience of their party and their odds at reelection (Lee 2009).

What, then, does this trend mean for lawmaking? If anything, it suggests that as the moderates continue to disappear, the remaining moderates should gain power, as there are fewer moderates to negotiate with. That is to say, President Obama had only a handful of possible Republican senators to negotiate with, making those senators infinitely more potent than their Democratic and Republican counterparts. Yet, all too often in the current environment, we see moderate senators losing their influence over the political process. On Republican centrists in the Senate, then Democratic Majority Leader Harry Reid describes:

> Several were publicly wavering. And some were consistently sending signals that they were with us, but when it came time to vote, they were not. [Republican] Arlen Specter of Pennsylvania is always with us when we don't need him. Lisa Murkowski of Alaska would tell me later that not voting for a Democratic troop-rest bill was the biggest mistake she ever made, only to then make the same mistake several more times. (Reid 2008, 6)

By Reid's account, moderates in the contemporary Senate are motivated less by public policy outcomes and more by the effect their vote would have on their political personas. Conventional logic would dictate that moderates should be able to not only push their agenda but also drive the proverbial bus. Indeed, even with the logic of political parties, scholarship on the US Congress focuses on the power of the pivotal voter that sits in the ideological center as the gear that turns the legislative machine. The evolution of the definition of a moderate senator has affected how they behave in the Senate.

Overview of the Book

This book reexamines the lawmaking game in the US Senate. I seek to bridge the gap between the electoral coalition-building nature of Senate politics and the unique situation for moderate Senators and the legislative decisions they make in the chamber. I assert that the differing electoral basis of moderate senators vis-à-vis their more ideological counterparts creates a legislative game in the Senate in which centrists are not the powerbrokers, and party leaders and ideologues carry the brunt of the legislative legwork. Indeed, moderate senators are more concerned with avoiding traceability on controversial legislation than they are concerned about maximizing their pivotal power. In this chapter, I have laid the groundwork for the question at hand: are moderates able to capitalize on their potentially pivotal role as centrists in the legislative game and break gridlock by maximizing policy outcomes to their preferred policy location, or are they marginalized due to the difficulty in their ability to survive in the Senate? With fewer moderates in play, theoretically their power should increase, but with improved partisan sorting in the populace, moderates may be thinking less about maximizing policy outcomes and more about their electoral vulnerability.

Studying the US Senate is a particularly thorny endeavor. With only one hundred senators to examine per legislative session (often more, in cases of sudden retirement, death, or resignation), empirical studies of the Senate are difficult. Furthermore, an examination of public records and voting behavior, while indeed necessary to any comprehensive study of Congress, is limited in its ability to harness the behind-the-scenes negotiations. These negotiations are of particular concern for this study at hand. As a result, I employ a mixed methods approach. First, I examine visible legislative behavior that is easily traceable for voters. Chapter 3 takes a comprehensive look at this type of congressional behavior by examining the number of amendments proposed over the span of ten years using *Congressional Quarterly*'s key votes from 2003 to 2012 as well as the language used in floor speeches by moderates on key legislation. Looking at the situation over a large period, I find that moderates frequently shied away from proposing amendments and regularly used language in speeches that were appealing to their cross-pressures. Chapter 3 then takes a more in-depth look at legislative behavior. It looks at centrist behavior on two highly visible bills, the Affordable Care Act of 2009 and the Medicare Expansion Act of 2003. Specifically, the chapter looks at how moderates spoke on the bill on the floor of the Senate, how many amendments they proposed, and how they voted on the final legislation. Given the individualistic and "wild west" nature of floor activity in the Senate (Harry Reid's unprecedented use of the amendment tree notwithstanding), we should expect to see senators who want to make an impact propose amendments. Indeed, Chapter 3 illustrates that partisans and leaders were prolific in the amendment activity, while moderates neglected the activity. Still, the argument could be made that moderates win behind the scenes when the bill is written and thus have no need to file amendments. As a result, Chapter 3 then turns to floor activity on speeches—the logic here is that if moderates did win in the backroom negotiations and are happy with the legislation, they should take to the floor to defend it. Again, we see that moderates eschew this behavior as well.

Chapter 4 then turns to voting behavior, examining how moderates vote on key legislation. As argued in Chapters 1 and 2, the expectation from the media and scholars alike is that the pivotal voters are typically those that sit in the ideological center of the chamber. As a result, we should expect to see moderates vote only for legislation that they find palatable, and vote against all else. Using data collected by Project Vote Smart, capturing the issue positions of many senators, we see that all too often this is not the case—centrists get "railroaded" by leaders and vote with the majority, even when the law goes against their stated position. Chapter 4 then examines the logic behind centrist voting decisions and how they make decisions on how to vote on salient and controversial legislation.

The second way I examine the role of moderates in the Senate is by looking at the "behind-the-scenes" aspect of lawmaking and deal brokering through interview data from 2013. Indeed, backdoor politicking and negotiating could account for different power dynamics, and as such, I conducted elite interviews with the legislative directors for senators of the 113th Congress in the summer of 2013. I conducted nineteen interviews over the span of two weeks in Washington, DC. The interviews were mostly structured but concluded with a semi-structured, open-ended discussion of the power dynamics within the Senate. Gaining access to elite interviews has been and continues to be an increasingly difficult endeavor (see Baker 2011; Beckmann and Hall 2013; Curry 2015) and many Senate offices now have official policies prohibiting their staff members from engaging in any interview process with academics or otherwise without express consent from the senator and their chief of staff. As such, I used a snowball technique for gaining access by gaining access with senators whose offices I had acquaintances with. While not random, the process has been used with some success by others (see Curry 2015; Esterburg 2002). I then asked the legislative director, at the conclusion of the interview, to suggest others who might be willing to speak with me, and if they would allow me to "name drop" and tell the legislative director that I spoke with the previous director. While this process is not perfectly random, it did allow for a selection of senators that included members of the leadership, rank-and-file Democrats and Republicans, as well as moderates.

The amount of information that was gained from these face-to-face interviews cannot be overstated. While it may have been possible to obtain more responses through structured, mailed or even phone surveys, face-to-face interviews combined with the semi-structured, open-ended nature of the survey instrument allowed the legislative director to explain the nature of negotiating, leadership dynamics within each party, and decision-making in the Senate. I expand on the surveys in the two interview chapters, Chapters 5 and 6.

Chapter 5 looks at the behind-the-scenes maneuvering by Senators on three bills debated and voted on in 2013: the debt-ceiling bill known commonly as "No Budget, No Pay," the "Gang of Eight" comprehensive immigration reform bill, and an agriculture bill. The chapter relies on interview data collected in 2013 from legislative directors for nineteen senators. As argued in Chapters 1 and 2, the expectation from the media and scholars alike is that the pivotal voters are those who sit in the ideological center of the chamber. As a result, we should expect to see moderates prioritize the No Budget, No Pay Act and the immigration bill, spending most of their time and resources on these bills. Indeed, if they are pivotal, they should report satisfaction with each bill's final content and legislative process. I find that on average, moderate respondents were less likely to report satisfaction with the overall outcome of the legislative process, despite the time and effort put into the process.

Chapter 6 builds on the discussion and results provided in Chapter 5. Chapter 6 also incorporates information obtained from legislative directors about the three bills mentioned above. The chapter answers the question, Do senators view themselves or other senators as influential? This chapter answers the question of whether backroom dealing is how moderates use their power. That is to say, do legislators consider moderate preferences to build a large enough coalition to pass legislation? Interview data suggests that while leaders do try to protect moderates, coalitions are built with the opposing side, not with centrists. Indeed, legislators rarely view moderates as the most powerful senators in the Senate and are seldom lobbied for their vote.

Throughout the book, I also use information provided by six former senators who agreed to speak to me in 2017. Former Senators Mary Landrieu (D-LA), Mark Pryor (D-AR), Lincoln Chafee (R-RI, though he changed his party identification to independent, then Democrat, and eventually Libertarian), Mark Begich (D-AK), Byron Dorgan (D-ND), and Norm Coleman (R-MN) all spoke to me via telephone about the project providing key insights into decision-making and how they behaved in the Senate. Their insight is valuable to each of the chapters, as they offered an understanding of how voting decisions were made when they could push leadership to change legislation, and how they tried (and in some cases, failed) to survive the pressures facing them.

Finally, I conclude with a comprehensive summary of how moderates operate in the Senate. While this book does not offer a guide for how moderates can survive the ideological center, it does paint a picture in which moderates face pressures that their ideological counterparts do not. As such, I offer implications regarding how these unique electoral circumstances and pressures impact the study of the Senate, electoral politics, and American politics in general. In the following chapter, I present my theory for how moderates operate in the Senate.

2

Marginalized in the Middle

A Theory of How Centrists Have Moderate Influence

In 1986, first-term Republican senator Arlen Specter ran for reelection in his home state of Pennsylvania. Though he eventually won with 56 percent of the vote, he was initially viewed as vulnerable. With growing economic turmoil in his state and a voter registration advantage numbering 800,000 for the Democrats, two young and qualified Democrats salivated at the chance to challenge the electorally weak Specter: Don Bailey, the state's auditor general, and Bob Edgar, a six-term member of Congress from Philadelphia. Even Republicans viewed Specter as a political liability as popular Republican governor Richard Thornburgh considered a primary challenge to Specter.

Although Thornburgh eventually declined the opportunity to challenge Specter in the Republican primary, Specter did have to face Edgar in the general election. What began as a formidable challenge to Specter's incumbency quickly defused when Specter reframed his record in the Senate, describing himself as "the most independent Republican" and declaring, "My vote is not determined by President Reagan, and I shy away from such labels as liberal or conservative." Indeed, as Richard Fenno (1991) put it in his examination of Specter's early career, "As a practical matter, that meant [Specter] vot[ed] with the Reagan administration on some matters and vot[ed] against the Reagan administration on other matters. As his home state observers had noted at the outset, he was 'the one up there on a tightrope'" (157).

Specter's balancing act is not unique for senators in the ideological center. In fact, most senators who sit in the center avoid being labeled as ideological and instead favor terminology like "independent" or "a maverick." Indeed, this strategy may be what moved Specter from being a vulnerable Senate candidate up for reelection to a virtual lock. But why did Specter have to eschew his party, his popular president, and his ideology to win?

At first blush, it seems that Specter behaved as a true moderate; he did not side with either party but instead blazed a third, moderate path. Fenno's assessment offers a different explanation, however—Specter did not genuinely

Life in the Middle. Neilan S. Chaturvedi, Oxford University Press. © Oxford University Press 2021.
DOI: 10.1093/oso/9780197599723.003.0002

grasp a position that was centered ideologically, but instead, his "moderate path" was a result of picking and choosing positions from both Democrats and Republicans.

Specter's 1986 plight describes much of what moderates experience in today's Senate. Like Specter, most moderates come from states not with moderate constituents, but with ideologically divided ones. For Specter, the key was to preserve a liberal constituency in Philadelphia with the more conservative areas of northwest Pennsylvania. Given these electoral circumstances, Specter had to build a weak coalition that was vulnerable to party image and economic conditions.

This form of coalition building is, of course, not without consequence. Given that moderates like Specter have such weak electoral backgrounds to rely on, they cannot possibly exert political power to influence the agenda one way or another, as doing so would likely adversely affect one piece of their electoral coalition. In this chapter, I outline a theory for why moderates are not genuinely moderate but are electorally conflicted. Indeed, like Specter, most moderates must walk the proverbial tightrope during the legislative process to yield any electoral success.

The Basic Framework: A Policymaking Game

As mentioned in Chapter 1, the strength of the democratic principles behind the Senate has been a topic of debate, mainly due to its supermajoritarian rules to overcome a filibuster. Scholars and observers continue to debate the merits of such a system, arguing that it puts the power of moving the agenda on a small number of swing voters. As I have built up to, this requires further examination.

Let's begin by reexamining the legislative process. While the US Senate has 100 members, not each member is equally powerful. Proponents of the public choice approach argue that we should only be concerned with a handful of senators. That is, if we were to simplify the legislative process to three (or in the case of divided government, four) players, the median voter, the filibuster pivot, and the president, we would have a sequential game, as illustrated in Figure 2.1, the Pivotal Politics Model.

The game begins when a member of Congress proposes a bill. Given that it takes a simple majority to pass a bill, the contents of the legislation must first be satisfactory to the median voter, here represented as m. If the median voter

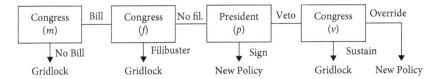

Figure 2.1. The Pivotal Politics Model

is dissatisfied, there will be no bill and gridlock will be the result. If, however, the median voter is satisfied, then the proponents of the bill must guard against a filibuster by satisfying the sixtieth senator that would invoke cloture, here represented as *f*. If the supporters of the bill are unable to appease this senator, then gridlock will again be the end outcome. If, however, they can satisfy this senator, then the bill is sent to the president for his veto or signature. Of course, if the president signs the bill then new policy emerges, but in the instance of divided government, the president may veto a bill, sending it back to Congress for a veto-override, in which the sixty-seventh senator now becomes the key player in the legislative process (Krehbiel 1996; 1998; Brady and Volden 1998).

Again, at its core, this theory of lawmaking in the US Senate emphasizes that only a handful of senators are actually pivotal to the passage of new legislation. Key to the process is the group of senators who sit between the fiftieth and the sixtieth vote on the ideological continuum. That is to say, the ideological moderates should then hold the key to new legislation. Indeed, scholars outside of formal modeling have come to a similar conclusion. John Kingdon's (1989) seminal study on congressional voting argues that members of Congress do not have enough time to research every policy area thoroughly. Richard Hall (1996) adds to this assessment in his study of congressional participation, arguing that only a select few legislators play a significant role while very few ever serve as principal authors. Indeed, as others have pointed out, successful lobbying should not target every member, but only the members whose votes are needed (see Beckmann 2009; Groseclose and Snyder 1996; Snyder 1991, in addition to the previously mentioned pivotal politics literature).

Still, early in the legislative game, presidents are seen lobbying and mobilizing their party's leadership. As Bond and Fleisher (1990) put it, "many important decisions in Congress are made in places other than floor votes and recorded by means other than roll calls" (68). Beckmann (2009) argues that the president, his supportive leadership in Congress, and the opposition leaders do much of the legwork in the legislative process. While this and many other theories still lean on the fact that centrists in the US Senate are integral to the policymaking process, there seems to be more evidence to support the idea that centrists are essential, but not powerful. That is, the work that the leadership puts into the legislative game may be more critical than the pivotal voters.

Lee (2009) argues for a similar framework for policymaking in the Senate, claiming that ideology and, by extension, the ideological placement of senators has less to do with policymaking than with partisanship. That is to say, political parties work to simplify the political process by deferring to leaders on many types of votes, especially procedural ones to score more "wins" for their "team." Curry (2015) argues that in the House of Representatives, the leadership controls the agenda through a monopoly on the control of information. At first glance, this is the problem. If ideologically moderate senators are deferring to their leadership instead of exerting their theoretically substantial political power, the assumptions behind gridlock and policy suggest that it is not senators in the middle who are pivotal, but another group, if any such group exists. In the following sections, I address the assumptions behind the belief in powerful moderate senators and outline a theory on their actual influence and the implications behind this.

Assumptions

Assumed in the models that put moderates at the forefront is that the policy space for any policy issue is one-dimensional. That is, members of the US Senate can be organized on a single continuum ranging from liberal to conservative. Regarding the legislative process, it is also assumed that for each policy there is an exogenous status quo point. Figure 2.2 illustrates two possible policy spaces for a conservative president.

Since legislators can be aligned by their respective ideologies, the placement of the filibuster pivot and median pivot would both have to be on the "correct side" of the status quo. That is, to move the status quo to a new destination, both pivots need to approve of moving the policy to a new location. In Figure 2.1, under the assumptions made about ideology, the status quo could conceivably move anywhere in the shaded area. In Figure 2.2, if we were to assume the same players and their ideological preferences, the status quo would not move to the president's more conservative preference, as both

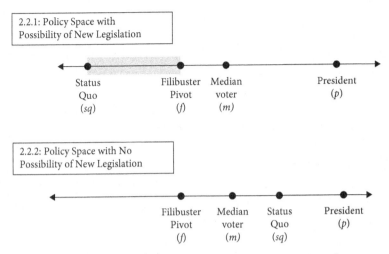

2.2.1: Policy Space with
Possibility of New Legislation

Status		Filibuster	Median		President
Quo		Pivot	voter		(*p*)
(*sq*)		(*f*)	(*m*)		

2.2.2: Policy Space with No
Possibility of New Legislation

	Filibuster	Median	Status	President
	Pivot	voter	Quo	(*p*)
	(*f*)	(*m*)	(*sq*)	

Figure 2.2. One-Dimensional Policy Space for Conservative President

the median voter and the filibuster pivot have ideological preferences that are more liberal than the president's preferences.

However, underlying these conclusions are the assumptions that each senator's ideal ideological position (1) can be mapped on an ideological continuum and (2) remains consistent across issues. This assumption is, of course, not without empirical support. Keith Poole and Howard Rosenthal's (1997) scoring algorithm, NOMINATE, measures the ideologies of each legislator as a single ideal point on an ideological continuum scale (Poole and Rosenthal 1997, 12). Assumed here is that legislators will vote with the policy option that is closest to their ideal ideological location. Calculated using roll call votes on non-unanimous votes on all issues regardless of content, the NOMINATE measures accurately measure ideology on a left-right dimension (Poole and Rosenthal 1997). The legitimacy of this measure is only buttressed by their high correlation with more traditional measures of ideology. When compared to scorecards by interest groups such as those done by the Americans for Democratic Action and the US Chamber of Commerce, the NOMINATE measures mostly hold up to interest group ratings (Burden, Caldeira, and Groseclose 2000; Lee 2009; McCarty, Poole, and Rosenthal 2006).

Still, there is a reason to question the validity of ideal ideological points. For example, Heckman and Snyder (1997) find that measuring party and regional loyalty accounts for the majority of ideological preferences.

Using dummy variables for Southern and Northern Democrats, and for Republicans, Heckman and Snyder find that the NOMINATE measures are more or less measures of these variables. Furthermore, when party-switchers are put under the microscope, their ideal ideological points shift violently from one ideology to the other as they become more loyal to their new party (McCarty, Poole, and Rosenthal 2003, 2006; Nokken 2000). Indeed, Frances Lee (2009) argues, "not every issue considered in Congress raises ideological questions, at least as 'ideology' is conventionally understood in American politics. As broad as 'liberalism' and 'conservatism' are as concepts, they cannot be expanded to cover every policy issue" (183). She goes on to argue that much of the conflict that observers see as ideological polarization is more about partisan strife rather than ideological misgivings.

It is off of these theoretical contributions that I propose a theory on the influence of moderates in the US Senate. Building on the work of scholars who have questioned the validity of ideal point ideology scores, I argue that partisans may have ideal points that are ideologically polarized but that measuring the ideal ideological location for moderates is much more difficult. Unlike their partisan counterparts, moderates do not have ideologically homogeneous preferences that can reflect a clear ideological point on a liberal to conservative continuum. Instead, moderates are elected from ideologically heterogeneous constituencies that force them to create volatile coalitions made up of differing interests. As a result, their placement in the "middle" of the Senate is suspect at best, and to propose that they sit in pivotal positions and have influence over the agenda should also be called into question. Moderates in the Senate should care less about maximizing their policy outcomes and more about minimizing the consequences of those outcomes. In the following section, I outline a theoretical explanation for why moderates behave cautiously in the legislative arena and propose a theory for how moderates are marginalized in their legislative and electoral predicaments.

Marginalized in the Middle: A Theory of Moderate Influence

In Chapter 1, I discussed Mayhew's (1973) assessment of the goals of members of Congress known as the "Electoral Connection." To summarize quickly again, Mayhew argues that among their many goals, members of Congress are concerned foremost with reelection. As a result, they must focus on keeping their constituents happy, mainly by representing the groups that make up the constituency that elected them (Fenno 1978). Though there are debates in the scholarly community about the effectiveness of legislators representing their constituency's interests (see the discussion in Chapter 1), it is difficult to dismiss the notion of representation entirely. It is fair to assume that legislators to at least some degree match their constituency's ideology.

Downs (1957) and Black (1958) assert that if voters can be organized on a one-dimensional policy space, the ideal point would be the median voter. Expanding that to the study of congressional behavior, representatives should respond to the median voter's preferences, as that is the ideal ideological point for a representative to represent as it captures the most significant portion of her constituency. Thus, the median voter theorem argues that legislators have single-peaked preferences that correspond to the median voter within their constituency. I illustrate the median voter theorem in Figure 2.3.

Of course, to assume that each constituency is perfectly balanced and that constituents line up in a fashion in which legislating from the middle would yield the most votes would be faulty at best. Americans continue to sort themselves ideologically and vote more consistently with their ideology as matched more accurately to their partisanship. Fewer and fewer constituencies look like Figure 2.3.1 and more and more like Figures 2.3.2 and 2.3.3. That is, legislators are representing increasingly homogeneous (though not necessarily polarized) constituencies. Indeed, as Table 2.1 demonstrates, senators from the ideological left and right tend to come from states that are solidly left and right.

Note that of these ten states, there are no swing states. None of the three candidates won states in the liberal column or lost states in the conservative column. That is to say, the states represented by the most liberal senators are mostly liberal, while the states that are represented by conservative senators are more conservative than not.

So then what of the moderates? In Chapter 1, I presented a table listing the top ten most moderate senators in the 116th Senate. Let us revisit this group again here, with more detail, as presented in Table 2.2.

In this table, the explanation for why these states elected moderates is, in some cases, less evident than in others. For example, it is conceivable that traditional swing states like Virginia or the emerging swing state of Arizona elect moderates like Mark Warner or Mark Kelly, respectively.

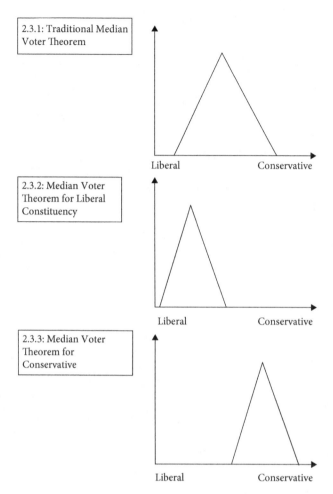

Figure 2.3. The Median Voter Theorem

But less intuitive are states that do not swing. That is, why would a state that is aligned with the Republican Party, like Alabama or West Virginia, elect Democrats like Heidi Heitkamp or Joe Manchin? For that matter, why would a state like Maine, which voted in the low 40 percent range for the Republican candidate at the presidential level, elect (and reelect) a Republican in Susan Collins?

As stated earlier, the Pivotal Politics model requires that members have single-peaked preferences that can be easily aligned on a liberal to con-servative consortium. To be fair, this is (mostly) true for the vast majority

Table 2.1. Comparison of the Most Liberal and Conservative Senators in the 116th Senate

Senator	State	Rank Based on DW-NOMINATE Score	Percentage Voting for Trump (20)	Percentage Voting for Trump (16)	Percentage Voting for Romney
Top Five Most Liberal					
Warren (D)	Massachusetts	1st	32	33	38
Harris (D)	California	2nd	34	32	38
Booker (D)	New Jersey	3rd	41	41	41
Sanders (D)	Vermont	4th	31	30	31
Hirono (D)	Hawaii	5th	34	30	28
Top Five Most Conservative					
Lee (R)	Utah	1st	58	45	73
Paul (R)	Kentucky	2nd	62	63	61
Cruz (R)	Texas	3rd	52	52	57
Braun (R)	Indiana	4th	57	57	54
Sasse (R)	Nebraska	5th	59	59	61

* Bernie Sanders is an independent who caucuses with the Democrats, despite running for the Democratic presidential nomination in 2016. He is a self-described Democratic Socialist.

of senators who fit this design, as illustrated in Figures 2.3.2 and 2.3.3. Most senators are elected from states that the media would traditionally refer to as "red" and "blue" states. But to assume that moderates are only elected from states with moderate ideologies is a mistake. Indeed, even assuming that they are all elected from "swing" states would also be an oversimplification. Moderate senators in the modern area come overwhelmingly from one of two states, the "partisan-lean states" and the "swing states."

Partisan-Lean States

Senators Manchin, Pryor, Donnelly, Landrieu, and Heitkamp and the like were all elected from states that are not viewed traditionally as swing states. So why are these states electing them? Or to be more specific, what distinguishes these states from traditionally "red" and "blue" states such that

Table 2.2. Comparison of the Top Ten Moderates in the 116th Senate

Senator	State	Rank Based on DW-Nominate Score	Percentage Voting for Trump (20)	Percentage Voting or Trump (16)	Percentage Voting for Romney
Joe Manchin III	West Virginia	1st	69	68	62
Doug Jones	Alabama	2nd	62	62	61
Krysten Sinema	Arizona	3rd	49	48	54
Susan Collins	Maine	4th	44	45	41
Angus King	Maine	5th	44	45	41
Tom Carper	Delaware	6th	40	42	40
Mark Kelly	Arizona	7th	49	48	54
Mark Warner	Virginia	8th	44	44	48
Lisa Murkowski	Alaska	9th	53	51	55
Jon Tester	Montana	10th	57	56	55

they choose moderates while others do not? Of the senators in Table 2.2 who are not elected from the dual-peaked swing states, there appears to be little logic to their election at first glance, other than the fact that they come from states in which the opposing party is strong. Take for example, Joe Manchin, the Democratic senator from West Virginia. In each presidential election, West Virginia voted overwhelmingly for the Republican presidential candidate. How then could a Democrat be elected if Republicans dominate the state?

West Virginia and a handful of other states for that matter are unique. While their electorates favor one party over the other, these states hold a unique set of circumstances in which they may be inclined to elect a member of the opposite party. These circumstances could include a family legacy (the Landrieu family in Louisiana, for example), a scandal for the incumbent party (Doug Jones defeating Roy Moore who was accused of sexually assaulting a number of minors), or a famous politician with ties to state politics (Olympia Snowe and Susan Collins in Maine or John Breaux in Louisiana, for example). I call these states, partisan-lean states. I illustrate them graphically in Figure 2.4. In these states, there is a clear advantage for one party or ideology, and it is, in one sense, a single-peaked preference.

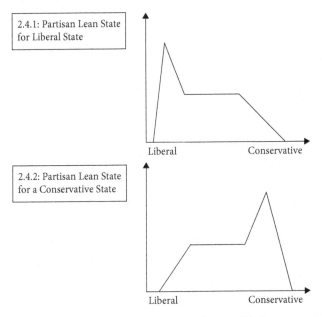

Figure 2.4. Partisan-Lean States for a (a) Liberal State, (b) Conservative State

It does not, however, capture the ideal point to gain the support of all the voters in every scenario.

That is to say, there are enough moderates to build a coalition with the weaker party to elect a moderate senator. For example, Olympia Snowe and Susan Collins can be elected from Maine because even though Maine traditionally elects liberal Democrats, a coalition of Republicans and weak partisan moderates can push them to electoral victory. Like dual-peaked swing states, however, these senators are also not genuinely ideologically moderate.

On his blog fivethirtyeight.com, statistician Nate Silver describes these states using the economic term of elasticity. Silver argues that states vary in their elasticity or their sensitivity to political conditions or changes in the nature of the times. He describes the "classic example" of an elastic state as a state like New Hampshire because of the state's large proportion of independent, swing voters. One example of a state that is inelastic is a state like Mississippi, which has few independent, swing voters, and many ideologically conservative Republicans and few liberal Democrats.

However, there exist some states that are surprisingly elastic that we would traditionally consider partisan states. Indeed, according to Silver's typology,

Rhode Island, New Hampshire, Maine, Hawaii, and Vermont rank the highest as "elastic" states. While all five of these are among the "bluest" of states, each state can elect Republicans. Silver explains it:

> Alaska, for instance, is sort of the polar opposite of Rhode Island—it has quite a lot of independent voters, but the Republican candidate usually wins because the Republican base there is larger than the Democratic base. But Alaskan voters are flexible enough to keep Republicans on their toes. A relatively liberal Democrat, Mark Begich, was narrowly elected to the Senate in Alaska in 2008 because Republicans had a problematic incumbent in Ted Stevens and because the national environment was very favorable for Democrats that year.[1]

Using individual-level data from exit polls conducted during the 2008 election, Silver (2012) examined nearly 100,000 voter responses. Running a logistic regression, Silver estimated the probability of a voter voting for Obama based on demographics. For example, he predicts a "66-year-old Latina Catholic living on a fixed income who describes herself as a conservative Democrat might have about a 75% chance of voting for Mr. Obama." He also uses the model to predict swing voters as well. For example, "a high-income white independent moderate voter who has an advanced academic degree and lives in a suburb in the South might have about a 45% chance of [voting for Obama]."

Based on these "swing voters" who have a nearly 50 percent chance of voting for Obama, Silver creates a scale of elasticity. The scale runs from a high value of 1.29 for Rhode Island to a low value of .45 for the District of Columbia. He estimates that for every change by a single percentage point in Obama's national standing, the state's support for Obama would change by their elasticity score.

Again, since the ideal position is not the center, these senators must build unstable coalitions of moderates and their base. In these states, senators are still vulnerable to a strong primary election challenge, but in the general election, the senator must be moderate enough to gain broad support to build a coalition—something Blanche Lincoln struggled with in 2010. Indeed, this measure of elasticity helps explain how West Virginia, a deep red state, can elect a Democrat like Joe Manchin, and how Rhode Island, a deep blue state, elected members of the Chafee family for so long. Given that the opposing party remains powerful, they will likely have to take positions from the opposing ideology as well on occasion.

It should be made clear here that there are a number of studies that examine statewide ideology (see, for example, Berry et al. 1998; Boehmke et al. 2004; Brace et al. 2002; Cohen 2006; Erikson et al. 1993; Gelman and Little 1997; Hofferbert 1966; Lax and Phillips 2009; Mooney and Lee 1995; Pacheco 2011; Park et al. 2004; Weber et al. 1972). However, I am less concerned with the overall statewide ideology—indeed, if a state is dual-peaked and polarized, in the aggregate, a statewide ideology measure would show an ideologically moderate state. As a result, despite the value in these studies, I instead examine the issue of state ideology through Silver's methodology.

In any case, the previous assumptions of the median voter theorem applying to all senators do not apply. That is, unlike ideological senators who have one clear constituency to represent, moderates must build extremely volatile coalitions with imprecise preferences. This means that instead of representing a "moderate" ideological position, they must instead balance their congressional participation by borrowing from both liberals and conservatives. Because of this, much of the nuance behind this predicament is lost on broader lawmaking theories.

Still, this only represents some of the states that elect moderates. After all, inelastic states like North Carolina and Florida have also elected moderates in the past. So what accounts for this? North Carolina and Florida both represent states that are inelastic, meaning there are few independent swing voters, but there are enough partisans on both sides to elect members from either party, allowing them to swing from one party to another.

The Swing States

Moderates can also be elected from swing states or states that have nearly equal numbers of both Democrats and Republicans. To assume, however, that voters could be easily drawn as having a single-peaked ideology would be negligent to the nuances of the electoral climate in these states. To be specific, states that are traditionally referred to as swing states are not swing states because they represent an ideologically moderate constituency, but because the electorate itself is torn concerning partisanship. This phenomenon is illustrated in Figure 2.5.

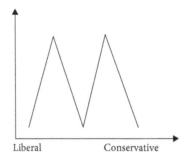

Figure 2.5.   The Dual-Peaked Swing State

Instead of having one distinct, "single-peaked" preference to represent, senators from states that are divided in partisanship have to address the concerns of two different preferences. This is, of course, precisely divergent from what ideological senators have to experience. Senators from these dual-peaked states have to strike a balance between the two sides if they are to maintain their weak electoral coalition. Of course, traditional measures of ideology, such as the DW-NOMINATE scores, or even the interest group scores would fail to measure this difference. As a result, senators that have traditionally been viewed to be moderate are anything but.

The aggregation of their vote choice in Congress merely reflects an effort to balance two distinct constituencies with divergent preferences.

As I mentioned in Chapter 1, Fenno's (1978) constituencies for this type of state are more complex. For a "run-of-the-mill" senator, their concerns should be their primary constituency, made up of their ideological base, and their general constituency made up of their base and other supporters. For senators from dual-peaked states, they still have the same concerns, but the calculus behind their decisions is much more complex. If a senator from a "run-of-the-mill" state is having trouble with her base, then she can run to her base and vote ideologically. If the same senator is vulnerable in the general election, she can moderate her positions to build a broader coalition. A senator from a dual-peaked state does not have the same luxury, however. Regarding measuring her reelection prospects, she can choose two legislative strategies. From her election, this senator could strike an odd ideological balance: running too close to the middle or opposite ideology will result in a primary challenge, while running too close to the base would yield a strong general election challenge. Ideally, she would have to strike some balance like that found by Arlen Specter throughout most of his career.

Table 2.3. Moderate Typology

Type of State	States
Swing States	Colorado, Florida, Iowa, Nevada, New Hampshire, North Carolina, Ohio, Pennsylvania, Virginia
Moderate Democrat/Conservative Republican	Alabama, Alaska, Arizona, Arkansas, Georgia, Idaho, Indiana, Kansas, Kentucky, Louisiana, Mississippi, Missouri, Montana, Nebraska, North Dakota, Oklahoma, South Carolina, South Dakota, Tennessee, Texas, Utah, West Virginia, Wyoming
Moderate Republican/Liberal Democrat	California, Connecticut, Delaware, Hawaii, Illinois, Maine, Maryland, Massachusetts, Michigan, Minnesota, New Jersey, New Mexico, New York, Oregon, Rhode Island, Vermont, Washington, Wisconsin, Minnesota

Alternatively, the senator in question could choose a legislative strategy that endears her to the ideological pole of her party to excite the base to turn out for her. This balancing act is a dangerous strategy, as there would likely be some backlash, but not one without its merits. Scholarship on elections demonstrates that, indeed, politicians who choose ideological extremes over ambiguity and moderation can increase support within their party (Peress 2011; Rogowski 2014; Tomz and Van Houweling 2008). Of course, this may work better for swing state senators than partisan-lean state senators.

Using the presidential vote share for the Democratic candidate for the 2012 and 2008 presidential elections, we can classify the states based on the typology described earlier. Table 2.3 lists this classification.

Of course, this classification is not without its faults. As mentioned, many very popular politicians have carved out moderate governing strategies in Congress and have maintained them despite the nature of their constituency. Nevertheless, a comparison between this typology and the DW-NOMINATE scores shows a great deal of accuracy in predicting where moderates and polarized senators come from. This is presented in Table 2.4. The typology listed above correctly predicted 90 percent of the top ten most moderate senators in the 112th and 110th Congresses, and 80 percent in the 111th and 108th Congresses.

Given that the overwhelming majority of moderate senators come from states where the ideological makeup is either contradictory or antagonistic,

Table 2.4. Percentage of Senators Correctly Predicted by Moderate Typology by DW-NOMINATE Scores

Congress	Top Ten Most Moderate
112th	90%
111th	80%
110th	90%
109th	60%
108th	80%

moderates must exercise their power as the vote to break a filibuster or pass legislation with extreme caution. As such, throughout the rest of the book, I refer to moderates under the typology of the state that elected them.

To be sure, swing state senators are in a different position than are partisan-lean state senators. Unlike partisan-lean state senators, swing state senators may enjoy a reasonably large base that they can motivate to turn out on their behalf. Again, turning to the measure of elasticity, certain swing states are inelastic in that they have few independent swing voters, but are still swing states as they have somewhat equal numbers of Democrats and Republicans. This bipolar configuration is a large reason for why we often see one state represented by two ideologically polarized senators. For example, for much of the latter part of the twentieth century, Tom Harkin, a liberal Democrat, and Charles Grassley, a conservative Republican, represented Iowa. Similarly, today, Sherrod Brown, a liberal Democrat, and Rob Portman, a relatively conservative Republican, represent Ohio.

The broad base that these senators enjoy allows for some flexibility. Some senators, like the ones already mentioned, may be able to play to their base and win elections by merely keeping their core constituents happy. Others, however, may view this is a much riskier situation and may operate as partisan-lean senators. If executed correctly, both strategies have the same level of success. For example, the recent slew of Democrats who have represented Virginia have chosen a path of moderation, and all of them have enjoyed high approval ratings (including Jim Webb, who retired before running for reelection). I will discuss this further throughout the book and in greater detail in Chapter 6. Note that while I do argue that swing state senators can strike either an ideological note or a moderate note,

I do not further distinguish between the two—indeed, those who strike the moderate note do so in similar ways as those senators from partisan-lean states, while those senators who take the ideological position find themselves rarely in positions more akin to rank-and-file members. In the following section, I outline a strategy for these electorally vulnerable senators to achieve reelection.

Moderate Strategies

If moderates are elected by building volatile coalitions, how can they possibly survive and retain their seat in future elections? As mentioned, the worst option for moderates would be to represent the ideological center. In dual-peaked swing states, representing moderate interests would serve only to anger the left and the right. In partisan-lean states, it could activate a base that would yield a strong primary challenger or anger the opposition yielding to a strong general election challenger. As noted, in 2010, Blanche Lincoln, a Democrat from Arkansas,[2] experienced just this fate. By running to the middle, she sufficiently angered her base enough to yield a strong primary challenge from Bill Halter, the much more liberal lieutenant governor of the state. While she was able to stave off Halter's challenge, she ultimately lost to Republican John Boozman, a much more conservative candidate (Muskal 2010).

So then how can the so-called group of moderate senators avoid the same fate as Blanche Lincoln? Proponents of traditional theories in which moderates are influential due to their ideological placement would argue that the best way to avoid electoral defeat is to exert power over policy decisions. Given the more nuanced explanation I have given about what constituencies elect these moderates, it would likely be problematic to use this method. In his seminal study of Congress, R. Douglas Arnold (1990) argues that many members of Congress seek to avoid traceability on salient issues, as the costs associated with them can be detrimental with voters, even in cases where the relative good outweighs the bad. This logic rings even more valid for senators in the middle. Because they have to maintain unstable coalitions that have differing and often opposing values, it is best for them to avoid any sort of traceability on most salient issues.

So then what strategies can be employed to preserve their incumbency? If these senators are trying to maximize their ideological flexibility while minimizing traceability, they should look to use four strategies. I illustrate these strategies in Figure 2.6.

To understand their actions fully, I split these strategies in two: the on-stage legislative game, in which senators shape and defend the legislation, and the behind-the-scenes legislative game, in which senators negotiate and push their influence on legislation. In the onstage legislative game, many senators can choose to be inactive, not only by choice but out of necessity. Again, as mentioned earlier, Kingdon (1989) argues that most members of Congress are inundated with numerous issues and legislation that they usually cannot engage legislation until it's on the floor, and even then, many neglect to do so.

Also, one of the primary concerns should be traceability. Can voters see the senator's fingerprints on the legislation? To avoid this scenario, moderates can employ one of four strategies. First, they can *delegate* their

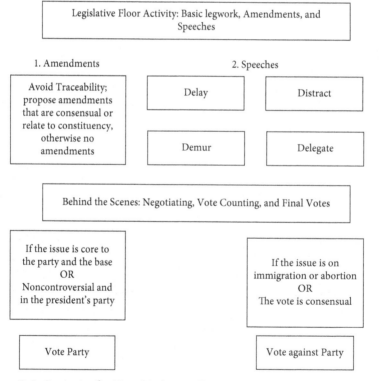

Figure 2.6. Strategies for How Moderates Try to Survive the Ideological Center of the US Senate

position to the party leadership. The logic behind this choice is to maximize the party's strength nationally to avoid both primary challengers and strong general election challenges. Borrowing from the Cartel Theory literature on the House of Representatives, here, senators choose to support their party's position to pass legislation regardless of their constituency's or even their policy preferences (Cox and McCubbins 1993; 2004). Of course, this strategy cannot always be used since many constituencies may find such an explanation unacceptable. For example, on a bill that advances budget cuts, Mark Begich (D-AK) justified his vote in favor of a bill that would sharply cut federal social spending in his state by playing up the fact that the bill increased the share of oil revenues to Alaska. This is, of course, a valid strategy for senators who sit in the middle. When party loyalty does not appease voters, senators can *distract* their constituencies by focusing on the consensual portions of the legislation rather than the direct costs of the legislation.

Still, what are moderate senators to do when the direct costs of the bill are clear and salient? Particularly salient bills that are getting high media attention or bills where no party has a clear partisan dominance of the issue regardless of ideology, like immigration and abortion, are particularly problematic for moderates. On these pieces of legislation, senators should (and do) use two strategies to avoid traceability. They can either *delay* their decision and make demands, which are often vague, to change the legislation or they can *demur* and avoid taking a clear position on the legislation. In either case, the goal of the senator is to prevent traceability and to get attention in the early game part of legislating.

Furthermore, on legislation that can have a clear impact on the party's ability to govern, especially when in the president's party, moderates must vote to defend their party. Indeed, this may have been part of Blanche Lincoln's problem—some Democrats viewed her as a Democrat in name only who voted against core party bills. Still, moderates must maintain some distance from their party as well—like Arlen Specter, they have to walk the tightrope to balance their constituencies. As a result, on hot-button issues like immigration and abortion, or on issues where both parties vote in agreement, moderates should seize these opportunities to vote against their party and demonstrate independence. Of course, there is evidence to support the idea that legislators play this hedging game. Yoshinaka and Grose (2011) find that legislators frequently hedge when they do not know what their constituents prefer. As such, I contend that moderates use this strategy as a survival method.

Conclusion

Of course, the strategies mentioned are not foolproof strategies, but they are strategies that senators in the middle must employ to survive the volatility of their electoral coalitions. Because of this, it is inconceivable that senators that sit on or near the "pivots" (i.e., the median voter and the filibuster pivot) are powerful at all. In fact, in many cases they can be "rolled" by party leaders on close votes—though unlike their colleagues in the House, vulnerable centrist senators can be rolled by either party, depending on which side is offering the stronger electoral challenge.

To return to the initial example given of Arlen Specter, it is because he avoided traceability on highly salient issues and beat a drum of independence that Specter was able to turn a potentially lost Senate seat into an easy victory. Still, his future career was met with electoral ambiguity and weak power. As Lincoln Chafee (2008) argued in his book, Specter "took no leadership role in representing the moderate point of view. He acquiesced [to the administration], and others followed his example" (7). Indeed, he ended his legislative career by switching parties and becoming a Democrat, only to lose in a primary to a more liberal Democrat.

In the following chapters, I test this theory by using empirical evidence first to demonstrate the electoral argument and then later the legislative argument. In the next two chapters, I focus on the legislative stage. How do senators behave when there is an official record that notes their behavior? In the subsequent chapters, I then focus on the behind-the-scenes dynamic. Are senators more powerful off stage than on? That is to say, are centrist pivotal players able to invoke more legislative power behind closed doors? I split each section by focusing first on the legislative early game, in which senators lobby and shape legislation, and then focusing on the legislative endgame, or when the senators vote.

3

Floor Action

Proposing Amendments and Speeches

Based on our discussion thus far, moderates face a distinctively precarious political position: they are elected from states that force them to build volatile coalitions. Not surprisingly, these reelection-minded members face political situations that have forced them to adopt survival strategies. Of course, this proves to be problematic for the overall lawmaking process. When presidents and leaders want to pass their landmark proposals, they have to find a way to round up at least some of these moderates to help pass their legislation, making them theoretically and realistically important. Can these legislators translate that importance into real political influence on public policy?

In this chapter, I examine the effects moderates have on legislation. Again, I argue in this chapter that moderates are less policy maximizers than they are electoral survivors in that their drive to preserve their electoral coalition undercuts their drive for policy influence. On salient legislation, instead of exacting control, moderates will instead yield to party leadership and employ various strategies to minimize the damage these bills could do to their electorally precarious coalitions. I will discuss the various activities that legislators take part in on the floor during the legislative game. I then discuss the details of two cases I examine in detail, respectively, focusing on the status quo and the key players. I follow this with an in-depth examination of the congressional behavior of moderates, including their voting and nonvoting behavior on both bills. My results show that moderates do indeed avoid influencing power and instead engage in activities that will lower their traceability on the bill.

Participation in Congress

The process by which the US Senate passes legislation has changed dramatically since the early 1950s. What was once a body that operated mainly in

Life in the Middle. Neilan S. Chaturvedi, Oxford University Press. © Oxford University Press 2021.
DOI: 10.1093/oso/9780197599723.003.0003

committees is now a body that works both in committee action as well as floor action (Sinclair 1989). In his study on Senate legislating, Matthews (1960) demonstrates that the Senate worked under the norms of apprenticeship, legislative work, specialization, and courtesy. Shortly after (Sinclair estimates around the 1970s), a new, more active form of legislating prevailed in which floor activity became the norm. Senators are proposing more amendments on the floor rather than in committee, with a distinct effort to impact either the bill itself or influence fellow party members (Sinclair 1989; 1995; Smith and Flathman 1989). Indeed, Sinclair (2017), in describing a "New World of U.S. Senators," outlines the process as problematic but characteristic of the modern Senate. She writes:

> The offering of many, not necessarily germane, amendments on the floor is a signature characteristic of the individualist Senate. When major bills are considered, dozens of amendments are routinely offered. Budget resolutions frequently see more than forty amendments offered and pushed to a recorded vote; on the FY 2010 budget resolution, there were thirty-eight roll call votes on amendments. The 2009 economic stimulus bill and the 2010 financial services reform bill (Dodd-Frank) were also subject to amending marathons, with twenty-six amendment-related roll calls on the former, twenty-eight on the latter, and many more amendments disposed of without roll calls. (Sinclair 2017, 9)

Richard Hall (1996), in his work examining members' participation in Congress, argues that "Constituency influence, in short, should operate not only on legislators' revealed preferences but on the intensities that they reveal in their decisions about when and to what extent they will participate in particular matters before their chamber" (58). Considering scholarship on lawmaking in the modern Senate, this would suggest that legislators should use some form of early-game congressional participation as an effort to both symbolically and substantively represent their constituents. As a result, I examine two distinct aspects of legislating: the proposing of amendments and floor speeches. Each is significant, although in uniquely separate ways. With the Senate's rules for amending bills reasonably open, amending bills offers senators the opportunity both to shape the bill and to express their position on the policy in question. Similarly, speeches give senators the chance to communicate their position.

As noted, the amendment process has changed rapidly in the US Senate. Already a fairly chaotic process, in which Senate rules allow for any member to offer an amendment to any bill, scholars note that the process has grown increasingly chaotic as minority party members use it as a method to force majority party members into facing difficult votes (Lee 2011). Again, others have found that senators are more than willing to propose amendments to rework policy proposals directly on the floor (Sinclair 1982; 1989). While the majority leader may have some unwieldy tools at his disposal to restrict floor amendments, they are typically far too difficult to use and are seldom exercised (Schiller 2000). Floor amendments in a grander sense are regulated more by informal bargaining and formal unanimous consent agreements (Ainsworth and Flathman 1995).

Certainly, there is an evident proliferation of Senate amendments in the modern era, but it is not without reason. Floor amendments provide utility for senators who choose to exercise them. Eric Schickler and Frances Lee (2011) argue that floor amendments serve three purposes for senators (regardless of party position or status): they allow for individual senators to change pending legislation to fit their preferences, they help senators shape the public's perceptions on the senator's performance and reputation, and they can be used for partisan electoral campaign purposes in which the minority party can critique the majority.

As a result, I use floor amendments to assess the activity level of members of the Senate. If, in fact, a Senator is active and influential, she is likely to, at the very least, propose amendments that would fulfill one of the three goals listed earlier, the most important of which for this study, of course, being changing legislation to fit the preferences of the senator in question.

Still, we should note that floor amendments are not solely used to fulfill one of the goals I have enumerated. Floor amendments can also be used to obstruct legislation or derail the discussion (Davidson et al. 2017). Indeed, moderate senator Claire McCaskill (D-MO) claimed that—Senate Minority Leader Mitch McConnell (R-KY) used the amendment process to make the legislative game more difficult for her. She claimed that "[McConnell was trying] to figure out some way to put something on the floor that would get me to vote against my own mother."[1] While some senators may use the amendment process to affect elections, others may use it to kill legislation altogether. These so-called poison pill amendments are written to render the underlying bill ineffective or unpalatable (Davidson et al. 2017). Republican senator Saxby Chambliss admitted, "the fact of the matter is, too, that we have some folks who are bound and determined to come up with some wild and crazy amendments rather than doing the business we were sent here to do in a very serious way."[2]

As a result, then Senate Majority Leader Harry Reid filled the "amendment tree," in which he limited the number of amendments that could be brought to consideration and left many in the minority unable to successfully have their amendments considered.[3] Still, even though this process limits the number of amendments that can be considered, it does not prevent senators from *submitting* amendments. Indeed, filing amendments puts any amendment that a senator proposes into the *Congressional Record*. In doing so, senators can fulfill two of the three previously mentioned goals by signaling constituents and providing fodder for future campaigns.

In addition to floor amendments, I also examine floor speeches. While less impactful on the legislation itself, floor speeches are not without significant costs and benefits. The benefits of floor speeches are fairly straightforward: they provide senators with the ability to signal constituents and key players in Washington on their policy positions to help clarify and build their reputation (Hill and Hurley 1999). While the activity is certainly symbolic, speeches serve as a form of position-taking not only to clarify but also to gain support among one or more constituency groups (Eulau and Karps 1977; Fenno 1978; Mayhew 1974; Oppenheimer 1974). Furthermore, speeches can also provide policy cues for other senators or even serve to influence them on matters of policy (Cox and McCubbins 1993). Godbout and Yu (2009) also find that minority members of the Senate use speeches to express their displeasure with legislation to signal both party members and their constituents.

Still, while speeches are necessarily beneficial to most senators, they do not come without drawbacks. As Hall (1996) argues, even nominal actions have costs. Speeches made on the floor of the Senate are recorded in the official *Congressional Record* and can be used not only to court constituencies but to alienate them as well. For many senators who are trying to avoid traceability, the notion of making a speech would be reprehensible. Given this, I use speeches to test the Marginalized in the Middle theory. If indeed moderates are powerful, key players, they should influence the agenda by pushing legislation that they favor. Given their placement on the ideological spectrum, moderates are potentially pivotal on each bill. If they are pivotal, we should see actions that signal their legislative power. Table 3.1 outlines the expectations of a powerful senator and a marginalized senator.

Table 3.1. Expectations for Floor Activity for a Powerful Senator and a
Marginalized Senator

Type of Action	Powerful Senator	Marginalized Senator
Proposing Amendments	Moderates will attempt to amend the bill to their liking (unless they are pleased with the bill as is)	Moderates will remain quiet to avoid traceability to the bill regardless of how they feel about the bill
Making Floor Speeches	If they are pleased with the bill, they should speak in favor, if they are displeased, they should speak against	Moderates will remain quiet to avoid traceability to the bill, regardless of how they feel about the bill

The overall goal of moderates, based on their weak electoral coalitions, should be to avoid any attention from their constituents on highly salient bills. While they will inevitably be held responsible for their vote, if they can avoid influencing the early shaping of the bill and its advocacy or opposition for it, they can at least cushion the backlash that they will inevitably receive from their vote.

Congressional Quarterly Key Votes from 2003 to 2013

Popular imagery of the Senate depicts a "Wild West" style legislature, in which any one senator can throw the proverbial wrench into the system by filibustering, using a procedural hold, or proposing an amendment (to name a few methods of delay). However, a look at the bigger picture may suggest that that the Senate is less chaotic, and works in an environment of organized chaos. Figure 3.1 illustrates this basic conclusion, at least about amendments. Examining every *Congressional Quarterly* "key" vote from 2003 to 2013, Figure 3.1 shows that when it comes to amendments, the most active members are not those who are situated in the middle, but those who sit at the poles of their respective ideological persuasions.[4]

Those sitting in the center of the chamber propose fewer amendments than their colleagues. While it might seem notable that conservatives in this figure are proposing more amendments than either moderates or liberals, this is mostly because the Democrats controlled the chamber for three out of the five Congresses examined. With Republicans dissatisfied with the

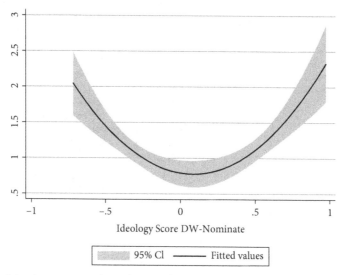

Figure 3.1. Average Number of Amendments Proposed on CQ Key Votes from 2003–2013

overall content of a given bill, it is likely that many took to the floor to offer an amendment either to protest the bill or in an earnest effort to change the bill to their liking.

Still, moderates are proposing fewer amendments than their ideological colleagues. Why is this the case? I hypothesize that senators that are sitting in the middle are those who have built weak electoral coalitions based on the dynamics of their state. Figure 3.2 looks more closely at the statewide constituencies and the consequences that they propose.

On average, senators from partisan-lean and, to a lesser extent, swing states proposed fewer amendments than their counterparts, with two exceptions. In the 110th Congress, swing state senators offered nearly one more amendment on average than either partisan lean-state senators or their other counterparts. Indeed, partisan-lean state senators marginally offered more amendments than others did as well in that session. This may be because the 110th Congress was the first Senate in which the Democrats had an outright majority in the chamber during the Bush administration (the eighteen months after the Jim Jeffords party switch notwithstanding).[5] Even still, it may be the result of the swing state caveat introduced in Chapter 2, in which swing state senators are not taking the marginalized position and are instead acting like their more partisan counterparts. If that is indeed the case,

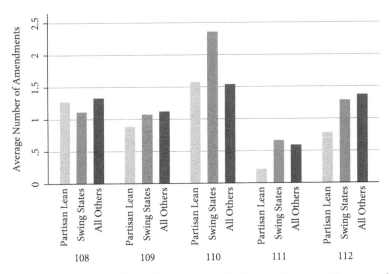

Figure 3.2. Average Number of Amendments by Type of State and Congress for CQ Key Votes from 2003–2013

we should expect to see swing state senators offer more amendments than their partisan-lean state colleagues.

Even when controlling for other variables like the party of the senator, whether they were a leader or not, a committee member or not, and which Congress was being studied, moderates were predicted to file fewer amendments than their more polarized colleagues.[6] Figure 3.3 presents the predicted marginal effects for the number of amendments senators file on these key bills.

As the image indicates, senators at the middle are predicted to file, on average, less than one amendment, though a movement from the middle to the ideological pole yields a change of approximately 1.5 amendments. That is, senators sitting at the ideological pole are predicted to file nearly two more amendments than their moderate colleagues. Most striking, however, is not the difference so much as the overall value of the number of amendments filed by moderates. Indeed, even when controlling for party, leadership, Congress, and committee membership, moderates are predicted to file less than one amendment on key legislation over a ten-year span.

As mentioned, it can sometimes be difficult to generalize among such a large population as well. Around this time, statewide politics was also shifting to match national politics. For example, Robert Byrd, the senior

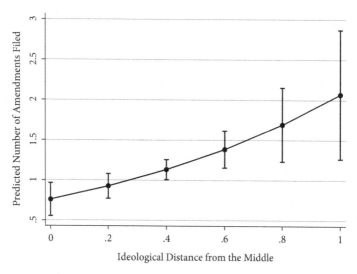

Figure 3.3. Predicted Marginal Effects for the Number of Amendments Senators Filed on CQ Votes from 2003–2013 by their Ideological Distance from the Middle (DW-NOMINATE)

senator from West Virginia, would be labeled as a partisan-lean state senator; however, over much of the period covered here, putting him in the same class as Lincoln Chafee would be a mistake. Byrd spent nearly fifty-one years in the Senate and was a brand that was recognized, despite his partisan and even ideological incompatibility on most issues with his state. So, given the extremes here, it may be more useful to examine this under a more rigorous, empirical look using case studies.

Case Studies

Among a handful of issues that every administration deals with, healthcare is a salient issue that often arises. Every modern president (from Franklin Roosevelt on) has faced some facet of healthcare reform. In their book examining healthcare politics in the White House, Blumenthal and Morone (2010) claim:

The health reform story illuminates almost every aspect of the presidency. Because health care reform is excruciatingly difficult to win, it tests presidents' ideas, heart, luck, allies, and their skill at running the most complicated government machinery in the world. (2)

Indeed, passing healthcare legislation, an issue that divides Democrats and Republicans ideologically as much as any issue, requires not only new policy proposals but also a keen ability to build legislative coalitions large enough to pass landmark legislation. As a result, I examine the two largest healthcare policy proposals in the 2000s era: the Affordable Care Act and the Medicare Modernization Act.

I first examine the Affordable Care Act, President Barack Obama's landmark legislative victory of his first term. It squares well as a case study for this theory, as the Obama administration, faced with extreme opposition from the Republican minority in the Senate, had a short window to corral sixty Democrats to vote for cloture to vote on the bill. If moderates are the pivotal players, then President Obama and the Democratic leadership would be utterly reliant on a handful of moderate Democrats who would settle their fate. Indeed, the small number of remaining moderate Republicans could also provide the pivotal votes to overcome a filibuster by opponents of healthcare reform.[7]

I then move on to the Medicare Prescription Drug Improvement and Modernization Act (referred to hereafter as the Medicare Modernization Act). While certainly not as comprehensive as the Affordable Care Act, the Medicare Modernization Act was still a salient and high-profile bill. Until the Affordable Care Act, the Medicare Modernization Act was the single largest reform to Medicare in its thirty-eight-year history. The situation surrounding the Medicare Modernization Act differs from that of the Affordable Care Act due to the legislative environment surrounding the issue. Unlike the Affordable Care Act, in which Obama and the Democratic leadership reached out mostly to Democrats and a small handful of Republicans, here, the George W. Bush administration could ill afford to ignore Democrats with their slim 51–49 majority in the Senate.

The Affordable Care Act

In 2009, after his path-defining victory to the White House, Barack Obama set his sights on two pieces of legislation that he promised on the campaign trail: economic stimulus and healthcare reform. Winning 54 percent of the popular vote, and having 236 Democrats in the House of Representatives and 58 Democrats in the Senate(including two independents caucusing with the Democrats), Obama's new administration was primed to pass sweeping healthcare reform (Beaussier 2012). Still, Democrats in the Senate were two votes short of the sixty-vote majority needed to invoke cloture and get past any Republican filibusters. This situation changed, however, when Al Franken was declared the winner of his Senate race in Minnesota (on July 7, 2009) and Arlen Specter switched parties, and signaled he would join in the cloture vote.

Still, the road to reform was not easily paved, with public support for sweeping healthcare reform at 55 percent in the summer of 2009, which was the highest percentage it would ever reach (Blumenthal and Morone 2010). After months of negotiations, proposals, and campaigning, House Democrats passed a version of the national health reform bill 220–215. The Senate Democrats, however, lost their sixtieth vote when liberal stalwart Ted Kennedy succumbed to cancer. While the Democratic leadership briefly considered courting moderate Republican Olympia Snowe, they quickly determined that this would be fruitless, as the Republican leadership was already pressuring her to vote with them (Blumenthal and Morone 2010). Foreshadowing the argument that moderates are beholden to their elec-toral circumstances, the Democratic leadership opted to wait for Kennedy's temporary replacement to be named to regain the sixty-seat majority while whipping the other fifty-nine members of their caucus in place, instead of courting other centrist Republicans. While it took significant concessions (Joe Lieberman I-CT forced the leadership to drop the public option), the leadership was able to maintain a coalition long enough to end the Republican filibuster and pass their version of healthcare reform.

Overall, this case provides an example of an incredibly salient piece of leg-islation that was heavily debated and talked about by members of Congress, Washington insiders, and the media. If we are to see the theoretical influence of moderates in play, it should be plain to find in this legislation, in which the Democratic leadership had to yield to moderate Democrats to gain their sup-port on the legislation. Furthermore, once on board, moderate Democrats, according to the theory, should make speeches to support the legislation, as they find the bill suitable or the bill should have sufficiently changed been to their liking. In the following sections, however, I demonstrate that this is anything but the case. Moderates viewed this piece of legislation as a poison pill that could not be amended in a fashion to their liking. Nevertheless, they voted for the legislation and supported their party and president. Of course, this lines up with what I theorized in Chapter 2, so first, I will briefly lay the background for the empirical examination.

The Status Quo

Despite its importance for predicting coalitions and strategies for legislative success, political scientists have struggled to locate the status quo *ex-ante* (Beckmann 2009; Smith 2007). As a result, we must instead look at the environment and voting coalitions *ex-post* to estimate with any accuracy where on a given issue the status quo lies.

We can, of course, estimate with some certainty that the status quo before the Affordable Care Act was conservative, if not very conservative. This is not to say that conservatives did not have preferences for healthcare reform outside of whatever the status quo was, but simply that the status quo on healthcare policy reflected the conservative ideal of limited government involvement. Simply looking at the voting coalition that passed the reform, no Republicans voted for the bill in either the House or Senate. Observers would argue, however, that this unified opposition was less about ideology and more about partisan politics, as the bill mirrored reform efforts by Republicans in the early 1990s as well as the Republican state healthcare plan instituted by then Governor Mitt Romney in Massachusetts.[8] Even still, there is evidence to suggest a very conservative status quo.

Evaluating the US healthcare system from a comparative perspective, Wilensky (2009) argues that among nineteen wealthy democracies, the United States is the "odd man out" because of its lack a national healthcare system, large private sector, and lack of government regulation over the use of costly procedures that yield few benefits. That is to say, the United States lacks government involvement to regulate costs and provide insurance for the uninsured.

Turning to domestic politics, the Congressional Budget Office estimated that 55 million Americans were without healthcare coverage due to the cost of coverage, immigration status, or by their own accord. This put much of the burden of the costs of healthcare for the uninsured upon taxpayers. Furthermore, by forgoing the liability of the uninsured, a problem that would require either a mandate or universal coverage, and by extension, a great deal of government involvement, there were no regulations in effect that would prevent health insurance companies from denying coverage to those with pre-existing conditions or those with high risks of disease. This in itself moves the status quo to an even more extreme point, as many Republicans voiced support for the so-called patient's bill of rights (Dickerson and Waller 2001).

Theoretically, this would indeed be the time that the Democratic president would have the most leverage to push healthcare policy to their preferred position. That is, with a unified government, the Obama administration would have the most leverage at this moment in time to push for its preferred policy, as the gridlock interval would be relatively small. Still, in terms of making *ex-post* predictions as to the effect of this status quo on congressional leadership and centrist legislators, the Democratic leadership preferred a liberal if not much more liberal alternative. Many centrist legislators were torn, however, between moving the status quo to the middle, where popular proposals like the patient's bill of rights sat, or leaving it at the extreme so as to not anger core constituents who preferred little government intrusion. To examine this further, let us first look at the key players, or at least the theoretically key players, who were involved in the passage of the Affordable Care Act.

The Key Players

As noted, the 111th Congress was composed of a majority of Democrats in both the House and the Senate. Figure 3.4 illustrates the ideological distribution of senators for this session. The Democrats used the short window in which they had sixty votes in their party to pass the reform bill, but at multiple points, it seemed as though they would not have the votes needed to break the Republican filibuster.

For Obama, pushing his agenda in the Senate should, in theory, be eased by the presence of Harry Reid as the Senate majority leader. Ideologically, the two are almost marching lockstep. However, even with a large number of Democrats, Obama and Reid had to appease all of them in some form. Indeed, while most of the Democratic caucus is centered toward the middle of the liberal ideology, Obama and Reid had a handful of moderates who would likely view the Affordable Care Act as a difficult vote. Even still, they had few, if any, Republicans to work with, as the number of moderate

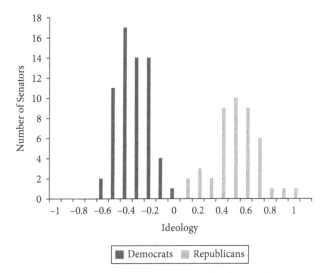

Figure 3.4. Ideological Distribution of Senators for the 111th Congress (2009–2011)

Republicans was few and there were no potential crossover Republicans (i.e., there were no Republicans who were more liberal than the most conservative Democrat). As such, following the theoretical framework of the Pivotal Politics model, Obama and Reid must appease a few key players with little room to deviate. These players are listed in Table 3.2.

While the leadership certainly had to appeal to their entire caucus, few if any that were sitting in the middle were making a clear distinction in what they needed to vote yes. Furthermore, the Democratic caucus was far from homogeneous ideologically. To view it in spatial voting terms, the senators who sat from the fifty-first vote to the fifty-fourth vote, or between Michael Bennett and Mary Landrieu, were separated only nominally regarding ideology. However, by the fifty-fifth vote, or Mark Pryor, the Democratic caucus becomes much more conservative, according to Poole and Rosenthal's DW-NOMINATE scores. Still, as they kept their silence, the leadership remained fairly confident they could win a cloture vote if they could win over Ben Nelson, the proverbial sixtieth vote.

Seemingly the leadership had little other recourse than to appease Nelson. As mentioned, the Democratic leadership did consider courting Susan Collins as the sixtieth vote but quickly backed away as they realized that the

Table 3.2. Key Players for the Affordable Care Act and Their Ideological Positions

Players	DW-NOMINATE Score	Distance from the President
The President		
Barack Obama	−.42	–
The Senate Leadership		
Harry Reid (Majority Leader)	−.40	.02
Mitch McConnell (Minority Leader)	.51	.93
Pivotal Voters		
Michael Bennett (D-CO) 51st	−.25	.17
Ben Nelson (D-NE) 60th	−.03	.39
Senators between the Pivots		
Kay Hagan (D-NC) 52nd	−.24	.18
Mary Landrieu (D-LA) 53rd	−.24	.18
Mark Pryor (D-AR) 54th	−.22	.2
Claire McCaskill (D-MO) 55th	−.21	.21
Jim Webb (D-VA) 56th	−.21	.21
Max Baucus (D-MT) 57th	−.19	.23
Blanche Lincoln (D-AR) 58th	−.163	.256
Evan Bayh (D-IN) 59th	−.11	.309
Potential Replacements to 60th Vote		
Susan Collins (R-ME) 61st	.04	.46
Olympia Snowe (R-ME) 62nd	.04	.46
George Voinovich (R-OH) 63rd	.11	.53
Lisa Murkowski (R-AK) 64th	.20	.62
Richard Lugar (R-IN) 65th	.31	.73

Republican Party leadership was pressuring her to vote no. While the prospect of a senator backing down to party pressure makes practical sense, theoretically, this makes less sense. Legislators in the middle should be clamoring to be the pivotal vote because this would mean that on an important matter of public policy they would get their preferences met. None of the five Republican alternatives to the sixtieth vote listed in Table 3.2 attempted to garner much attention from the Democratic leadership or the president. Indeed, the feeling seemed to be mutual, as the leadership put all of its eggs into its own caucus's basket.

Already, this is counter to the conventional wisdom on Senate politics. The administration and party leadership should have had a plethora of options to leave Nelson behind. Of course, theoretically, they would have had to appease the ideological desires of any replacement. For example, to gain the vote of either Collins or Snowe, the leadership would have had to make the bill more conservative. Furthermore, theoretically, Collins and Snowe, and for that matter, any other Republican who could conceivably replace Nelson should embrace being a part of the process as this allows them to pass public policy that fits their preferences and to claim credit for moderating an otherwise partisan bill. Snowe, Collins, or even Voinovich, representing the swing state of Ohio, could reap benefits from constituents who would prefer a more comprehensive healthcare bill. But all three players remained on the sidelines throughout the debate. Still, this is too much of a cursory assessment. A more systematic assessment using measures of legislative participation could help in gaining traction to answer the question at hand.

Committee Work

One possible way in which moderates may have been able to have an impact is through committee work. The two Senate committees tasked with writing and marking up the bill were the Senate Health, Education, Labor, and Pension Committee (HELP), and the Finance Committee. The HELP Committee initial draft was record on June 9, 2009, and the committee markup of the bill occurred between June 17 and July 14 of that year. Unfortunately, the HELP Committee's draft did not have a markup report that allows us to look at how senators on the committee behaved.

The Finance Committee, however, did release and continue to maintain records on the markup report for their version of the bill. The committee also received a large share of media attention with the first conversations held between a "Group of Six": three Democrats, Max Baucus (MT), Jeff Bingaman (NM), and Kent Conrad (ND); and three Republicans, Mike Enzi (WY), Charles Grassley (IA), and Olympia Snowe (ME). The Group of Six was tasked with negotiating the Finance Committee's version of the bill but ultimately could not reach an agreement (Cannan 2013). With the group unable to come up with its own bill, Baucus proposed his own draft on September 16, following an address before a joint session of Congress by President Obama on September 9. The Finance Committee's markup began on September 22, considering in total 564 amendments.[9]

The Finance Committee of the 111th Congress was composed of Max Baucus as the chair (D-MT), with Democrats John ("Jay") Rockefeller IV (WV), Kent Conrad (ND), Jeff Bingaman (NM), John Kerry (MA), Blanche Lincoln (AR), Ron Wyden (OR), Charles Schumer (NY), Debbie Stabenow (MI), Maria Cantwell (WA), Bill Nelson (FL), Robert Menendez (NJ), and Thomas Carper (DE), and Republicans Charles Grassley (IA), Orrin Hatch (UT), Olympia Snowe (ME), Jon Kyl (AZ), Jim Bunning (KY), Mike Crapo (ID), Pat Roberts (KS), John Ensign (NV), Michael Enzi (WY), and John Cornyn (TX). Of particular interest here are the moderates on the committee, Blanche Lincoln of Arkansas and Olympia Snowe of Maine, both listed in the previous table as either key players, or potentially key to the passage of the bill.[10] If moderates are indeed powerful, these four in particular should be especially powerful as they sit on the Finance Committee that was tasked with forming this legislation. Table 3.3 lists the number of amendments proposed and passed by each member of the committee.

At first glance, the two moderates on the committee seem like outliers, although Snowe appears to be much more of an outlier than Lincoln. For the Democrats, Stabenow and Rockefeller each proposed the most of the group at twelve apiece, though Menendez proposed eleven and Kerry ten. For the Republicans, we see many more amendments proposed, though this is likely a sign of their overall displeasure with the bill. For the most part, with the exception of Grassley and Hatch, no other Republican had more than two amendments passed (with most having passed zero amendments). Snowe, however, proposed and passed three amendments. The relatively few number of amendments proposed suggests that either Snowe was avoiding participation on the record or that she was displaying a general happiness with the content of the bill. Furthermore, her success rate in having passed all her amendments suggests that Snowe's proposals were either seen as reasonable by her Democratic colleagues (or enough to gain a majority vote) or viewed as necessary to gain her vote.

Still, Snowe's voting record on the amendments suggest that she was far more willing to vote with her Republican colleagues, suggesting

Table 3.3. Number of Amendments Proposed and Passed by Each Committee Member during Committee Markup of the ACA

Committee Member	Number of Amendments Proposed in Markup	Number of Amendments Passed in Markup
Democrats		
Max Baucus	3	3
John Rockefeller IV	12	5
Kent Conrad	2	2
Jeff Bingaman	4	2
John Kerry	10	3
Ron Wyden	6	4
Charles Schumer	9	4
Debbie Stabenow	12	9
Maria Cantwell	4	2
Bill Nelson	5	3
Robert Menendez	11	7
Thomas Carper	3	3
Republicans		
Charles Grassley	12	5
Orrin Hatch	15	4
Jon Kyl	16	0
Jim Bunning	9	2
Mike Crapo	7	0
Pat Roberts	11	0
John Ensign	12	2
Michael Enzi	8	2
John Cornyn	18	0
Key Moderates		
Blanche Lincoln	7	3
Olympia Snowe	3	3

similar displeasure with the bill. Among seventy-three recorded votes on the amendments, Snowe voted with her party forty-three times. That is almost equally divided, yet it still suggests that she was not completely satisfied with the bill. Indeed, while she voted in favor of moving the bill out of committee, she was pressured enough to vote against a very similar version of the bill when it hit the floor. Blanche Lincoln, by comparison, voted with her party sixty-nine out of seventy-seven times, defecting only eight times. Still, these are only two moderates. Indeed, an analysis of the floor action will go on to demonstrate just how effective moderates were in shaping their bill on the floor and beyond committee action.

Legislative Floor Action: Proposing Amendments

The amendment process is an incredibly important form of participation, even if the amendments ultimately fail to pass. Indeed, one of the major goals in amending legislation is to shape the legislation to one's personal preferences, but for many senators, this may not be the end goal. For some, it may be to influence voters as a signal of their actual position on the issue.

In this section, I examine who proposed amendments to the Affordable Care Act. Using the official *Congressional Record*, I examine every amendment proposed, regardless of passage, during the debate on the bill. I then aggregate the number of amendments per senator. Here, I am less concerned with the actual content of the amendment than I am the overall act of proposing an amendment. The reason for this is that to offer an amendment suggests a desire to impact the policy proposal through substance or through debate. However, by not offering an amendment, this suggests that the senator is either pleased with the bill in its current form, or has little interest in making an impact on the policy itself. Figure 3.5 illustrates the number of proposed amendments by ideology, here calculated as the DW-NOMINATE measure.

This first, bivariate analysis of the data suggests that those in the middle are less likely to propose an amendment. What seems more likely is that partisans of both sides propose more amendments. Furthermore, although the bounds are fairly spread out, conservatives seem to be much more likely to propose amendments than moderates or liberals, though again, both liberals and conservatives sponsored more amendments. The best explanation for this is that Republicans were likely either trying to influence the bill, or (perhaps more likely in a partisan environment) attempting to force Democrats into difficult votes by proposing ideologically polarizing amendments in an effort to use their vote against them in future elections (see again the discussion on poison pill amendments). Even still, they may be using the process to signal voters of their displeasure with the bill and their efforts to reform the legislation.[11]

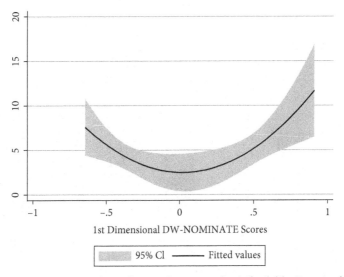

Figure 3.5. Average Number of Amendments to the Affordable Care Act by Ideology

Most important here is that the senators who should be theoretically proposing the most amendments are notably not doing so. Moderates are exhibiting surprising restraint in their amendment activity. Indeed, the senators who should be theoretically pivotal are not exhibiting typical behavior with the proposal of amendments. Figure 3.6 demonstrates the average number of amendments by pivot position. When we look specifically at the senators closest to the median pivot, or the forty-fifth to the fifty-fourth senator, and the senators that are closest to the filibuster pivot, or the fifty-fifth to the sixty-fourth senator, we see similar results.

Figure 3.6 illustrates that the theoretically most important players in this particular legislative game, the senators sitting closest to the filibuster pivot, were the ones who were least active in their proposals of amendments. While the senators sitting closest to the median pivot were more active, they were not the pivotal members for this particular bill, as the Republican leadership had threatened a filibuster long before the bill hit the Senate floor. The most active senators were the Republican leadership, followed by Republican and Democratic rank-and-file senators, and then the senators closest to the median pivot. Even still, this is a relatively conservative estimate as I look at the top ten senators closest to the median pivot and filibuster pivot, respectively.

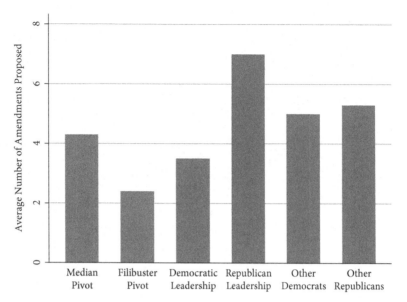

Figure 3.6. Average Number of Amendments Proposed to the ACA by Position of Power

As Table 3.2 demonstrates, these ten senators are not necessarily close to each other ideologically.

To examine this in more depth, I run a negative binomial regression predicting the number of amendments a senator proposes. To measure the effect of ideology, I construct a variable that measures the distance from the ideological center by taking the absolute value of the senator's ideology, thus constructing a measure that measures the distance from "0," or the center of the DW-NOMINATE scale.

As others have pointed out, often congressional participation can boil down to a partisan battle (see, for example, Lee 2009), so I again control for partisanship by including a dummy variable in which senators that are Republicans receive a code of "1" while Democrats receive a code of "0." I then interact the term with the distance from the middle variable, creating an ideological measure for Republicans (the interaction term "Distance Middle X Republican") and Democrats (the original "Distance from the Middle" variable).

Also, as I have mentioned, party leaders may use early game politicking as a means to influence and protect their party and its members, so I include a control variable for party leaders. Finally, I likewise control for committee members who sat on the Finance Committee, as many may seek to influence the policy after the committee meetings because they are policy specialists and likely care a great deal about the policy itself. The results of this regression are presented in Table 3.4.

The results of the negative binomial regression largely confirm the initial conclusion of the descriptive results, at least for Democrats: ideologically polarized senators are much more likely to propose amendments than moderate senators, even when controlling for leadership, and committee members. That is to say, the further the Democratic senator is from the ideological center, the more amendments they are likely to propose. Indeed, the interaction term measuring ideology for Republicans is insignificant, suggesting that there is no statistical relationship between ideology and the number of amendments proposed for Republicans. This, of course, should not be surprising. Since even moderate Republicans were out of play for the Democratic leadership, we should not expect to see anything distinguishable between centrist and extreme Republicans. However, if centrist Democrats

Table 3.4. Number of Amendments Proposed on the ACA, by DW-NOMINATE Score (Negative Binomial Regression Results)

	Model 1		Model 2	
	Coefficient	Standard Error	Coefficient	Standard Error
Distance from the Middle (DW-NOMINATE)	2.07*	1.14	1.97*	1.15
Republican	.12	.63	.3	.7
Party Leader	.18	.52	.23	.53
Committee Member	.67**	.25	.27	.71
Distance from the Middle X Republican	1.35	.85	−1.15	1.59
Distance from the Middle X Committee Member			.9	1.52
Constant	.55	.36	.60	.47
Log Likelihood	−258.95641		−258.78158	
N=	100		100	
Pseudo R-Squared	.03		.03	

*P<.1, **P<.05

were pivotal, then we should see a negative relationship, in which moderate Democrats propose more amendments to legislation than their more polarized counterparts.

To be specific, I calculate the expected number of amendments proposed when the value of the distance from the middle is moved from the minimum value to the maximum value. For senators who are neither leaders nor committee members, and are Democrats, the expected number of amendments proposed increases by approximately nine amendments when changing the ideology variable from the minimum to the maximum. This is, of course, a non-trivial amount. Figure 3.7 illustrates this relationship.[12]

These results indicate that moderates were, as hypothesized, less likely to propose amendments than their more ideological counterparts. Interestingly, the difference between Republicans and leaders and their peers was not statistically significant. However, committee members continued to propose amendments, suggesting that policy specialists who care about the legislation continue to affect their proposals through the lawmaking process. Again, of interest is that moderates proposed approximately three amendments on average, compared to their just slightly more ideological colleagues (i.e., those who were within .4 units away from the center), who were predicted to propose approximately seven amendments. This suggests that there is a real behavioral difference.

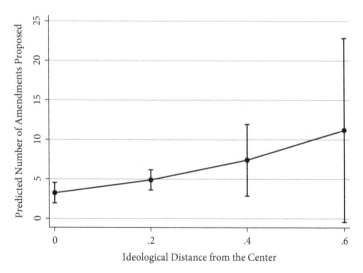

Figure 3.7. Predictive Margins for Number of Amendments Proposed to the ACA by Democrats, with 95% Confidence Intervals

Table 3.5. Number of Amendments Proposed to the ACA, by Pivot Position (Negative Binomial Regression Results)

	Coefficient	Standard Error
Median Pivot	.07	.36
Filibuster Pivot	−.86**	.38
Party Leader	.28	.53
Committee Member	.77**	.25
Republican	−.009	.23
Constant	1.38**	.20
Log Likelihood	−259.46212	
N=	100	
Pseudo R-Squared	.03	

*P<.1, **P<.05, ***P<.01

One possible explanation could be that some of the behavioral differences are being caught in the committee member variable. That is, committees may have a larger number of moderates on them due to their essential role in the legislative game (see, for example, Shepsle and Weingast 1987). I test this alternative explanation by interacting the committee member term with the distance from the middle term and present the results in Table 3.4. Here we see that this is not the case, as the interactive term is not statistically significant. This suggests that even when on committees, moderates still shy away from proposing amendments on the floor.

Even looking specifically at the pivot positions, we see similar results in a multivariate analysis. Table 3.5 shows the results of a negative binomial regression for the specific pivot positions.

Again, the pivotal position for this piece of legislation was the filibuster pivot, where we should see those senators closest to that position offering more not less regarding amendments or efforts to change the bill to their liking. However, compared to their colleagues, the senators sitting near the filibuster pivot offered fewer amendments on average.

Why is this the case? Figure 3.8 maps out the number of amendments proposed to the Affordable Care Act by Democrats by their ideological distance from the middle and what type of state they represent using the typology from Chapter 2. While there is a great deal of variation among all three types of states, the ideologically moderate Democrats, who incidentally also

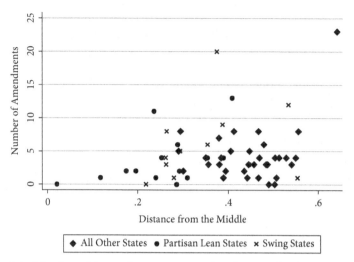

Figure 3.8. Number of Amendments Proposed to the ACA by the Senator's Ideological Distance from the Middle

proposed the fewest amendments, all represented either partisan-lean states or swing states. This finding, of course, suggests that the cross-pressures that are unequally applied to these senators vis-à-vis their more polarized counterparts affect their behavior in the chamber.

Still, while certainly persuasive, this evidence may suggest one of two possibilities. It may suggest that moderates are, in fact, less powerful than theoretically proposed, or that backroom deals and the early shaping of the bill were satisfactory for moderates, allowing them to avoid the amendment process altogether. If this is true, then we should see moderates partake in another form of congressional participation: speech-making. That is, we should see moderates pushing their legislative accomplishments on the Senate floor.

Legislative Floor Action: Proposing Speeches

While certainly different in substance from amendments, speeches afford senators the opportunity to make clear their thoughts and presumptions on legislation. Speeches provide them an opportunity to make clear their position to their colleagues as well as to their constituents. Of course, since these speeches are officially transcribed in the *Congressional Record*, they can serve as a double-edged sword of sorts, as their signaling may induce negative reactions among some of their constituents, which would trigger strong electoral opposition. Also, it could provide campaign material for the incumbent but could backfire as well in the form of campaign fodder for their opponent's negative advertising.

As a result, if moderates are as hamstrung as I hypothesize, they should avoid any attachment to the bill, as having roots in the bill could anger the volatile electoral coalitions they have built. Still, speeches are a powerful tool that should not be undermined, as they do provide information on political positions for voters and other members of Congress.

As with the amendments, I again compiled a dataset from the congressional record of the number of speeches each senator made. Here I am concerned both with the number of speeches made as well as the content of the speech, as, again, I am concerned not only with the action of making a speech but also whether moderate senators took a clear position when making the speech. Figure 3.9 provides another descriptive cut of the data.

As with the amendment data, again, it seems that moderates were less likely to make speeches on the Affordable Care Act than their more ideological counterparts. Different from the amendment data presented earlier, however, is that conservatives gave many more speeches than both moderates and liberals (though liberals still gave more speeches than moderates did).

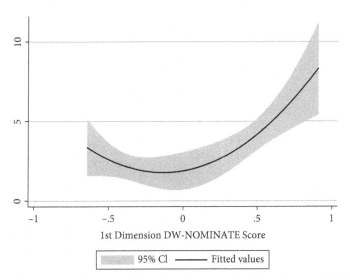

Figure 3.9. Average Number of Speeches Made on the Floor for the ACA, by ideology

This is likely because conservatives wanted to clearly express their displeasure with the bill. It could also be because more conservative members may have been attempting to not only take a position with their constituents but to sway public opinion to ultimately kill the bill entirely. For liberals, they likely spoke out in favor or defense of the bill.

Again, this seems to suggest that moderates are only questionably pivotal in the Senate. If indeed the assumptions made about proposing amendments were wrong, and backroom politicking prevailed, the expectation should be that moderates should not only push the legislation, but they should take credit for it as well. One of the best ways to do this would be to go to the floor of the chamber and make this clear.

Figure 3.10 looks specifically at the pivot positions and finds that both pivot positions were inactive in their speech activity on the floor of the Senate. Indeed, the leadership of both parties was most active, but both pivot positions participated less than backbencher Democrats and Republicans. This likely reflects an effort by the leadership to shield their members from having to publicly support or oppose the legislation, but even still, both Democrats and especially Republicans spoke up when compared against the senators who sit closest to the median and filibuster pivot positions.

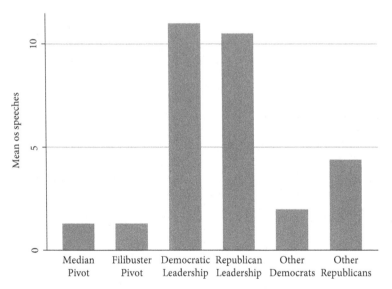

Figure 3.10. Average Number of Speeches Made on the Floor for the ACA, by Pivot Position

Table 3.6. Number of Speeches on the ACA Made, by DW-NOMINATE Score (Negative Binomial Regression Results)

	Coefficient	Standard Error
Distance from the Middle (DW-NOMINATE)	2.0*	1.07
Republican	.56	.63
Party Leader	1.40**	.39
Committee Member	.44**	.22
Distance Middle X Republican	−.22	1.38
Constant	.27	.35
Log Likelihood	−207.42594	
N=	100	
Pseudo R-Squared	.08	

*P<.1, **P<.05, ***P<.01

I again examine this more in depth by running another negative binomial regression that allows us to control for more variables, this time predicting the number of speeches made. I use the same control measures that I used in the previous model. The results of this regression are presented in Table 3.6.

Again, the results confirm the descriptive presentation of the data. As with proposing amendments, the further a Democratic senator is from the ideological center, the more speeches that senator will make, even when controlling for partisanship, leadership, and committee membership. Again, the ideological distance from the center had no statistically significant relationship with the number of speeches made by Republican senators, demonstrating that, as with the amendments, it was Democrats, and specifically centrist Democrats, who were in vulnerable, cross-pressured positions. Since the Democrats were in the majority and the legislation was fueled by the Democratic leadership and President Obama, it then makes sense that centrist Democrats choose to marginalize their power, as the attention is mostly on them rather than their Republican colleagues. For a standard Democrat who is neither a party leader nor a committee member, the number of speeches made on the floor of the Senate increases by approximately eight when the distance from the middle is changed from the minimum value to the maximum value. Figure 3.11 illustrates this relationship. The relationship here is much "flatter," in that it takes much more movement on the ideological

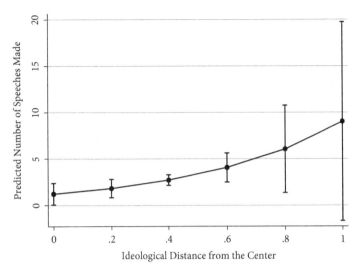

Figure 3.11. Predictive Margins for the Number of Speeches Made on the ACA, by Democrats

spectrum to increase the number of speeches offered. Again, the value of interest is that moderates on average are offering nearly zero speeches on the Affordable Care Act.

Interestingly, with speeches, Democrats were predicted to make fewer speeches than Republicans. Again, this is likely because of the strong opposition the Republicans put up to the healthcare bill itself rather than a matter of swaying opinion or position taking. Also, party leaders were likely to make more speeches than non-party leaders. This is also likely to provide other party members with cover to either vote for or against the bill. In fact, it may be an example of cartelization in the Senate in which party members are deferring to their leadership to provide not only guidance but a public image for the party platform (see Cox and McCubbins 1993; 2004). Also, committee members were also likely to speak more on the bill, probably to push the work that they did in committee, or to fight against the work that they were unable to complete. Table 3.7 demonstrates the results of a negative binomial regression for the number of speeches made by pivot position. When we zero in on the senators who are closest to the pivot positions, just as with the amendments, we again see that those senators sitting closest to the filibuster pivot were silent. This suggests that those senators who are vital to the passage of key legislation

Table 3.7. Number of Speeches Made on the ACA, by Pivot Position (Negative Binomial Regression Results)

	Coefficient	Standard Error
Median Pivot	−.47	.38
Filibuster Pivot	−.85**	.37
Republican	.52**	.19
Party leader	1.47**	.39
Committee Member	.53**	.22
Constant	.67**	.15
Log Likelihood	−207.23651	
N=	100	
Pseudo R-Squared	.08	

*P<.1, **P<.05

are less interested in pushing the agenda than they are avoiding it altogether. Indeed, Republicans, party leaders, and committee members were all predicted to have delivered more speeches than those senators closest to the filibuster pivot.

Looking again at Figures 3.9 and 3.10, while ideologues made more speeches than moderates, moderates did make speeches. While few and far between, it is important to examine the content of the speeches made—after all, if only a handful of them proved to be pivotal, then perhaps only a handful of them would make a speech for or against the bill. However, if moderates are weak, we should see them employ a strategy outlined in Chapter 2. Table 3.8 examines the content of the five moderates who made speeches.

When moderates did make speeches—and of the fifteen possible moderates listed in Table 3.2, only five did—none of them made a speech that was in clear support or opposition to the bill. Returning to language from Chapter 2, these senators chose strategies that would detract from the traceability of their position on the legislation. Each of them chose to find a way to either *demur*, or talk about the bill without making it clear how they would vote (Voinovich), or to *delay* and make references to changes that they wanted without any specifics (Lincoln and Bill Nelson). Landrieu *delegated* her authority to her party and chose to simply talk about supporting the president and the need for healthcare reform despite having her objections to the bill.

Table 3.8. Types of Speeches Moderates Gave for Affordable Care Act

	Support	Opposition	Delay	Delegate	Demur	Distract
Ben Nelson (D)	–	–	–	–	–	2
George Voinovich (R)	–	–	–	–	1	–
Blanche Lincoln (D)	–	–	1	–	–	–
Mary Landrieu (D)	–	–	–	1	–	–
Bill Nelson (D)	–	–	1	–	–	–

Ben Nelson, the pivotal sixtieth vote, was in a much more difficult position, as media attention focused primarily on his vote. As a result, Nelson *distracted* voters by focusing on the parts of the bill that he supported while acknowledging the elements of the bill that he did not support. There is, of course, the logic behind each of these strategies. For Voinovich and Bill Nelson, the costs of the bill were clear—states would have to expand their Medicaid coverage to a larger group of people, a cost that many "big state" governors were wary of being able to cover. Given that their costs were clearer than others, they had to choose a strategy that would afford them time by not giving a clear position on the legislation. Blanche Lincoln, already under fire from the left and the right in her home state and preparing for reelection, also had to use a strategy that would afford her the most time to decide on how to vote, while simultaneously avoiding much attention. For Landrieu and Ben Nelson, both were able to win over some policy concessions despite losing ground in other ways. As a result, both senators had to employ a strategy that would make clear their reasoning for voting for the legislation but also signaling that they had reservations with the bill itself.

While many of these senators went on to make speeches supporting or opposing once the legislation had been voted on, before the vote took place, if moderate senators were making speeches, it was to give themselves cover and deniability rather than pushing the legislation one way or another.

Side Negotiations versus Policy Outcomes: A Case against Pivotal Moderates

As I have mentioned (and will continue to discuss), understanding the true influence of individual senators is an incredibly difficult aspect of lawmaking to ascertain. Thus far, I have used proxies like the amendment process and speech-making to demonstrate that on this particular legislation, moderates shied away from the process. Still, the case could be made that behind-the-scenes politicking and backroom negotiations could have played a more significant role in the legislative process than what I have examined here. For example, it could be argued that much of the end result of the debate of the bill was actually favorable for moderates, indicating a legislative victory for the collective group. This is difficult to say with much certainty, however. Many of the more liberal proposals such as the public option and the option to buy into Medicare were dropped due to opposition from Senator Joe Lieberman (I-CT) (see Cannan 2013). As mentioned, while Lieberman is often viewed in the aggregate as a moderate, this is mostly due to his conservative voting record on foreign policy and liberal voting record on domestic policy. Here, he took a more moderate, if not conservative, position due to the overwhelming presence of the healthcare industry in his state. Furthermore, Committee hearing transcripts suggest that, at least at first, some of the efforts to moderate the bill were an effort to gain Republican votes to pass a bipartisan bill. For example, lamenting ranking member Charles Grassley's comments on the breakdown of bipartisan negotiations, Kent Conrad argues:

> The fact is that many things that Republicans wanted to see left out of this have been left out. There is no public option. There is no employer mandate. There is tax reform to go after Cadillac plans to reduce overutilization. There is clear language to prevent those who are here illegally from benefiting from these initiatives. There is also a clear directive to prevent Federal funding from being used to fund abortion. There is also clear language to encourage medical malpractice reform in the States.[13]

Indeed, my interviews with retired senators suggest that there was quite a bit of negotiation that occurred behind the scenes. Still, the story does not indicate that moderates can negotiate payouts or move policy. For example, when I asked former senator Mary Landrieu about the so-called Louisiana Purchase, an amendment to the Affordable Care Act that gave allegedly gave Louisiana an extra $700 million for Medicaid in exchange for her vote, Landrieu denied this storyline as patently false. Landrieu described the situation differently:

> [Then] Governor Bobby Jindal called the entire Congressional delegation into his office and described the budget shortfall on Medicaid that the state

would experience as a result of insurance payouts for [Hurricane] Katrina. He asked the entire delegation to lobby the federal government to get this money. Since I was in the majority, I called Senator Reid [the majority leader] and asked if [the healthcare bill] would be an excellent place to put this amendment. He obliged.

Of course, after scrutiny from Republicans and the media, including Republicans in Louisiana like Bobby Jindal, Reid, and the leadership removed the amendment from the bill.

So was Landrieu able to move policy? Perhaps. According to Landrieu, she was able to negotiate into the bill a provision that allowed adults under twenty-six to be covered under Medicaid if they were previously under foster care, as they would not have parents who could provide coverage for them otherwise. While certainly not a small provision (the addition did cover a portion of the population that is often overlooked), the provision moved the bill to *the left* rather than to *the center*. Even still, the provision got little attention and yielded few, if any, electoral benefits for Landrieu. Furthermore, the payoff was not policy-oriented so much as it was oriented toward her state. That is to say, at best, Landrieu's concession was not a policy concession, but rather a side negotiation on a payout for her state.

Indeed, this lack of influence by potentially pivotal voters is not unique. Another potentially pivotal moderate Democrat, Mark Pryor (D-AR), said that the leadership never "doubted his vote."

Medicare Modernization Act

The Medicare Prescription Drug, Improvement, and Modernization Act (2003), while still covering healthcare and, for that matter, a very salient issue in healthcare, was much less controversial than the Affordable Care Act. Still, it was a bill that required broad support for its passage, as the Democratic minority was largely opposed to many aspects of the bill. Again, it provides a robust test of the power dynamics in the Senate, as the bill mathematically requires party leadership to reach to moderates in both their party as well as the opposition.

After he was inaugurated in 2001, Republican president George W. Bush sought to reform Medicare by incorporating aspects of free market competition and private insurance into the largely government-run program for prescription drug coverage whereby those who could afford it could purchase more comprehensive plans while more destitute seniors would be assisted by the government (Pear 2002). Democrats saw this as an attack on the notion of equality that was inherent in the program since its founding. Ted Kennedy even went on to proclaim, "It's going to become increasingly apparent through the summer that Medicare reform is not going to take place" (Pear 2001).

The road to passing a comprehensive Medicare reform bill for prescription drugs would inevitably be an uphill battle for the Bush administration and its allies. To begin his presidency, Bush and the Republicans enjoyed a majority in the House with 223 votes to the Democrats' 209 votes. The Senate, however, was evenly divided at 50 senators apiece, though Vice President Dick Cheney, as the tie-breaking vote, did give the Republicans the technical majority. This changed quickly after Republican Jim Jeffords of Vermont switched parties and became an Independent choosing to caucus with the Democrats, giving the Democrats the majority in the Senate in early June of 2001 (Noah 2001). Unlike Obama, who enjoyed a sixty-seat majority in the Senate, without a similar majority, Bush would have to work with members of both parties to pass his legislative agenda. As a result, this allows for a less partisan test than the previous case's atmosphere, as the pivotal votes for passage must come from the opposition.

Early on, Bush's domestic agenda hit the back-burner, with Democrats controlling the Senate and the events of September 11, 2001, and the Republican leadership had little stomach for a long and potentially unpopular debate on Medicare reform (Blumenthal and Morone 2010). Still, the House of Representatives was able to pass a version of Bush's proposal, but the bill quickly lost steam after running into the Democrat-controlled Senate. These circumstances changed, however, by January 2003. Partially due to President Bush's desire to build a resume of legislative success to run on in 2004, Bush resumed his lobbying efforts to pass a Medicare reform bill. Another circumstantial change that perhaps had even more of an effect was that by November 2002, the Republicans had retaken the Senate with a 51–49 majority. Early on, it seemed the bill would pass as a bipartisan bill that was championed by leaders in both parties as well as a handful of moderates. In the Senate, the liberal Ted Kennedy joined Senate Majority Leader Bill Frist in defending the bill, with moderates Max Baucus (D-MT) and John Breaux (D-LA) also supporting the bill early (Blumenthal and Morone 2009). However, House of Representatives quickly amended the bill, yielding an ideologically conservative conference bill. As a result, the Republican leadership in the Senate lost Kennedy as well as a handful of liberal Democrats but Frist was able to hold on to a bipartisan coalition of sixty-one votes to invoke cloture, and fifty-five votes to pass the bill.

Though less salient and controversial than the Affordable Care Act that would follow, the Medicare Modernization Act provides another test for the power and influence of moderates in the Senate. Again, if moderates are indeed powerful, we should see them not only shape the bill through the amendment process but speak on the bill to push the legislation.

Status Quo

As with the discussion of the status quo with the Affordable Care Act, estimating the status quo here is just as difficult, if not more so, as there was a greater sense of bipartisanship on this bill. Still, we can ascertain some elements of the status quo by examining both the voting coalition as well as the conditions that Medicare operated on before the passage of the act.

Before the passage of the Affordable Care Act, one of the federal government's primary areas of influence on healthcare was Medicare. Void in the program was comprehensive coverage for pharmaceutical care, however. In most circumstances, providing for pharmaceutical care and expanding Medicare would probably be a move from a conservative status quo to a new liberal status quo, but the actual provisions of the bill make it difficult to reach this conclusion. Indeed, as scholars have pointed out, the bill uses free market elements and private insurance to cover most of the gap in coverage (Oberlander 2007). Furthermore, the bill was written with a gap in coverage known commonly as the "doughnut hole," in which coverage stopped at $2,250 and then resumed at $5,100 (Moon 2006). Both of these provisions moved a mostly public program to a public program with private elements. This makes it difficult to classify this as a genuinely liberal bill. Indeed, this is expanding a fairly liberal policy (after all, Medicare is a federally run program offering healthcare to a portion of the population) using conservative principles.

With regard to an *ex-post* analysis, based on the coalition that was built to pass the bill, it is clear that the legislation was conservative. That is to say, with Ted Kennedy leading a filibuster with twenty-six other liberal senators to attempt to stop the bill, Republicans, or perhaps more aptly, conservatives were leading the charge to pass the legislation. As with the Affordable Care Act, let us first examine theoretically key players.

Key Players

In stark contrast to the previous case study, the Bush administration had a much tougher, though much more typical, path to passing legislation, as most presidents do not enjoy sixty-seat majorities in the Senate. Bush was more conservative than the Senate majority leader, Bill Frist, though Frist did work arm in arm with the administration. Unfortunately for Bush, the first pivotal voter, the fifty-first senator, was already on the opposite side ideologically, even if he was a fellow Republican: Lincoln Chafee (R-RI) was much more liberal and ideologically further from the president, and his party's leader.[14] To make matters worse for the Bush administration, after Chafee, they ran out of reliable allies, as every vote after Chafee was a Democratic vote. Furthermore, the pivotal sixtieth vote to end debate was Joseph Lieberman, the Democrat from Connecticut and former vice-presidential rival to the Bush-Cheney ticket in 2000. These key players in addition to the other potentially key players are listed in Table 3.9.

Bush also did not have many replacements for either the fifty-first vote, in which only Ben Nelson could serve to replace the often-perfidious Chafee, as the others were ideologically further from the middle. He faced a similar situation with the filibuster pivot in which any replacement to the sixtieth vote would have been much more liberal than Lieberman. As a result, Bush had to build a broad coalition from the beginning, which his administration largely did by reaching out to Ted Kennedy (whose support they eventually lost as they began to appease their base).

So again, given the difficulties that the Bush administration should have in building a large coalition of ideologically dissimilar senators, we should see potentially pivotal voters clamoring for a chance to be influential on the legislation. If, however, the Marginalized in the Middle Theory is

Table 3.9. Key Players for the Medicare Modernization Act and the Ideological Positions

Players	DW-NOMINATE Score	Distance from the President
The President		
George W. Bush	.52	–
The Senate Leadership		
Bill Frist (Majority Leader)	.40	.12
Tom Daschle (Minority Leader)	−.37	.89
Pivotal Voters		
Lincoln Chafee (R-RI) 51st	−.05	.57
Joseph Lieberman (D-CT) 60th	−.27	.79
Senators between the Pivots		
Ben Nelson (D-NE) 52nd	−.06	.58
John Breaux (D-LA) 53rd	−.11	.63
Max Baucus (D-MT) 54th	−.22	.72
Blanche Lincoln (D-AR) 55th	−.22	.74
Evan Bayh (D-IN) 56th	−.23	.75
Tom Carper (D-DE) 57th	−.23	.75
Mary Landrieu (D-LA) 58th	−.24	.76
Mark Pryor (D-AR) 59th	−.26	.78
Potential Replacements to 60th Vote		
Bill Nelson (D-FL) 61st	−.30	.82
Joseph Biden (D-DE) 62nd	−.30	.82
Herb Kohl (D-WI) 63rd	−.31	.83
Kent Conrad (D-ND) 64th	−.32	.84
Ernest Hollings (D-SC) 65th	−.32	.84

correct, then moderate senators should again shy away from shaping and pushing the bill as they did with the Affordable Care Act. Indeed, right at the start, this goes against conventional wisdom, as the administration sought Kennedy's support rather than seeking the support of moderate senators.

Legislative Floor Action: Amendments

Looking at a descriptive cut of the data, we again see a trend similar to what we have seen throughout this chapter. Figure 3.12 demonstrates that liberal Democrats were proposing more amendments than moderates or even conservative Republicans. The confidence intervals are comparatively much larger than what we saw with the Affordable Care Act, although this is probably because the number of amendments that were proposed for this bill was much lower than for the Affordable Care Act.

As a result, I focus my attention on the probability of proposing an amendment over the number of amendments. Again, I direct my attention at the act of proposing an amendment rather than the content of the bill, as that is the action that gives evidence of congressional behavior and a desire to affect the policy agenda.

To further understand the behavior of moderates in the Senate, I run a logistic regression model predicting the probability of proposing an amendment. As with the previous model, the variable of interest is the distance from the ideological center, calculated again using the DW-NOMINATE measure. I also include control variables again, controlling for party, which is a dummy variable in which a "1" corresponds to being a Democrat while a "0" corresponds to being a Republican; a measure of party leaders; and a measure

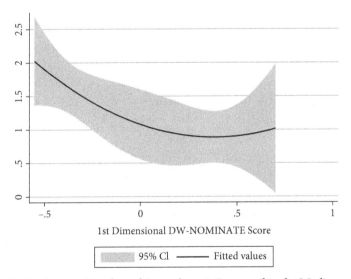

Figure 3.12. Average Number of Amendments Proposed to the Medicare Modernization Act, by DW-NOMINATE Score

for committee members. Finally, to measure the specific impact of centrist Democrats against centrist Republicans, I again interact the Democrat dummy variable and the "distance from the middle" variable. The results of this model are presented in Table 3.10.

Similar to the previous case, which measured the number of amendments proposed, a Democratic senator's ideological distance from the center has a statistically significant and positive effect on the senator's probability of proposing an amendment. That is, ideologically polarized Democrats are more likely to sponsor an amendment than moderate senators. Given the difficulties in interpreting raw logistic regression coefficients, I present the changes as probabilities. Substantively, these results suggest real effects for senators. For the Republican senator who is not a party leader or a relevant committee member, the probability of amending a bill increases by .66 for a change from the minimum value to the maximum value in the distance from the ideological

Table 3.10. Probability of Proposing and Amendment to the Medicare Modernization Act (Logistic Regression Results)

	Model 1		Model 2	
	Coefficient	Standard Error	Coefficient	Standard Error
Distance from the Middle (DW-NOMINATE)	.25	1.84	2.20	2.15
Democrat	−2.46**	1.47	−2.86*	1.69
Party Leader	−1.06	1.11	−1.12	1.11
Committee Member	1.19**	.61	4.42**	1.85
Distance from Middle X Democrat	8.84**	3.80	9.41**	4.43
Distance from the Middle X Committee Member			−8.24**	4.15
Constant	.93	.66	−.73	.84
Log Likelihood	−58.553274		−56.314215	
N=	100		100	
Pseudo R-Squared	.11		.15	

*P<.1, **P<.05, ***P<.01

center for Democrats. Both these results are consistent with the expectations that moderate senators do little to shape policy or affect the overall agenda.

Again, since the potentially pivotal members were mostly Democrats, we should expect to see this relationship. Furthermore, Democrats were also more likely to propose an amendment than Republicans because they disapproved of the bill and were trying to shape it to their liking, or were forcing Republicans into politically difficult votes as the Republicans would do with the Affordable Care Act. So again, we see that partisan politics plays a role larger than ideological appeasement with moderates. Figure 3.13 illustrates the relationship between the probability of proposing an amendment and a given Democratic senator's ideological distance from the middle.

While the probability of proposing an amendment is relatively low for moderate Democrats, the probability increases dramatically as we move toward the ideological pole of the party and plateaus around the middle of the liberal ideological spectrum.

One possible explanation for this behavior can be seen when I interact the committee member term with the distance from the middle term. Here, the interacted variable is both positive and statistically significant. This suggests that moderates on the referred committees were more likely to propose an amendment on the floor than their counterparts. This behavior suggests that moderates, when on committees, still behave as their counterparts would in terms of legislative participation, in that committee members tend to be most active on the floor as well (Hall 1996). Furthermore, it suggests that the moderates that are participating in floor activity are participating less as a pivotal legislator and more as a specialist in the policy area.

But again, the case can be made that backroom politicking prevailed, and moderates largely received what they wanted early in the bill as Senators Baucus and Breaux supported the bill early on. If this is the case, and moderates were indeed pleased with the bill, then we should see them support the bill through floor speeches. The following section looks at this floor activity in the form of speeches in depth.

Legislative Floor Action: Speeches

As with the amendments, the number of speeches that were made on the Medicare Modernization Act is much lower than the number made for the Affordable Care Act; thus, examining the probability of making a speech is once again more appropriate than the number of speeches made.[15] I am also once again concerned with both the probability of making a speech as well as the content. If moderates are pleased with the content of the bill, they should make speeches supporting or opposing the legislation. If, however, there are problems with the content, they should employ one of the strategies that were outlined in Chapter 2.

To examine the issue in depth, I run another logistic regression with the same variables from the previous model. The results of this model are presented in Table 3.11.

In this model, the distance from the ideological center for Democrats is just outside of statistical significance, but still the coefficient is positive on the probability of making a floor speech on the Medicare Modernization Act. However, since the number of speeches is so few for the Medicare Modernization Act, a logistic regression model may not provide us with the detailed results needed to draw a conclusion.

Instead, we can turn to the content of the speeches to find an answer to the question at hand. Indeed, five of the fifteen possible pivotal voters did make speeches. However, none of the five spoke in outright favor or opposition to the bill. The content of their speeches is listed in Table 3.12.

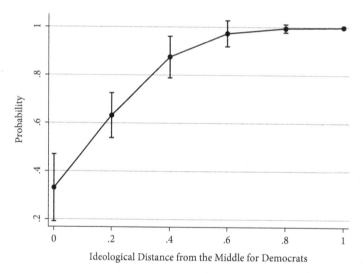

Figure 3.13. Predictive Margins Measuring the Probability of Proposing an Amendment to the Medicare Modernization Act, with 95% Confidence Intervals

Table 3.11. Probability of Making a Speech on the Medicare Modernization Act (Logistic Regression Results)

	Coefficient	Standard Error
Distance from the Middle (DW-NOMINATE)	1.37	.188
Democrat	−1.96	1.38
Party Leader	.49	1.2
Committee Member	.86	.57
Distance from Middle X Democrat	4.32	3.47
Constant	−.17	.75
Log Likelihood	−63.931196	
N=	100	
Pseudo R-Squared	.06	

*P<.1, **P<.05, ***P<.01

Each moderate senator who made a speech on the bill avoided outright supporting or opposing the bill and instead opted to distract, focusing on parts of the bill that they supported over parts that they opposed. Arlen Specter (R-PA) said in his speech, "We already know that there are many criticisms directed to this bill at various levels. . . . One area of concern is the so-called 'donut-hole,' which requires a recipient to pay the entire cost of drug coverage." Later, however, he says, "I am pleased that this bill contains a number of improvements for the providers of health care to Medicare beneficiaries," but then again questions the bill's merits by saying, "I would note that I do have concerns with this legislation with regard to oncological Medicare reimbursement and the premium support demonstration project for Medicare Part B coverage" (*Congressional Record*, November 23, 2003).

Indeed, this political double-talk, where Specter seems to disagree with large parts of the bill but is still speaking in support of it, was echoed by his other moderate colleagues. If Specter and the other moderates were listened to and had the legislation shaped based on their preferences, there should be no room to speak about disagreements in the bill. Still, all five moderates who spoke on the bill ultimately chose to emphasize their displeasure with some of its aspects.

Table 3.12. Types of Speeches Moderates Gave for the Medicare
Modernization Act

	Support	Opposition	Delay	Delegate	Demur	Distract
Olympia Snowe (R)	–	–	–	–	–	1
Ben Nelson (D)	–	–	–	–	–	1
Susan Collins (R)	–	–	–	–	–	1
Arlen Specter (R)	–	–	–	–	–	1
John Breaux (D)	–	–	–	–	–	1

Conclusion

In this chapter, I have examined the influence of senators who are largely viewed as pivotal to the legislative process on policymaking. Specifically, potentially pivotal voters sitting in the middle should be able to exact influence, a notoriously thorny concept to measure. Here, I have looked at two highly visible aspects of legislative participation in the filing of amendments and the making of speeches on the Senate floor. If moderates are pivotal, then we could see some activity in the floor amendment stage of lawmaking. Instead, this chapter demonstrated that on key votes, and in particular, on two highly salient healthcare bills, moderates tend shy away from such activity. Still, this could suggest that these potentially pivotal voters were already satisfied rather than, as is hypothesized here, that these senators were more concerned with reelection than policy outcomes.

The debate activity on the floor, however, suggests this not to be the case. Indeed, moderates offered fewer speeches on the floor, eschewing an opportunity to take credit for a policy that they were happy with if they were indeed happy with it. Even when they did speak, they did so in a manner that protected and justified their vote rather than a manner that suggests a victory on policy outcomes.

Still, this is merely one piece of the legislative puzzle. In this chapter, I look only at key legislation and look in depth at only healthcare legislation. It is conceivable that moderates have more power and are pivotal in other policy areas. Furthermore, legislative floor action is also only part of the puzzle. In the following chapters, I build on the findings here that begin to suggest that power in the middle is not so much pivotal as it is marginal. In the following chapters, I look at voting decisions as well as the "behind-the-scenes" negotiations that dictate power and lawmaking in the US Senate.

4

Legislative Decision-Making

Final Voting Strategy for Potentially Pivotal Players

> "Centrist" senators are more willing to support bipartisan bills. Like
> Blanche Lincoln, an Arkansas Democrat who wanted bipartisan
> support for the massive 2010 healthcare bill, at a time when she
> was facing reelection the next year in a state that had voted for the
> Republican Presidential nominee, Senator John McCain, by 20 per-
> centage points over the Democratic nominee, then-Senator Barack
> Obama. The healthcare bill did not attract any Republican support
> and Lincoln wound up casting a deciding vote for it and losing her
> election, though that vote was hardly the only cause. For the Senate's
> majority party, working with the minority party is essential. And
> so is working with today's opponents who may become tomorrow's
> allies.
>
> —Former Senate Majority Leader Tom Daschle (D-SD)

The narrative provided by Senator Daschle in the epigraph seems to indicate that Daschle viewed the partisan vote on the healthcare bill as particularly damaging for centrists like Lincoln who faced the consequences of their
voting behavior. Daschle's logic suggests that centrists rely on bipartisan
support for cover—for example, Daschle argues, "Support from members
of both parties muzzles partisan radio and TV talk-show hosts and 'special
interests,' or advocacy groups, aligned with one side or the other" (Daschle
and Robbins 2013, 18). This summation yields problematic assumptions as
to the power of centrists. After all, political science scholarship argues that
pivotal voters should act as the proverbial MVPs (Most Valuable Players) of
the legislative game. If moderates were able to act as these pivotal players,

Life in the Middle. Neilan S. Chaturvedi, Oxford University Press. © Oxford University Press 2021.
DOI: 10.1093/oso/9780197599723.003.0004

they should not need bipartisan cover, but instead should force legislation to their preferred point.

In the previous chapter, I used two case studies to demonstrate that centrists in the Senate are more likely to hedge and hide on key legislation than to take the lead. That is, they do not exhibit the signs that active senators who are trying to impact public policy would. For example, they rarely offer floor amendments to shape legislation. It could, of course, be argued that centrists, in particular, do not need to propose amendments because, in their pivotal status, their preferences have already been met before the legislation has hit the floor through logrolling and backroom politicking. If this is true, these centrists should then at least be taking clear positions and offering support of the legislation through floor speeches. Again, Chapter 3 demonstrates this not to be the case.

Of course, based on the explanation in Chapter 2, this makes sense, as there is a logic that moderate senators must heed when making decisions on how to vote on legislation. When speaking to the group of retired senators, I asked all of them the same question: "How were you able to balance being a [member of their party] while representing a state [with the opposing ideology]?"

Senator Byron Dorgan (D-ND) illustrated a tightrope walk that moderate senators engage in:

BD: It is a balancing act. The people that support you do so because they like you and know you. [For me] it was a small state, and they gave me some room—but you can't stray too far either. If you vote contrary to what they want, you won't stay there (in office) too long.

Based on Dorgan's assessment of the caution that moderates must use in their voting calculus, it is unremarkable that they often shy away from participating on salient legislation. Still, his explanation also demonstrates that there is a considerable amount of danger in how one votes on legislation. Lincoln Chafee (R-RI; later a registered Libertarian) echoed this sentiment but added some advice as well:

LC: You have to strike a balance, especially if you want to get reelected. If you're getting out of step, you have to explain the reason for your vote. Communication is very important.

Mark Begich (D-AK) went further and argued that moderates need to look at the state's ideology to decide how to vote. Describing his state and how he voted, Begich said:

MB: From a presidential standpoint, [Alaska] votes Republican, but state-wide it has elected Democrats, Independents, and Republicans. For example, Anchorage has voted for both Democratic and Republican mayors about equally. I consider myself an independent Democrat—I believe in Democratic issues, but I consider myself independent which allows me to represent Alaska by going against the party. I'm conservative on positions like oil and gas, gun rights, and supporting the military, but I am also a believer in climate change. I view climate change from an economic standpoint [for Alaska].

Indeed, this all follows hand in hand. Moderates are walking a tightrope, on which they are members of their party with allegiances and preferences toward their party's views and interests; yet they also have to balance those preferences with the preferences of their constituents who are going to disagree with the senator's party's positions with regularity. As such, moderates cannot stray far from the state's ideology unless they can communicate why they voted against their constituents, as Chafee argues, or else risk losing reelection.

Still, this may only be one strategy. One Republican that I spoke to, Norm Coleman (R-MN), took a different stance on finding a logic to his voting patterns. Coleman argued that senators are elected to follow the trustee model of representation:[1]

NC: In the end, we have a representative democracy—that doesn't mean you take a poll on every issue; you try to do what's right. Sometimes your constituents agree, sometimes they don't. Sometimes your party agrees, and other times they don't.

Coleman's attitude indeed suggests that he had some room to operate and that he did not need to look over his shoulder constantly. Indeed, he suggests that he seldom looked to his constituents for guidance on how to vote. Still, this strategy (or lack thereof) may have consequences. For example, later in our discussion, I asked Coleman about his loss to Al Franken.

NC (me): Looking back at 2008, is there anything you could have done to change the outcome of the race and beat Al Franken?

NC (senator): The conservatives in Minnesota didn't show up. Had I not voted for the TARP vote (the Troubled Assets Relief Program) it wouldn't have been close. I think it cost me about 100,000 votes. People were very emotional and passionate.[2]

As such, it seems that moderates need to fear how constituents might view their vote constantly. Indeed, while Coleman argues that he did not consult with his constituents on every issue, it is noteworthy that he assesses his base's turnout as a result of one vote as the cause for his loss in 2008. That is to say, like the others, Coleman seems to have noticed that straying too far from the base has its consequences. As such, party loyalty can play a large role in a centrist senator's voting decisions, especially when the vote is on an issue that is key to the party and their president. For example, Lincoln Chafee expressed dismay when talking about Republican centrists and their response to George W. Bush's tax plan.

LC: In my 30 years of public service—that moment was the most disappointing of my career: when the moderates didn't stick together. If we had said no, we could have been the powerbrokers and changed American history, but they didn't want to exert power—everything was seniority so I couldn't push it and he should have been more adamant. [We] moderates did roll over with the tax cuts—just didn't stand up—it was just me and John McCain. Why? They wanted to be team players—they put that higher than their allegiance to the country—even though they had their doubts as to the wisdom of the policy decisions.

Here, Chafee is referring to his centrist colleagues Arlen Specter, Olympia Snowe, and Susan Collins. While he notes that they could have been powerbrokers, it is likely that none of the three would revisit these votes, as they were central to the Bush agenda. If they voted against the tax bill, it likely would have killed Bush's agenda early in his presidency, delivering a critical blow to the Republican brand.

Regional issues also reign supreme. Senator Mary Landrieu (D-LA) seemed to echo this sentiment when I asked her the same question:

ML: I sided with the Democratic Party 70–80 percent of the time and voted consistently with Democratic principles—things like access to education, criminal justice reform, etc. I was open on trade issues more so than the left, but that is because Louisiana is the largest port system in the world. I had to be radically pragmatic—not hunkered down in ideological corners but willing to move across the aisle to help get things done.

Even still, regional issues may provide moderate senators some clarity on how to vote—if it helps the state economically, it is an easy way to gain support among constituents. More difficult are issues like Coleman's TARP vote—votes that are salient and visible to voters and affect many constituents.

It is still conceivable that this explains only part of the puzzle, however. Indeed, if senators are always concerned with voters tracing their vote to the passage of a particularly unpopular bill, they may sidestep speech-making activity even if they support the end product. This scenario would run against the legislative picture that I have painted thus far, but upon further review, this caveat does not accurately portray what Senate voting behavior looks like. In this chapter, I examine first whether moderates are policy maximizers. That is, I look to see if moderates can push their ideology on legislation, or at the very least, get a payoff. I then examine the logic behind voting decisions for moderates in the Senate. To explore this issue, I begin by examining voting on the two case studies discussed in Chapter 3. I then follow with an examination of voting behavior on key legislation, demonstrating that moderates are unable to push their ideology, nor are they able to get significant policy payoffs in exchange for their vote.

Case Studies: How Did Senators Vote on the Healthcare Bills Examined Previously?

Regardless of whether they are voting for or against their party, if moderates are marginalized in the middle, they should be deferential to whatever option gives them the most ideological flexibility. As such, preferences on salient issues take a back seat for moderates. To examine this, let us first turn to the case studies reviewed in Chapter 3. Based on the results presented in the previous chapters, on the floor, moderates are either unwilling or unable to exert much political power through congressional participation. The argument could still be made, however, that the result is what is the most important. That is, as long as the senator achieved their goals on the legislation, their participation and position taking are secondary. After all, theoretically, pivotal senators exist regardless of their electoral circumstances, and even if they are weak regarding their power, they still must be appeased for party leaders to earn their vote. However, this appears to be less than accurate. Indeed, looking at the vote choices of centrist senators, it would seem to be that not only do moderates not participate in shaping legislation but in many cases, their policy preferences are just not met.

To examine whether senators voted against their policy preferences, I investigate answers from Project Vote Smart, a nonprofit organization that performs surveys with members of Congress asking for their positions on salient issues. Project Vote Smart is a nonprofit, nonpartisan group that collects information about candidates through questionnaires distributed before the election. Questionnaires are quite comprehensive, and each question focuses on a particular policy with a resemblance to a roll call vote. Rogowski (2014) notes the possibility that staffers or others affiliated with the candidate may be completing the surveys, or that the responses are an effort to muddle the legislator's record, but he also finds that the survey data correlates very highly with DW-NOMINATE scores as well as the perceptions of constituents. Indeed, while the argument can be made that these positions are signals to supporters and are not actually sincere policy preferences, if we were to assume that these answers were simply motivated by a desire to be reelected— having positions on highly salient issues public would allow highly knowledgeable voters, interest groups, and opponents the ability to hold them accountable in the following election if they did not vote according to their stated preferences. That would suggest that when these politicians voted against their stated positions, they were either exhibiting poor political skills, or, as the book argues, were rolled by their party.

While many candidates refuse to answer the questions for fear of retribution from voters, many do answer the survey questions, providing political scientists with at least some data on the policy preferences of legislators. Other studies have used these data with some success as well (for example, see Dahlberg 2001; Koch 2002; Lupia and Philpot 2005; and Rogowski 2014, among many others). Every survey contains questions that use either ordinal responses or yes or no responses to evaluate candidates on a variety of issues from taxes, budgets, international affairs, and policy initiatives.

Table 4.1 presents the fifteen potentially pivotal voters, their vote, and whether it matched their preferred position.[3]

It should be noted that a handful of senators refused to provide information on their policy position on healthcare so an assessment cannot be made.

Table 4.1. Vote Choice on the Final Bill for the Affordable Care Act

Senator	Vote	Preferred Position?	Explanation for Position	Type of State
Michael Bennett (D-CO)	Aye	Yes	–	Swing
Kay Hagan (D-NC)	Aye	n/a	–	Swing
Mary Landrieu (D-LA)	Aye	Yes	–	Partisan Lean
Mark Pryor (D-AR)	Aye	No	Opposition to govt. regulation	Partisan Lean
Claire McCaskill (D-MO)	Aye	Yes	–	Partisan Lean
Jim Webb (D-VA)	Aye	n/a	–	Swing
Max Baucus (D-MT)	Aye	Yes	–	Partisan Lean
Blanche Lincoln (D-AR)	Aye	No	Opposition to govt. regulation	Partisan Lean
Evan Bayh (D-IN)	Aye	No	Opposition to govt. regulation	Partisan Lean
Ben Nelson (D-NE)	Aye	No	Opposition to govt. regulation	Partisan Lean
Susan Collins (R-ME)	Nay	Yes	Supports universal healthcare	Swing
Olympia Snowe (R-ME)	Nay	No	–	Swing
George Voinovich (R-OH)	Nay	n/a	–	Swing
Lisa Murkowski (R-AK)	Nay	No	–	Safe
Richard Lugar (R-IN)	Nay	No	–	Safe

Of the twelve senators who provided a policy position, only seven voted according to their preference. Mark Pryor, Blanche Lincoln, Evan Bayh, and Ben Nelson all voted for the healthcare bill, despite making statements in opposition to increased government regulation of healthcare. Similarly, Susan Collins voted against the bill, despite the fact that she has made comments in support of universal healthcare.[4] So why would a potentially pivotal voter vote against her preferences on such a salient bill and vote with her party?

One possible explanation is that choosing to vote with your party guarantees that the party will provide a defense when it comes time to run for reelection, either through fundraising or through other resources. Another explanation is that moderate senators may prefer to defer to their party leadership on salient bills regardless of their preferences as a way to avoid traceability. Perhaps most convincing, though, each of the Democrats here was necessary for the passage of the Affordable Care Act. Not voting in favor of the bill would have led to a disastrous ending to a key aspect of the president's agenda and reflected poorly on the party as well as the president. As Lincoln Chafee put it earlier, sometimes senators must put their party ahead of other goals.

Noticeably, every Republican, including Susan Collins, who supports universal healthcare, voted against the bill. Why would a senator who supports the legislation (and for that matter, could have negotiated their way into a pivotal position, thereby increasing their negotiating power on the bill) vote against the legislation? Again, following the logic outlined earlier in this chapter, Collins would not win any increase in party reputation by voting for a key aspect of the opposition's president's agenda; if anything, this would do damage to her brand as a Republican among partisans in her state. Furthermore, with a moderate Republican base that opposed the bill and a liberal Democratic constituency that favored the bill, Collins was in a difficult position that could ultimately damage her chances within her constituency. Thus, the optimal position for her was to vote against her preferences and with her party.

It could be argued that some of these senators voted for the legislation because they were able to negotiate projects or earmarks for their states. Indeed, Ben Nelson was able to negotiate the so-called Cornhusker Kickback, which exempted Nebraska from certain provisions of the bill. While this certainly was an effort by the Democratic leadership to gain Nelson's support, it does not demonstrate centrist power in terms of moving policy. At best, Nelson was able to exempt his state, and only his state, from a handful of provisions. This suggests that the leadership accurately surmised that they could gain Nelson's vote not by moving the policy to his preferred point, but by giving him special provisions that applied only to him. Even still, the Cornhusker Kickback was removed in conference after numerous senators and members of the media criticized the move. Nelson eventually voted no on the reconciliation bill. Furthermore, as discussed earlier in the book, Landrieu's "Louisiana Purchase" was not a quid pro quo for her vote, and even if it was, it too was removed in conference.

Of course, the Affordable Care Act provides an example of moderates cowering away from the political limelight with regards to both activity and credit claiming. Indeed, the Affordable Care Act had no bipartisanship, was polarizing within the chamber and in the media, and was incredibly salient. What happens when the legislation is bipartisan? Do moderates follow the same logic? To answer this question, let's turn to the other case study, the Medicare Prescription Drug, Improvement, and Modernization Act.

Using the data from Project Vote Smart again, I examine the preferences of the fifteen potentially pivotal voters and their end votes. The results are presented in Table 4.2.

Though slightly more limited here, as only nine of the fifteen gave responses that could be used, of the nine, four voted against their preferences. Lincoln Chafee voted against the bill despite actually preferring most of the provisions of the bill. This decision was likely due to the more conservative elements of the bill that would potentially anger his liberal constituents in Rhode Island. Since he was not pivotal to the bill's passage, he could consider the constituency, and more important, sub-constituency issues that could impact his election prospects.

Furthermore, Democrats who considered themselves fiscal hawks who favored either shrinking the medical expenditures of the federal government voted in favor of the bill despite its being widely seen as a bloated spending bill. Being in the vulnerable position, these Democrats did not want to be seen voting against a bill that would increase benefits for the elderly. What is most notable, however, is that despite sitting at or near the pivotal position for passage, none of these senators was able to maneuver themselves into a position of influence. That is, the "winners" of the bill were not the moderates, but the framers of the bill and the Bush administration.

Also notable, each of the senators in both examples, with the exception of Herb Kohl (D-WI), came from states that are either partisan-lean states or swing states—meaning electoral vulnerability played a supreme role here in that it decreased the potentially pivotal political clout that these senators had and replaced it with partisan complacency.

Still, these tables only represent the pivotal behavior on two bills. In particular, the Affordable Care Act is a unique bill in itself in many ways, as it was the landmark bill for the Obama administration. As a result, many considerations could go into a moderate senator's decision to vote for or against the legislation, especially considering that the Senate was only able to muster up the minimum sixty votes required to invoke cloture. Furthermore, after Scott Brown, a Republican, filled Ted Kennedy's seat in Massachusetts, the Democratic leadership turned to the parliamentary tactic of reconciliation, in which only fifty-one votes are needed to pass the legislation. This change, of course, means that the leadership was either unwilling or incapable of

Table 4.2. Vote Choice on the Final Bill (Cloture Vote) for the Medicare Modernization Act

Senator	Vote	Preferred Position?	Explanation for Position	Type of State
Lincoln Chafee (R-RI)	Nay	Yes	Favors expanding drug care	Partisan Lean
Ben Nelson (D-NE)	Aye	Partially	Favors expanding drug care/lower spending on healthcare	Partisan Lean
John Breaux (D-LA)	Aye	Yes	–	Partisan Lean
Max Baucus (D-MT)	Aye	Yes	–	Partisan Lean
Blanche Lincoln (D-AR)	Aye	Yes	–	Partisan Lean
Evan Bayh (D-IN)	Nay	Nay	–	Partisan lean
Tom Carper (D-DE)	Aye	n/a	–	Safe
Mary Landrieu (D-LA)	Aye	Nay	Favors maintain Medicare spending/ no expansion	Partisan Lean
Mark Pryor (D-AR)	Aye	Yes	–	Partisan Lean
Joseph Lieberman (D-CT)	Nay	n/a	–	Safe
Bill Nelson (D-FL)	Aye	n/a	–	Swing
Joseph Biden (D-DE)	Aye	n/a	–	Safe
Herb Kohl (D-WI)	Aye	No	Favors decreasing federal spending on healthcare	Safe
Kent Conrad (D-ND)	Aye	n/a	–	Partisan Lean
Ernest Hollings (D-SC)	Nay	n/a	–	Partisan Lean

negotiating with Republican moderates—suggesting party politics was more at play on this particular bill than ideology.

Policy Maximizers, Partisan Warriors, or Something Else?

Early congressional scholarship mostly asserts that parties were weak, and that individuality reigned supreme in the US Senate. David Mayhew famously wrote, "The fact is that no theoretical treatment of the United States Congress that posits parties as analytic units will go very far" (Mayhew 1974, 24). Even in his early twentieth-century assessment of Congress, Woodrow

Wilson wrote of the Senate, "No one is *the* senator. No one may speak for his party as well as for himself; no one exercises the special trust of acknowledged leadership" (Wilson 1885).

In the 1990s, however, the literature on the weakness of parties was questioned, as scholars argued that parties do impact legislation (see, for example, Aldrich 1995; Rohde 1991; Sinclair 1995; Cox and McCubbins 1993; 2005). Furthermore, scholars have found that the impact of parties has not necessarily grown over time, but has always existed (Cox and McCubbins 1993; 2005). These conclusions, however, are largely made about the House of Representatives. As discussed earlier, Keith Krehbiel (1996; 1998) downplays the influence of party, especially in the Senate, by questioning the effect they have. In fact, Krehbiel argues that the logic behind the median voter theorem, and by extension, the Pivotal Politics Model, negates any effect that parties have on the institution.

Indeed, if centrists are truly pivotal, they should always be in winning coalitions. That is, since their votes are so crucial to the matter at hand, they should, more often than not, be on the side that wins (regardless of whether the bill passes or not). If the legislation moves too far away from their preferred point, the pivotal voter should vote against the legislation, or at the very least, threaten to vote against it to force changes to the bill. Second, if centrists are pivotal, they should have a higher rate of voting against their party. Again, given their vital position, they should have enough cachet to negotiate with both sides of the aisle.

Using data from the 108th to the 112th Congresses, Figure 4.1 illustrates the average percentage of time that senators vote with their party based on their proximity to the pivot points and the type of state they represent. Figure 4.1a shows that senators from partisan-lean states and swing states are less loyal than their safe state counterparts. Similarly, Figure 4.1b shows that the ten senators who sit closest to the respective pivot points are also less loyal to their parties than their more polarized counterparts.

On its own, however, this tells us little. If centrists are pivotal, they should vote against their party—after all, they should vote with the coalition that best suits their needs. Even still, if centrists are vulnerable, they too should vote against their party to create distance between them and their ideologues to signal their constituents that they are indeed independent. When we look more specifically at which senators are most in winning coalitions, we see a different picture altogether. Figure 4.2 shows which senators are in winning coalitions the most.

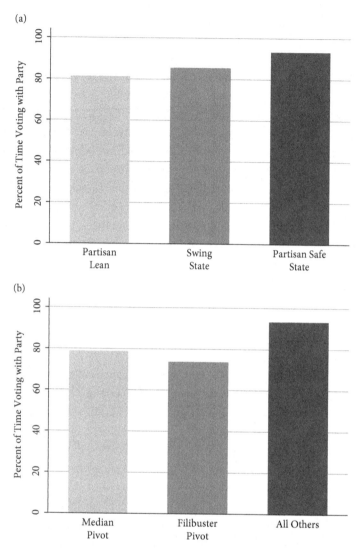

Figure 4.1. Senate Party Loyalty Based on (a) Type of State for the 108th–112th Congresses, (b) Pivotal Position for the 108th–112th Congresses.

Senators in the Median Pivot and Filibuster Pivot are coded as the ten senators closest to these positions (i.e., the 45th–54th senator for the median pivot and the 55th–64th senator for the filibuster pivot).

Looking at Figure 4.2b, there is some evidence to suggest that the senators who are sitting closest to the median pivot and filibuster pivot are in winning coalitions more often than their counterparts, but there is a significant difference between being in the minority party and the majority party. Indeed, there is almost no difference between the senators sitting closest to the median and filibuster pivots and their counterparts for senators in the majority. Senators in the minority who are closest to the pivots are in the winning coalition much more often than their counterparts. Still, this is somewhat unremarkable. After all, they are the senators who are ideologically closest to the majority, and as such, may vote with them on occasion.

Still, Figure 4.2a demonstrates that it is not necessarily true that all senators who are sitting closest to the median and filibuster points are part of the winning coalition. Partisan-lean state senators and swing state senators in the minority were less successful than not only their counterparts in the majority but also less successful than the senators in Figure 4.2b. That is to say, capturing the ten senators who are closest to the middle captures perhaps too many senators who all too often not pivotal. Indeed, safe state senators like Joe Biden (D-DE) in the 108th Congress, Richard Lugar (R-IN) in the 110th and 112th Congresses, and Charles Hagel (R-NE) in the 110th were all listed as one of the ten closest senators to the filibuster pivot, but were ideologically far enough away and from safe states that they did not have to play the same calculus as their vulnerable counterparts.

Frances Lee (2009) argues that the Senate is a body that has become increasingly partisan. Parties have an impact, and they seem to be most effective as a "cost cutter" to pass legislation. Ansolabehere et al. (2001) argue that while individual preferences do matter, party effects are highest on close votes, issues that are key to the party, and procedural votes, a finding that is largely corroborated by Lee (2009) as well.

Based on these findings, we can expect to see one of two outcomes. First, individuality can reign, in which senators vote only on their preferences. Pork barrel spending, pet projects, or incentives could buy them off, however. Or, we could see senators deferring to their parties to defer traceability and give the party more power to enact its policies. I argue that while preferences and individuality may be the norm for many senators, moderates are unique in this regard. Moderates should vote in a way that maximizes the number of options they have electorally. In many cases, that will involve voting against one's preferences and with their party as a means of maintaining party success or preventing the other party from being triumphant.

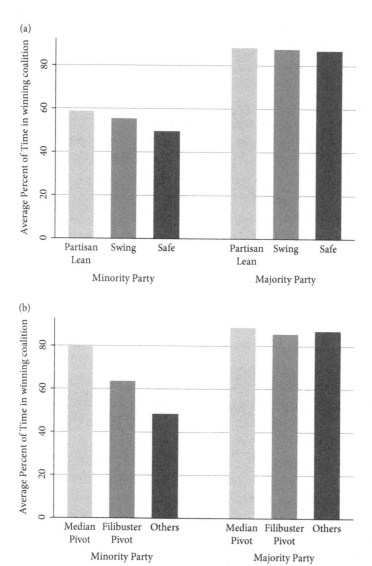

Figure 4.2. Average time a Senator Spends in the Winning Coalition (a) by Type of State for the 108th–112th Congresses, (b) by Pivotal Position for the 108th–112th Congresses

Senators in the Median Pivot and Filibuster Pivot are coded as the ten senators closest to these positions (i.e., the 45th–54th senator for the median pivot and the 55th–64th senator for the filibuster pivot). Here they are divided by party as well.

Again, using the answers provided in the Political Courage Test from Project Vote Smart, I look at eleven other bills from the 108th to the 112th Congresses to measure the impact of moderate preferences on legislation. I focus my attention on the congruence of policy preferences and outcomes on *Congressional Quarterly*'s collection of key votes, which are compiled based on three criteria: the vote must include a matter of controversy, a test of presidential or political power, and a decision of potentially great impact on the lives of Americans (Congressional Quarterly Almanac 1970).

To accurately assess the power of moderates, we must first estimate their preferences, which in itself is a thorny endeavor. The Political Courage Test is useful in one sense; the survey instrument is structured with the option to clarify any positions given and is offered multiple times. Still, there are areas of policy that are missing—notably, issues dealing with current events, or specific forms of policy (e.g., Wall St. reform) are not asked, nor is there any room for senators to fill in this information. Furthermore, the survey is completely optional; while Project Vote Smart does its best to pressure politicians publicly and privately, many senators do not answer the surveys. In other cases, senators filled out an earlier form but failed to update their positions later. While Project Vote Smart does try to fill in gaps by compiling statements and news stories on the policy area, voids remain. As a result, I only examine policy issues in which there are reliable opinions from most (though certainly not all) of the moderates in question. The bills examined are provided in Table 4.3.

To be as conservative as possible, I coded policy positions as loosely as could be reasonably allowed. That is, if the senator received nearly every-thing that their stated position said, I coded the bill as a policy match. Of the eleven bills, the Senate rejected five. More important, of the six bills that were passed, one was adopted with a very close vote. This vote should give us a situation in which moderates won the day by being the crucial votes for passage. Similarly, two votes were defeated by three votes and one vote (HR 8, the Estate Tax Bill, and S 493, the EPA Bill, respectively). These two votes should demonstrate instances where moderates were unable to negotiate preferable deals to move the policy to their ideal position. I look at specifi-cally the top twenty most ideologically moderate senators according to the DW-NOMINATE scores. Theoretically, these senators sit closest to the two pivot positions.

Table 4.4 demonstrates the proportion of votes corresponding to the number of times the senator voted according to her preferred policy position.

Table 4.3. Bills Examined for Preference Matching

Congress	Bill Number	Short Title	Content	Vote Total/ Result
108	S2061 (Cloture)	Medical Malpractice	Caps damage awards on medical malpractice suits	48–45, Rejected
108	SJRes40 (Constitutional Amendment)	Same-Sex Marriage Ban	Constitutional amendment banning same-sex marriage	48–50, Rejected
108	S3	Partial Birth Abortion Ban	Bans partial birth abortions	64–34, Adopted
108	SConRes23 (Amendment)	ANWR Drilling	Protect against drilling in ANWR	52–48, Adopted
109	S2611	Immigration Reform	Pathway to citizenship guest worker, border security	62–36, Adopted
109	HR8 (Cloture)	Estate Tax	Permanent repeal of the estate tax	57–41, Rejected
110	HR2419	Farm Bill	Extends subsidies and food stamps	81–15, Adopted
110	S3036 (Cloture)	Climate Change	Caps greenhouse gas emissions	48–36, Rejected
110	HR2	Minimum Wage Increase	Increases minimum wage	94–3, Adopted
112	S493	Prohibition on EPA Regulation	Blocks EPA from regulating CO_2 emissions	50–50, Rejected

The list contains eighteen senators who sat closest to the median and filibuster pivots. Note that senators repeat by Congress. Those that offered no policy positions are not listed.

Only four of the eighteen senators have "perfect" voting records in which they had no instances of voting against their preferences, one of which, Joe Manchin, has only one vote in the data set for the 112th Congress. Of the remaining three, Tom Carper, a Democrat from Delaware, is from a safe state. As a result, only two of the eighteen have voting records that can be described as consistent with their preferences on a series of votes that are also vulnerable.

Susan Collins voted against her stated preferences six out of a possible ten times, while some other senators voted against their preferences multiple times in more than one congressional session. Indeed, Mary Landrieu voted against her preferences at least once in each session.[5] Looking at the bill that passed by razor-thin margin, the amendment to S.Con.Res.23 to protect against drilling in ANWR passed by only two votes. This small margin should suggest that moderates were the most influential players, but were they? Oddly enough, despite being on the record as favoring opening up drilling in restricted areas like ANWR, Ben Nelson (D-NE) voted in favor of the bill, effectively voting against himself. What is even more baffling is that Nelson did not need to vote for the bill; that is to say, he was not the pivotal vote that passed the bill—there were fifty-two votes in favor of the bill even without Nelson. Similarly, Republicans Susan Collins (ME) and Gordon Smith (OR) both voted against the bill despite being on record as against drilling in ANWR.

Another point of interest is on legislation where senators could have played a pivotal role and moved legislation to their ideal point but failed to do so. HR 8, a bill in the 109th Congress, permanently eliminating the estate tax, only needed three more votes for cloture. Evan Bayh, a Democrat from Indiana, voted against the bill, despite having made statements in favor of eliminating the estate tax. Of course, the case could be made that Bayh's vote would only up the vote count to fifty-eight, two short of the sixty needed to invoke cloture—which makes Susan Collins's vote in support of cloture all the more contradictory to her preferences. Despite her preference to keep the estate tax, Collins voted to invoke cloture on a bill that would have eliminated it entirely, and was not even the pivotal vote for passage. Collins was hardly alone in this type of behavior. On the cloture vote for S2061 in the 108th Congress, a bill regulating medical malpractice suits, Gordon Smith voted against his preferences, in favor of a cloture vote that would fail. Multiple senators voted in favor of the immigration reform bill in the 109th Congress, despite having major opposition to the key components of the bill. This becomes even more confusing, as their votes were not needed for passage.

So why is this the case? It could be that instead of policy concessions, these senators received some earmark or special spending project for their state. The *Congressional Record* shows no such payoff for any of the bills examined here, though there could have been some payoff down the line (see Koger 2010). What seems more likely is that moderate senators are grasping the opportunity to demonstrate to their constituents that they can vote against

Table 4.4. Proportion of Votes Matching Preferences

Senator	Type of State	108th Congress	109th Congress	110th Congress	112th Congress
Max Baucus (D-MT)	Partisan Lean	4/4	1/2	2/3	1/1
Evan Bayh (D-IN)	Partisan Lean	4/4	0/1	1/2	N/A
Tom Carper (D-DE)	Safe	3/3	1/1	N/A	N/A
Lincoln Chafee (R-RI)	Partisan Lean	5/5	2/2	N/A	N/A
Susan Collins (R-ME)	Swing State	0/4	0/2	3/3	1/1
Mary Landrieu (D-LA)	Partisan Lean	2/3	1/2	1/2	N/A
Blanche Lincoln (D-AR)	Partisan Lean	3/4	1/2	3/3	N/A
Richard Lugar (R-IN)	Safe	5/5	2/2	2/3	1/1
Ben Nelson (D-NE)	Partisan Lean	2/3	2/2	2/3	0/1
Gordon Smith (R-OR)	Partisan Lean	3/5	2/2	3/3	N/A
Olympia Snowe (R-ME)	Swing State	3/5	1/1	3/3	0/1
Arlen Specter (R-PA)	Swing State	5/5	n/a	2/2	N/A
Mark Pryor (D-AR)	Partisan Lean	N/A	1/2	2/3	1/1
Lisa Murkowski (R-AK)	Safe	N/A	N/A	0/2	1/1
Scott Brown (R-MA)	Partisan Lean	N/A	N/A	N/A	1/1
Joe Manchin (D-WV)	Partisan Lean	N/A	N/A	N/A	1/1
Claire McCaskill (D-MO)	Partisan Lean	N/A	N/A	N/A	0/1
Bill Nelson (D-FL)	Swing State	N/A	N/A	N/A	0/1

Note: Some ratios do not match because senators answered some questions but did not answer others or were too ambiguous to provide a position.

their party. Indeed, being the pivotal policymaker is of little use; pushing legislation to the senator's ideal location may help, but on partisan votes, voting with one's party does little than subject the senator to the attack that she is a party shill. As such, moderate senators should care less about maximizing policy preferences, as seen here. Instead, they should seize opportunities to vote against their party to demonstrate independence—especially when their vote would not have been pivotal. As previously quoted, Harry Reid's reference to Arlen Specter voting with the Democrats only when they did not need his vote is particularly telling of how moderates operate. The effort seems to be that they should seek not the role of a pivotal voter, but instead strategically oppose their party when few costs are attached to the action. Given now that centrists frequently "lose" on their preferences, I now turn to the logic behind centrist voting decisions.

(Moderate) Senators' Voting Decisions

Kingdon (1977) lays out a basic logic to congressional voting. In his article, Kingdon illustrates an integrative model for legislative voting for members of the House of Representatives. The model provides an illustrative conditional flow chart of how members of Congress make voting decisions on legislation. For example, Step 1: if the bill is noncontroversial, Kingdon advises voting with the consensus; however, if it is not, Step 2: the legislator must examine if there is a conflict among actors in their field of forces or party leaders, constituency, and trusted associates. For senators in the middle, the model runs into trouble at Step 2.

All too often for centrists, especially those in partisan-lean states, their field of forces is at odds—their constituency and party leadership are frequently at opposite ends of the issues. Assuming, then, that the goals surrounding this piece of legislation pass a "critical threshold of importance," or a decision in which there would be relevant consequences to the legislator, a senator then must strategize the correct vote. Of course, in the Senate, we can assume that any vote that involves the filibuster pivot is likely a salient and major piece of legislation, as opponents may find it less than worthwhile to obstruct minor legislation (Wawro and Schickler 2006).

Kingdon then argues that the next step would be to examine if the goals that do pass the threshold have any conflict. That is, are there elements in the bill that are both agreeable and disagreeable with the senator's preferences?

If not, then the senator should vote based on their goals. Again, Senate moderates face difficulties, as their goals are often much more precise than their colleagues—senators from partisan safe states will have fewer goals that hit the threshold of importance because their constituencies are more consensual on their preferences. As we saw in the previous chapter, centrists all too often must find ways to justify their vote despite having legitimate problems with the bill.

If the senator fails to have a consensus among her goals on the legislation, then she must then consider her constituency. As mentioned in Chapter 2, given that sub-constituency politics is in play for many moderates, the consideration of constituency is a dangerous one. For swing state senators, the safe answer is almost always siding with the base—if the two constituencies are approximately equal in size, there is little incentive to vote against the senator's base—but what about senators from partisan-lean states? Indeed, the calculus for choosing whom to represent is difficult and is often based on perceived constituent interests (Miller 2010). Choosing their base would likely anger their opposition, but choosing their opposition may only be fruitful if the base is indifferent to the issue (Bishin 2008). Here moderates are in the precarious position of figuring out how to appease a constituency where one side will likely be angered.

Kingdon goes on to argue that if the constituency is not involved, which, given the nature of the bills that would be up for debate at this point, almost certainly will be the case, the legislator must examine their party's goals versus their policy goals. I argue, however that the considerations for the moderate senator are much more difficult and, as such, operate in a different order.

Figure 4.3 illustrates how the Marginalized in the Middle theory predicts legislative voting decisions are made in the Senate for moderates. Again, the senator's primary concern should be traceability—at no point does the senator want to be in a position in which they are the deciding vote for any piece of legislation that is not core to the policy goals of their party. Indeed, as mentioned earlier in this chapter, senators like Blanche Lincoln prefer bipartisan coalitions for landmark legislation, as it provides cover for their choices.

Another concern for the centrist senator should be their constituency and the "strange bedfellows" who must agree to keep them in office. For many moderate senators, constituency and party will play against each other consistently. So when should moderate senators vote with their constituency and when should they vote with their party? After all, moderate senators

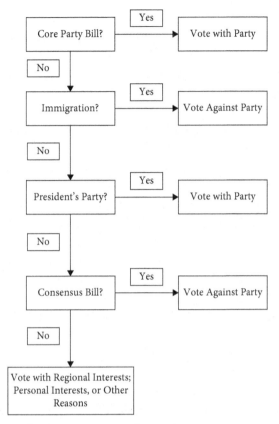

Figure 4.3. Logic for Voting Decisions for Moderates

need to strategize a way to distance themselves from their party while also staying within the party's core beliefs to not anger their base. Two issues that are particularly controversial are abortion and immigration. These two issues very often also provide senators with the ability to characterize themselves as moderates. Indeed, moderate Republicans more often than not are pro-choice and in favor of immigration reform, while moderate Democrats tend to favor abortion restrictions and have a more difficult time voting for immigration reform (see, for example, Brady and Schwartz 1995 and Jeong et al. 2011).

If the senator is from the president's party, one concern may be the party and the president's popularity. Indeed, if the president is unpopular, that should increase the senator's vulnerability—regardless of whether their reelection falls in an off-year or presidential election year. As numerous studies demonstrate, voters exercise their disapproval of the president's performance by voting against his co-partisans in the House and Senate, especially during midterm elections (Abramowitz 1984; 1985; Abramowitz and Segal 1992; Campbell and Sumners 1990; Cover 1986; Jacobson 1997; Kernell 1977; Marra and Ostrom 1989; Tufte 1975). Hibbing and Alford (1981) use survey data from the 1978 election and find that negative short-term views of the nation's economy can hurt incumbent members of Congress from the president's party. They argue, "Voters do not simply blame the president's entire party; rather they seem to assign blame selectively, based on objective responsibility" (Hibbing and Alford 1981, 437). That is to say, voters assign blame and credit to the incumbent senators from the president's party. Fiorina (1983) goes on to offer more evidence for this argument using a different methodology and five more election studies.

As a result, if the senator's vote is needed to pass the president's agenda, then the senator should vote to pass the bill, even if the senator's needs are not met. Indeed, voting against the president's agenda does more damage to the party's brand and increases the vulnerability of the president and fellow partisans nationally, and also risks the senator's support with their base.

The moderate senator's other opportunity to vote against the party and distinguish herself as independent is when the vote within the chamber is consensual. When there is bipartisan support for the legislation, moderates are safe to vote against their party if needed.

The exception to this rule, however, is if the senator has a constituency concern that is at odds with the party. For example, when President Obama and the Democratic leadership made it a priority to defeat the Keystone Pipeline, an oil pipeline that would run from Canada to the United States that some argue would have environmental ramifications, senators like Mary Landrieu of Louisiana had to vote in favor of the pipeline because her conservative constituency wanted her to. The senator should vote with that sub-constituency—regardless of their ideological bend. For example, on environmental issues Democratic senator Joe Manchin, who hails from West Virginia, should vote with the active sub-constituency of his state— the coal industry—even as they oppose much of what the Democratic Party stands for. Truly, this is more relevant for Democrats than Republicans as Republicans have fewer regional issues to deal with.

To test this logic, I again turn to *Congressional Quarterly*'s key votes. I compiled a data set of every key vote from the 108th Congress to the 112th Congress by potentially pivotal voters, or senators representing partisan-lean states or swing states. To simplify the analysis, I eliminated any bills that dealt with foreign policy, treaties or international agreements. I ran a logistic regression predicting when moderates vote with their party. A full list of the bills examined can be found in Appendix B.

Based on the model demonstrating the logic of voting decisions for moderates, I include a variable that measures whether the bill was a part of the party's core messaging. For Republicans, these bills included any bills that limited government regulation, environmental regulation, or the lowering or elimination of taxes. For Democrats, these bills included increasing environmental regulation and protections, government regulation, and the expansion of civil rights. I also included dummy variables for immigration bills. I also included a dummy variable for consensual votes, operationalized as any vote with more than sixty-five votes in favor or against the piece of legislation. Finally, I include a variable measuring possible regional conflicts.[6] Again, this may be only an issue for Democrats, as only Democrats were affected by this variable. The results of the regression model are presented in Table 4.5. For ease of interpretation, I report the odds ratios rather than coefficients.

The results of Model 1 demonstrate that centrist voters are much more likely to vote with their party on core party bills. That is, on bills that are closest to the party's platform, moderate senators vote with their party more often than not. On immigration bills, potentially pivotal moderates are more likely to vote against their party. Also, members of the president's party are also more likely to vote with their party. This falls in line with the expectations outlined earlier.

Finally, on consensual votes, moderates are, again, less likely to vote with their parties. Interestingly, regional conflicts have no statistically significant impact on the odds that a moderate will vote with their party. Again, this may be because of the few Southern Democrats in the data set who are the only moderates affected by regional issues. Still, there were no bills examined in this particular data set that changed moderate Republicans in the same way.

In Model 2, I added variables measuring the ten senators who sit closest to the median pivot and the filibuster pivot. Here, both coefficients are negative, suggesting that senators who sit closest to the median and filibuster pivots on the ideological spectrum are more likely to vote against their parties—another sign that moderates are mostly concerned with their ability to distinguish themselves from their party. Indeed, those sitting closest to the pivot positions are the most interested in separating themselves from

Table 4.5. Logistic Regression Predicting When Moderates Vote
with Their Party

	Model 1		Model 2	
	Odds Ratio	Std. Err.	Odds Ratio	Std. Err.
Median Pivot			.41***	.13
Filibuster Pivot			.57***	.1
President's Party	2.21***	.18	2.18***	.15
Consensus Vote	.38***	.03	.37***	.03
Regional Conflict	2.06	1.78	2.03	1.66
Core Party Bill	3.42***	.32	3.46***	.34
Immigration Bill	.22***	.03	.22***	.03
Abortion Bill	1.23	.25	1.24	.25
President's Party X Median Pivot				.36
President's Party X Filibuster Pivot			1.07	.31
Constant	2.54***	.22	3.02***	.22
Log Likelihood	3569.8382			
Pseudo R-Squared	.11			
N=	7,144			

*P<.1, **P<.05, ***P<.01

their parties. I also interacted the variables with the president's party variable to test how the senators from the president's party and the opposition party who sit closest to the median pivot and filibuster pivot positions behave. Interestingly, neither of the interacted terms is significant. This echoes the discussion at the forefront of this chapter, illustrated in Figure 4.2, demonstrating that the difference in voting behavior between the two parties is significant in that pivotal voters in the majority party do not act like pivotal voters in the minority party.

Conclusion

The purpose of this chapter has been to argue that even as moderates refuse to play the legislative game by not offering amendments or taking positions through floor speeches, they still are not getting what they want. Instead, they are actively choosing to not exert power and exhibit deference to others. The results from this chapter seem to suggest that moderates are not nearly as powerful as social science literature theorizes they could be. As I argued in Chapter 3, it is certainly conceivable that moderates do not propose amendments or make speeches on legislation because they already gain what they want before the bill even reaches the floor. Both case studies at the beginning of the chapter examining the Affordable Care Act and the Medicare Expansion Act demonstrate that moderates frequently vote against their preferred positions. Furthermore, they are not negotiating their votes and are not getting any payoff in the form of earmarks or park barrel spending. In doing so, they are protecting themselves while seemingly being "rolled" by their party leaders. Even after expanding the analysis to twelve bills over four Congresses, there was still evidence that moderates do not vote for bills based on their preferences and regularly vote in ways in which they are not looking to maximize their policy outcomes but minimize their electoral punishment.

If moderates are not powerful voters who shape legislation, what is the logic behind their voting behavior? The goals for moderates is that they must find a way to distinguish themselves from their party but also balance their votes to ensure that they "look like" their party. The easiest way for them to do this is to vote with the party on legislation that is closest to the party's base. Issues that define the party, like for Republicans, less government regulation, or more government regulation for Democrats, are the bills that moderates should vote for. On the other hand, hot-button issues that do not necessarily define either party, like abortion and immigration, are areas of legislation where moderates can distinguish themselves. Furthermore, bills that are relatively consensual, in which both parties agree to vote for the legislation, are another opportunity for moderates to vote against legislation to distance themselves from their party.

The implications for this fall on policy outcomes. Because of their inability to move legislation to their ideal points on all legislation, we can assume that much of the legislation that comes out of the increasingly polarized Senate is indeed polarized itself. Again, this is likely due to the electoral pressures today's moderates face. Unlike their ideological counterparts, moderates face pressures that force them to look at their electoral endgame rather than their legislative policy preferences.

Even beyond policy outcomes, the implications for these types of voting behavior suggest that on the "advice and consent" portion of the Senate's duties, party leaders are able to roll moderates as well. Indeed, while historically, voting on Supreme Court nominees has been relatively void of partisan behavior, recent votes have been extremely partisan. While President Obama's nominees, Sonia Sotomayor and Elena Kagan, were confirmed with bipartisan majorities (sixty-eight votes and sixty-three votes in favor, respectively), President Trump's nominees had a much more divided vote. His first nominee, Neil Gorsuch, was confirmed with 54 votes, in which all Republicans voted in favor of his nomination. Three moderate Democrats did vote in favor of his nomination (Heidi Heitkamp [ND], Joe Manchin [WV], and Joe Donnelly [IN]), but none of them was pivotal to his confirmation. His second nominee, Brett Kavanaugh, was approved by a much narrower margin (50–48) after multiple accusations of sexual assault. Susan Collins, viewed as the pivotal vote that could sink his nomination, held out her position until the final moment when she took to the floor in a full-throated endorsement for his nomination.[7] This sealed his nomination and allowed Joe Manchin to vote in favor of his nomination without being the pivotal vote to confirm. Finally, Trump's third nominee, Amy Coney Barrett, was confirmed by a vote of 52–48, in which every Democrat opposed the confirmation and every Republican voted to confirm, except Susan Collins—again, her vote against Barrett was not pivotal to her confirmation one way or the other. These voting patterns fit the larger voting patterns described earlier, in which moderates voted with their party if their vote was pivotal and against their party when they were not needed.

Still, we must temper what conclusions can be taken from this chapter. While this chapter's findings certainly do add to the findings in Chapter 3, they do not protect against the larger idea that back-room politicking of future promises may be happening. It may be the case that moderates can build up a larger cachet through logrolling—since moderate votes are necessary, the case could be made that moderates are "betraying" their party not because they need to distinguish themselves, but because they are trading votes for issues that are more important to them. In the following chapters, I examine interview data to examine the back-room negotiations in greater detail.

5

Behind the Scenes

Priorities, Time, and Overall Satisfaction with the Legislative Process

In Chapters 3 and 4, we took an in-depth look at participatory and voting behavior in the Senate and demonstrated that cross-pressured senators exercise very little power, at least on the surface. When sponsoring, amending, or defending bills, these senators rarely show their theoretical strength. Still, this is only what outsiders can view of the system. Given the nature of the Senate, political scientists must rely on data that only offer information that is "on the record." That is to say, much of the theoretical power that these so-called moderates have may be displayed behind closed doors where they can negotiate deals with colleagues and the leadership. It may even be the case that the leadership seeks out these senators under the understanding that it is these votes that they will require.

Indeed, it may be that moderates are workhorses, not show horses, that they do their work cutting backroom deals, secretly getting their preferred outcome while the media focuses on show horses that are arguing the merit of legislation publicly. In this chapter, I examine interview data from eighteen senators (via their legislative directors) in which I determine just how much work cross-pressured horses do behind closed doors. These interviews were semi-structured in-person interviews conducted at the offices of the senators in Washington, DC. Senators were chosen using the snowball method in which I solicited interviews with staff members familiar with the legislative history of their senator. The composition of those participating ended up as four swing state senators, five partisan-lean state senators, and nine rank-and-file senators. Of these partisan senators, three were members of the leadership, while the other six were rank-and-file senators who were ideologically unremarkable from the median of their caucus. As such, I refer to these six senators as rank-and-file senators throughout this chapter.

Gaining access in Washington, DC, has become an increasingly controversial and challenging endeavor. Many of the staffers I spoke with displayed

Life in the Middle. Neilan S. Chaturvedi, Oxford University Press. © Oxford University Press 2021.
DOI: 10.1093/oso/9780197599723.003.0005

an abundant amount of caution in their conversations with me. Six offices refused to speak with me at all. Among those that refused interviews, the staffers cited office policy as the reason for denying me access. Others cited situations in which legislative staff and even senators themselves were "burned" by individuals posing as academics who then used the information for personal gain. As such, to gain access I had to promise complete anonymity for the respondent as well as the senator. The only exception I was allowed was that I would be allowed to use region, party, or leadership status, but not in conjunction with one another, to preserve some amount of anonymity. Senate offices were approached initially by email and then followed up with either in-person or phone requests for meetings. Each office was given a confidentiality agreement as well. The full survey instrument and agreement is provided in Appendix C.[1]

The respondents were asked about their senator's position on the bill, the priority they had given to the topic, how much time their office spent working on the bill, and their overall satisfaction on the bill (among other questions that will be examined in Chapter 6). I asked the senators about three specific bills: H.R. 325, the bill to raise the debt ceiling (commonly known as "The No Budget, No Pay Act"); S.744, the bill that attempted to reform the immigration system; and S.954, the agriculture reform bill that also affected food stamps. I started each interview by handing the legislative director a copy of the privacy and consent forms to ensure that the interviewee was comfortable and trusted the instrument.

Table 5.1 presents the expectations of a powerful senator and a senator who is marginalized in the middle.

Again, we should expect to see that moderates are far from dominant in the legislative arena. Indeed, the name of the game is survival, and as such, their priorities should be focusing on bills that have a decent payout for their constituency with a very little risk of blowback while avoiding bills that are damaging to their weak electoral coalitions. When one legislative director of a moderate senator (LD) was asked about immigration, their response proved especially poignant:

LD: We're not a border state, and we don't have a large immigrant population. Why focus any of our time on immigration? All it could do is damage us back home with almost no payoff with the few liberals that were in favor of it.

Table 5.1. Expectations for Semi-structured Interviews for Priorities, Time, and Satisfaction with Legislation

	Powerful Senators	Marginalizing Moderates Theory
Priority Given to Legislation	No distinguishing expectations; powerful senators are theoretically powerful and thus can choose what to prioritize.	Bills that are highly salient should be low priorities; only bills that can positively or negatively affect politics back home should be a priority.
Time Spent on Legislation	Powerful senators can either take an active role or passive role, but they will win the vote.	Moderates will need to work just as hard as other senators, if not harder, to win votes.
Satisfaction with Legislation	Powerful senators are always satisfied as their votes are crucial for passage.	Moderates are frequently dissatisfied with outcomes; they are either defeated by broad coalitions or forced to vote against their preferences.

In the following discussion, I find that the responses that were given were largely in line with the findings of previous chapters. That is to say, cross-pressured senators often lost on bills regardless of how much time they spent on the bill. Furthermore, they spent just as much time as other senators and yielded no greater satisfaction on the legislation despite their theoretically pivotal role.

Cases in Varying Salience

The 111th Congress, running from 2009–2011, was productive in its passage of multiple bills, especially by today's standards. After passing a large stimulus bill, the Affordable Care Act, Wall Street Reform, and the Lilly Ledbetter Fair Pay Act, President Obama ran into legislative difficulties after the 2010 midterm elections in which the president's party took a "shellacking," as Obama put it,[2] when Republicans took control of the House of Representatives and won enough seats in the Senate to deprive Obama of his supermajority. Indeed, Democrats lost an atypical sixty-three seats in 2010 in the House, losing the majority as they retained only 193 seats. In the Senate, Democrats lost six seats but kept the majority with fifty-three seats.[3] The 2012 midterms did give Democrats one more seat, but they remained six away from the sixty votes needed to invoke cloture without having to reach out to Republicans. Still, the 113th Congress did take up some pieces of legislation that offer us a chance to examine the power of the senators who sit in the ideological center of the US Senate. The Senate specifically examined bills that controversially raised the debt ceiling, attempted to reform immigration policy, and reformed agriculture and food stamps policy.

As mentioned in previous chapters, pivotal voters may shift by issue. One drawback to the previous chapters is that only key votes, or highly salient votes, were examined. It may undoubtedly be the case that pivotal voters on budgetary issues may not align ideologically to be pivotal voters on less publicized issues or, even for that matter, more polarizing issues. As a result, I asked senators about three bills covering differing policy areas with varying levels of salience. I first asked senators about H.R. 325, the bill that raised the debt ceiling that the sponsors dubbed the "No Budget No Pay Act," in which members of Congress would not receive their pay unless they were able to agree on a budget. This bill is a unique case to examine for many reasons. First, the bill was highly salient and affected all constituencies regardless of region, state ideology, or otherwise. Second, it is an interesting comparison point between the other bills examined, as the bill originated in the House and was negotiated mainly in that chamber. It provides the opportunity to examine how senators can affect legislation when the other chamber is driving the debate.

The second bill I asked about was S.744, the Immigration Reform bill proposed by the "Gang of Eight." This bill also received quite a bit of fanfare from the media, but unlike the budget bill, this one was absent of participation from the White House and relied mostly on a small group of senators. The third bill I asked about was S.954, an agriculture bill that also cut funding for food stamps. This bill received almost no attention from the media until it was passed and signed by the president, and even then, it quickly faded from the nation's attention. Each bill offers a different take, as they vary in salience and policy area. Indeed, as illustrated in Figure 5.1, even when asked how much time they spent on each bill, staffers reported varying accounts, where nearly all of the senators interviewed reporting spending more time on the immigration bill, the most salient of the bunch; followed by the budget bill, in which most of the senators reported spending an average amount of time;

and then the agriculture bill, in which there was much more variance in the time spent, but averaged out to about an average amount of time for all of the senators who participated in the survey.

There is also some disparity in the level of priority given to each bill, allowing for a broader comparison. After all, it is conceivable that different legislators play key or pivotal roles in different policy arenas. Figure 5.2 demonstrates that on average, senators viewed the immigration bill as the most important of the three issues, followed closely by the budget bill, and then the agriculture bill.

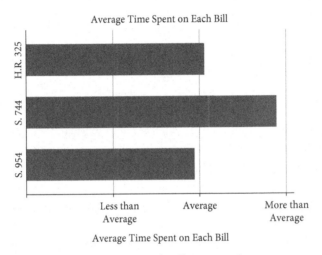

Figure 5.1. Average Time Spent on Each Bill Examined

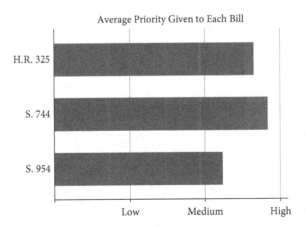

Figure 5.2. Average Priority Given to Each Bill Examined

Of course, one of the reasons the budget bill was viewed as such a high priority was that it fundamentally affected the government's ability to govern. As one rank-and-file senator's legislative director put it:

> LD: It was a huge priority, but there wasn't much for us to do. We had to play into the House leadership and watch a handful of Tea Party Republicans and the Senate leadership deal with each other. Most of the time on this bill was the leadership and those few Republicans, not the rest of us.

In the following sections, I go into greater detail about each bill examined and the overall impact it had on all of the senators who were interviewed.

"No Budget No Pay"

To galvanize public support behind what many referred to as a gimmicky bill, Dean Heller (R-NV), the sponsor of the Senate version of the No Budget No Pay Act of 2013, said, "If you don't do your job in America, you don't get paid. In Washington, D.C. there should be no difference."[4] In reality, the bill was a compromise between Republican leaders in the House and President Obama to temporarily allow the Treasury Department to continue to borrow money to pay for American debt even after expenditures would hit the artificially set debt ceiling until May 19, 2015. In return for allowing the government to continue to pay its debts, congressional Republicans received the provision that the pay for members of Congress would be suspended if they were unable to approve a new budget.

Much of the debate on this bill took place in the House of Representatives, where congressional leaders were struggling for power with a small group of Tea Party Republicans who threatened to shut down the government unless President Obama met certain conditions. Indeed, Senate Majority Leader Harry Reid said, "I understand, and we all understand the Tea Party plays a big part in what goes in the House, and they need a gimmick or two to get things done over there, but to spare the middle class another knock-down, drag-out fight, we're going to proceed to work on this legislation and get it out of there as quickly as we can."[5] On January 23, the House passed their version, and true to his word, Reid took up the bill immediately and passed their version on January 24.

While much of the debate and controversy did take place in the House, to say that the Senate sat idly by to the debate would be an overstatement. As Figure 5.1 demonstrates, most senators reported spending more time than average on the No Budget No Pay Act. Indeed, even when the bill was brought to the floor, the Senate debated, and ultimately rejected, four Republican amendments prior to passage: first an amendment that would have required a dollar in cuts for every dollar increased in the debt ceiling, a second that would have initiated automatic continuing resolutions if Congress could not agree on appropriations bills, a third that would have required the secretary of the treasury to prioritize federal spending in the event that Congress failed to raise the debt ceiling, and a final, non-germane amendment that would have prohibited the sale of defense items to Egypt.[6] Though the bill came from the Republican leadership in the House, a spokesman for Mitch McConnell noted the Senate Republican leadership opposition to the bill, saying, "Leader McConnell and other Senate Republicans had several amendments aimed at forcing Washington to cut government spending, but all were defeated by Democrats. As a result, the leader simply couldn't support the bill."[7] The bill went on to pass in the Senate by a 64–34 vote.

Table 5.2 lists the senators that voted across party lines, twelve Republicans and one Democrat.

Again, traditional theories of lawmaking would dictate that the key votes would need to come from the middle of the chamber. Democrat Joe Manchin, the most conservative member of the Democratic caucus according to the DW-NOMINATE measure, should have been able to negotiate his preferences here and pushed policy in a way that was similar to the behavior of Tea Party Republicans in the House. If the logic behind a legislative win is that moderate senators "win" votes when they vote yes, Manchin's defection from the Democratic leadership suggests that the senator suffered a legislative loss.

Indeed, Reid's caucus had fifty-five Democrats, but Manchin's defection left him with fifty-four votes, six shy of the number needed to invoke cloture. Some votes did come from the center of the chamber with moderate Republican senators Collins (R-ME), Murkowski (R-AK), and Ayotte (R-NH) joining Democrats in voting for the bill. It is difficult to call these legislative victories for this group. Looking at the list of senators who crossed party lines (and the overall count of votes), Reid had little need for those votes or of Manchin's vote, as he got more than enough support from rank-and-file

Table 5.2. Senators Voting against Their Party Leadership on No Budget No Pay (HR 325)

Name	Party	State	Type of State	Ideological Rank (DW-NOMINATE)	Vote
Kelly Ayotte	Republican	New Hampshire	Swing State	60th	Aye
Roy Blunt	Republican	Missouri	Partisan	75th	Aye
Thad Cochran	Republican	Mississippi	Partisan	61st	Aye
Susan Collins	Republican	Maine	Partisan Lean	56th	Aye
Lindsey Graham	Republican	South Carolina	Partisan	64th	Aye
Dean Heller	Republican	Nevada	Swing State	67th	Aye
John Hoeven	Republican	North Dakota	Partisan	69th	Aye
John McCain	Republican	Arizona	Partisan	63rd	Aye
Lisa Murkowski	Republican	Alaska	Partisan	57th	Aye
Richard Shelby	Republican	Alabama	Partisan	92nd	Aye
John Thune	Republican	South Dakota	Partisan	83rd	Aye
Roger Wicker	Republican	Mississippi	Partisan	73rd	Aye
Joe Manchin	Democrat	West Virginia	Partisan Lean	55th	Nay

Republicans like Roy Blunt (R-MO), Thad Cochran (R-MS), John Hoeven (R-ND), Richard Shelby (R-AL), John Thune (R-SD), and Roger Wicker (R-MS). He did not even need the votes of those senators closer to the center (but not quite close enough to be considered moderate) like John McCain (R-AZ) or Lindsey Graham (R-SC).[8] This suggests that even as the Republican leadership withheld support on the bill, there were enough partisans that supported the bill that those senators who were in the middle were less than pivotal. Furthermore, Manchin's defection was also minimized as a result of the partisan crossovers.

The No Budget No Pay Act, or H.R. 325, provides a case in which the House conducted the legislative train, not the Senate. While senators did report that the bill was important, at least as compared to the agriculture bill, and that more time was spent on the bill on average, the handful of amendments that were proposed were quickly voted down and the bill voted up.

The Gang of Eight and Immigration

Shortly after the 2012 election, a group of eight senators began negotiating a deal to pass comprehensive immigration reform. The group was composed of four Democrats led by Charles Schumer (D-NY), Robert Menendez (D-NJ), Michael Bennet (D-CO), and Richard Durbin (D-IL); and four Republicans, John McCain (R-AZ), Lindsey Graham (R-SC), Marco Rubio (R-FL), and Jeff Flake (R-AZ). Interestingly, many in the media incorrectly characterized this bipartisan group as moderate. Indeed, while the argument could be made that Rubio and Bennet represent swing states and could theoretically behave like cross-pressured senators, none of the members of the Gang of Eight could be considered moderate by any ideological measure. The bill was, however, a truly bipartisan bill as it borrowed heavily from both liberal and conservative viewpoints on immigration. The bill allowed for a path to citizenship but also strengthened immigration law enforcement. While hopes of immigration reform passing into law were low, initial efforts in the Senate were somewhat hopeful. Furthermore, in perhaps a strategic move from the White House, the Obama administration limited their lobbying efforts to push the bill and instead relied on the leadership of Harry Reid and the Gang of Eight.[9] Still, even those who were supportive of the bill fell short of supporting the bill consistently. Moderate swing state senator Kelly Ayotte endorsed the bill but did not commit to voting for cloture, arguing that the bill should still be debated.[10]

In this bill, fourteen Republicans voted in favor of the bill while no Democrats voted against the bill. Let us first presume again that Reid and the Democratic leadership retain every Democrat, which in this case, they were able to do. The Democrats would still need five Republicans to cross over to prevent a filibuster. Table 5.3 lists the Republicans who crossed party lines and voted in favor of the bill.

Again, even though Democrats won the fifty-fifth vote, along with the fifty-seventh through the sixtieth votes, they did not have a practical need to reach out to them for their votes because they were also getting votes from Flake, Graham, Hoeven, McCain, and Rubio, each of whom falls outside of the sixty senators in ideological ranking.

The immigration bill provides a case in which members of the Democratic leadership (Durbin, Schumer, and Harry Reid) worked with members of the Republican Party to write and negotiate a palatable bill for the Senate to pass.

Table 5.3. Senators Voting against Their Party Leadership on the Immigration Bill (S.744)

Name	Party	State	Type of State	Ideological Rank (DW-NOMINATE)	Vote
Lamar Alexander	Republican	Tennessee	Partisan	58th	Aye
Kelly Ayotte	Republican	New Hampshire	Swing	59th	Aye
Jeff Chiesa	Republican	New Jersey	Partisan Lean	60th	Aye
Susan Collins	Republican	Maine	Partisan Lean	55th	Aye
Jeff Flake*	Republican	Arizona	Partisan	66th	Aye
Lindsey Graham*	Republican	South Carolina	Partisan	64th	Aye
Orrin Hatch	Republican	Utah	Partisan	62nd	Aye
Dean Heller	Republican	Nevada	Swing	67th	Aye
John Hoeven	Republican	North Dakota	Partisan	69th	Aye
Mark Kirk	Republican	Illinois	Partisan Lean	57th	Aye
John McCain*	Republican	Arizona	Partisan	63rd	Aye
Marco Rubio*	Republican	Florida	Swing	81st	Aye

* Original "Gang of Eight" co-sponsors of the bill

Interestingly, the Gang of Eight itself would not provide enough votes to prevent a filibuster, as no centrists took part in the writing and framing of the original bill. As a result, the case would provide a test for which a bipartisan coalition of members of the Gang of Eight as well as the Democratic leadership reached out to in their efforts to pass the bill.

Agriculture and Food Stamps

Debbie Stabenow (D-MI), chair of the Senate Agriculture Committee, sponsored S.954, formally known as the Agriculture Reform, Food, and Jobs Act of 2013, which appropriated nearly $955 billion over ten years. The bill itself covered a broad variety of policy areas including food assistance for low-income families, foreign food aid, and crop insurance. While sponsored by the leading Democrat on the Agriculture Committee and supported by the Democratic leadership, Thad Cochran (R-MS) added some provisions meant to appeal to his party as well including an overall decrease in spending and a large cut to the food stamp program.[11] Still, the Republican leadership formally opposed the bill.

S.954 provides a unique case in that this is a bill that was a bipartisan bill—one that senators of both parties from states with a large agricultural sector were supportive of. Still, it was a controversial bill, as Senate Republicans added a provision that stripped funding for food stamps in return for continued subsidies to various agricultural sectors. As a result, Table 5.4 shows us a fairly eclectic set of senators who voted against their party leadership.

Fourteen Republicans from safe states voted in favor of the bill—though all fourteen were from heavily agricultural states. Furthermore, of the three

Table 5.4. Senators Voting against their Party Leadership on the Agriculture Bill (S.954)

Name	Party	State	Type of State	Ideological Rank (DW-NOMINATE)	Vote
Lamar Alexander	Republican	Tennessee	Partisan	58th	Aye
Roy Blunt	Republican	Missouri	Partisan	75th	Aye
John Boozman	Republican	Arkansas	Partisan	78th	Aye
Richard Burr	Republican	North Carolina	Partisan	77th	Aye
Saxby Chambliss	Republican	Georgia	Partisan	71st	Aye
Jeff Chiesa	Republican	New Jersey	Partisan Lean	60th	Aye
Dan Coats	Republican	Indiana	Partisan	72nd	Aye
Thad Cochran	Republican	Mississippi	Partisan	61st	Aye
Susan Collins	Republican	Maine	Swing	55th	Aye
Deb Fischer	Republican	Nebraska	Partisan	82nd	Aye
Lindsey Graham	Republican	South Carolina	Partisan	64th	Aye
Chuck Grassley	Republican	Iowa	Swing	76th	Aye
John Hoeven	Republican	North Dakota	Partisan	69th	Aye
Johnny Isakson	Republican	Georgia	Partisan	68th	Aye
Jerry Moran	Republican	Kansas	Partisan	85th	Aye
David Vitter	Republican	Louisiana	Partisan	87th	Aye
Roger Wicker	Republican	Mississippi	Partisan	73rd	Aye
Jack Reed	Democrat	Rhode Island	Partisan	13th	Nay
Sheldon Whitehouse	Democrat	Rhode Island	Partisan	5th	Nay

Table 5.5. Senators Who Did Not Vote on the Agriculture Bill (S.954)

Name	Party	State	Type of State	Ideological Rank (DW-NOMINATE)
Mark Begich	Democrat	Alaska	Partisan Lean	40th
Joe Manchin	Democrat	West Virginia	Partisan Lean	54th
John McCain	Republican	Arizona	Partisan	63rd
Lisa Murkowski	Republican	Alaska	Partisan	56th
Rand Paul	Republican	Kentucky	Partisan	99th
Mark Udall	Democrat	Colorado	Swing	38th
Mark Warner	Democrat	Virginia	Swing	46th

Republican senators from either swing or partisan-lean states, one, Chuck Grassley, was from an agricultural state. This suggests that representational and regional factors played a greater role in this bill than party politics. Since the Democratic leadership faced only two defections, they did not need to apply pressure to any moderate Republicans as many Republicans benefited from this bill, given the states they represented. Perhaps of more significant interest on this bill are the senators who did not vote on the bill at all. Table 5.5 lists these senators.

Of the seven senators who did not vote on the bill, three came from partisan states. Notably, John McCain (R-AZ) missed the vote, but with his long record of opposing agricultural subsidies, his absence is not particularly surprising on a bill that had widespread support. Four of the seven come from either cross-pressured or swing states, in which each of the four does not represent agricultural interests (or at least, do not count them as a large part of their electoral coalition). As a result, it is interesting to see here that even on a relatively innocuous bill that the media did not cover, cross-pressured and swing state senators still exhibit some caution in their vote choices. In the following sections, I explore this further.

Senatorial Behavior

When I asked about the priority put on legislation, one legislative director summarized it like this:

> All of the bills that we've talked about could be labeled as a high priority. If this were a media interview, of course, I'd say they were a high priority. But

the truth of the matter is that not only do we not have the resources to focus on everything, we simply don't want to focus on everything. Being seen on a bill with no payoff hurts us.

Indeed, even though this legislative director represented the thoughts of a rank-and-file Republican, this logic should ring truer for moderates who conceivably would have even more issues with no payoff. In the following sections, I examine the priorities, efforts, and overall satisfaction with the three pieces legislation that are the focus of this chapter.

Priority Given

For each bill, I asked the legislative directors to think back to the specific bill and what their senator's position on the bill was. I then asked what priority each senator put on the bill. Again, if moderate senators are truly pivotal to the process, they should put a priority on all legislation as they are in a position to "win" the legislative debate on every bill debated. However, the answers varied significantly, as demonstrated in Figure 5.3.

As the figure indicates, safe state senators tended to view the budget and immigration bills as high priorities, while the partisan-lean state senators viewed the immigration and agricultural bills as higher priorities, on average.

Indeed, the budget bill seemed to be a bill that was more of a partisan warrior bill than anything else, as we should expect it to be. As noted, the bill was a piece of legislation that has been passed routinely and only recently held up by Tea Party conservatives in the House of Representatives. Given that moderate senators are trying to minimize traceability, especially on controversial legislation like this that transcends region, ideology, and socioeconomics, moderate senators should refuse to play a significant role on this bill. This rang true with the interview respondents as well.

When I asked one moderate senator's legislative director about the priority his office put on this legislation, he scoffed at the idea that his office paid much attention to the legislation at all. He said:

LD: We viewed it as a low-priority bill. It was campaign fodder more than anything else. It helped a lot of the Tea Party folk . . . maybe some very liberal Democrats who wanted to be seen doing battle with them, but the rest of us . . . we didn't care.

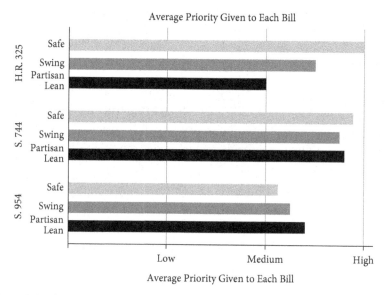

Figure 5.3. Average Priority Assigned to Each Bill by Legislative Directors

When I asked another moderate senator's legislative director the same question his response was:

> LD: This was simply not a priority for us. There were a lot of antics from Tea Partiers, but for the rest of us, this was a routine bill that we have been passing for decades.

These responses suggest that ideological battles, regardless of their salience and the media's attention, proved to be of little worth to moderate senators. Of course, highly visible ideological battles should be of little to no worth to moderate senators as they could do much more damage than good. For those who are cross-pressured, fighting a partisan battle would do much to shore up support for the base, but would likely activate the much larger opposition that the senator would face in the general election. Even swing state senators would likely galvanize support for a strong general election challenge. Still, others stayed out of the partisan battle to look like they were above the fray. As one moderate LD said:

LD: This was as gimmicky of a bill as you could get. We stayed out of it because it made the Republicans look dysfunctional. The only thing that can help us sometimes is when the other party looks bad.

Meanwhile, partisan leaders and the ideological rank and file were much more up front with their fervor for the bill. One liberal rank and file senator described the debate as "a serious policy issue that needed to be dealt with immediately," but also later conceded that the debate was "largely partisan." Lending support to the idea that participation and activity on a bill serve to support one's electoral prospects among the base, another liberal rank-and-file senator said that the bill was a high priority, as the senator's participation would score points back home, confirming the thoughts of one of the previous moderate LDs. Indeed, a member of the party leadership summarized it best by saying:

LD: This was the highest priority a bill could have. We took it upon ourselves to frame the debate for our caucus and make sure we passed the bill.

While collective choice logic would suggest that the optimal position would be to play the role of powerbroker, here this logic rings less true. For moderate Democrats, playing a large role and voting with the party may help with the base, but with high media coverage, it will activate the opposition. Even playing a pivotal role in voting with the opposition could ultimately hurt the Democrat with their base, or even hurt the party overall as it would make the party look dysfunctional as well—something that one of the LDs I interviewed talked about with the opposition party. For moderate Republicans, there is little incentive to play a visibly pivotal role for the Democratic leadership, as it would likely draw the ire of the Tea Party and other ideological elements in their constituency. Similarly, it is less than optimal for them to play the pivotal role for their leadership for the same reasons as the moderate Democrats. As such, it makes sense for moderate legislators to worry less about getting a legislative victory than to just avoid traceability on the issue.

On the immigration bill, each Senate office reported that they viewed the bill as either a medium or a high priority, but for wildly different reasons. As one moderate senator's LD summarized:

LD: We viewed this bill as a high priority simply because we had to worry about the party and our constituents. We knew that either way we were going to let someone down.

This hardly screams of political power. Instead, this suggests that moderates are pressured more than they can exert power. Indeed, if the senator had pivotal power, they should be able to push legislation to their ideal point, as party pressures would not matter. Given the fact that the legislative director felt pressure from the party in that there was a fear that they were going to disappoint the party if they did not vote with them, it suggests that the party leadership was not willing to play the legislative game as a powerful vote. Instead, it seems that the leadership was rigid in their requirements and what they were willing to add or remove from the bill.

Even when constituency did not play a large role, moderate senators still sat on the sideline. For example, another moderate LD said:

It's a medium-priority bill for us. We're lucky since we're not a border state. We know this is an important issue and the media's watching, but we're not going to play a large role here.

Again, this equivalent of a political "punt" works against the narrative of a powerful senator as it suggests that when able, moderates will avoid the political stage altogether. Here, a moderate senator is not particularly cross-pressured in that the senator's constituency does not view the issue as particularly controversial, yet the senator still maintains minimal involvement in the debate. Of course, the senator could be behaving cautiously with the presumption that their participation could activate a sub-constituency against them.

In contrast, each Democratic leader or rank-and-file senator reported the bill as being a high priority save one, who was supportive of the bill but had little incentive to participate since they were not a border state senator. Indeed, the rank-and-file senators viewed it as a high priority as it tugged at the Democratic coalition: labor and union interests versus immigration and minority communities. Members of the leadership were especially optimistic about the bill and viewed it as their highest priority outside of the debt ceiling bill.

The Republican leadership and rank-and-file senators I talked to had a slightly different view. While they all viewed it as a high-priority bill, they all viewed it as a priority to defeat the bill. As a result, one senator's LD said:

LD: We spoke to every member of our caucus including the Gang of Eight to defeat the bill. For us, the loss was twofold: we would lose with our base, while simultaneously giving the Democrats something to brag about.

This last line speaks against bipartisanship even when bipartisan agreements are in place. This of course also suggests that there is little room for deal-brokers who are not on solid footing with their constituents as party pressures would play an even more significant role here—a point that was alluded to earlier by a moderate fearful of the demands of party and constituency. Indeed, as the media incorrectly characterized the Gang of Eight as a group of moderates, the truth is that a group of eight moderates would likely have difficulty building a large coalition as even rank-and-file senators increased their lobbying efforts against this bill.

On the agriculture bill, while there were a few legislative directors who mentioned that they viewed this bill as a high priority bill to get passed, none of the moderates I interviewed had much of a desire to get involved directly. Indeed, even with cross pressures motivating action, moderate senators still avoided traceability on the bill.

One moderate LD reported:

We knew we had to get this passed for our farm community, but we thought hard about proposing an amendment on the food stamps. Ultimately, we decided against it because we didn't want to be targeted by the Republicans.

While this echoes a desire to play a pivotal role, again we see moderates shy away from the process in fear of becoming an easy target for the opposition. Of course, this runs against the conventional wisdom of moderates. In this particular case, this legislative director viewed the bill as a high-priority bill as they had constituents who were directly affected by the outcome of the bill. To prevent Republican obstruction, Democrats allowed Republicans to add in a highly restrictive measure regarding eligibility for food stamps. Despite the fact that the moderate senator opposed this measure, the senator refused to play a larger role and instead allowed the right wing of the Republican Party to play a larger role. As such, it is difficult to view moderates as pivotal here as, again, despite "winning" the vote (i.e., they did vote in favor of the bill and get agriculture subsidies for their constituents), they failed to move the bill to their ideal ideological point.

Time Spent

As mentioned in Chapter 3, much of a legislator's time goes into the basic legwork of understanding a policy area and deciding how to participate in the legislative process. While senators can specialize in certain areas, high-profile pieces of legislation like the ones discussed in this chapter are relatively immune to specialization. That is to say, on bills like the ones examined in this chapter, conventional wisdom would dictate that senators, especially ones who are pivotal to the lawmaking process, not defer to their party but instead focus their time on constructing strategy on the bill. Indeed, intuitively it makes sense for senators to spend a considerable amount of time deciding what their position will be and the extent to which they will participate. For each bill, I asked, "Thinking back to the debate on [the issue], how much of your office's time was spent on that issue compared to other legislation you were working on?" The results on average are presented in Figure 5.4.

Safe state senators spent the most time on the debt ceiling bill, while swing state senators and partisan-lean state senators spent the most time on the immigration and agriculture bills.

On the debt-ceiling bill, all five moderates I interviewed reported spending less than average or the average amount of time they would spend on a typical bill. One moderate Democrat's LD said that neither she nor her senator

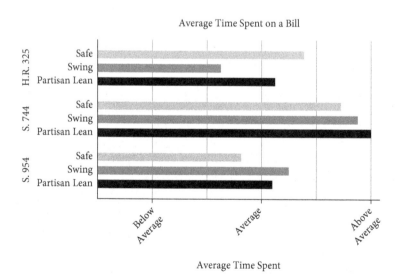

Figure 5.4. Average Time Spent on Each Bill

spent much time on the bill at all and relied solely on the advice of their legislative assistant. However, given the nature of the bill and the rhetoric behind the bill, conservative Republicans made a strong effort to toe the company line. As one LD reported, "it was all hands on deck."

Another LD for a rank-and-file Republican went on to say that they spent the bulk of their time focused on a legislative strategy to break the bill on the floor. They focused on writing amendments that would make the vote especially hard for vulnerable senators. Of course, the battle to vote on the amendment proved to be difficult, as Senate Majority Leader Reid filled the amendment tree, preventing this particular office from having any of their amendments voted on.[12] Still, it was clear that the priority was to at least demonstrate that the senator was putting up a strong fight against the legislation.

The Democrats, however, absent a rhetorical argument for their base, played less of a role, referring the legislation in most part to the leadership. Even then, members of the leadership deferred to Patty Murray (D-WA) and the other members of the Budget Committee along with the leadership in the House of Representatives. As one rank-and-file senator put it, "The Senate as a body added a few things, but we largely accepted the terms agreed upon in the House."

Most senators' LDs reported spending a great deal of time on the immigration bill, however. Among the partisan-lean state moderate senators, each one reported spending more time than average, but on average, felt that the time spent might have been for naught. For example, one non–border state senator described the negotiation process as particularly futile:

> NC (in response to the LD describing the amount of time spent on the immigration bill as "a lot"): How did the negotiations go from your point of view, given the amount of time your office spent on the bill?
>
> LD: [It was] fairly straightforward. They asked us what we needed to vote for the bill, and we told them. The problem was that we didn't really need anything.

Even when confronted with a situation in which they could have played a pivotal role, the senator demurred and failed to make substantive demands.

Still, other moderate senators viewed the process through a different lens, describing a negotiating point with little leverage. One moderate partisan-lean state senator described a particularly divisive process when I prodded for more information:

NC (again, in response to the LD describing the amount of time spent on the immigration bill as "a lot"): Did the office's work yield any positives regarding outcomes?

LD: We didn't like all of the bill, which was problematic for us because immigration is highly divisive back home, but we weren't going to be able to change it.

Even efforts to change the bill through amendments were thwarted for moderates.

LD (continues): We wanted more amendments. We planned on a few amendments that would have made the bill a lot stronger in our eyes, but we weren't even allowed to push them very far. Some senators just hold a systematic advantage.

When I asked for clarification, the legislative director made it clear that they were referring not to herself or their cohort of moderates, but to the leadership of both parties.

Swing state and partisan-lean state senators did report spending more time on average as compared to their safe state counterparts on the agriculture bill, however. Still, it does not seem to be that these moderate senators were using their power to sway the bill's contents to their direction. Instead, it seems that the bulk of their efforts was in trying to get the minimal benefit for their constituents despite the large costs attached to avoid Republican obstructionism. One exchange was particularly telling of the precarious position moderate senators were in on this bill.

LD: This bill was so important to us politically. We are, after all, a farm state and we desperately needed to get this through. Yeah, we didn't like that there were cuts to food stamps, but the blowback we would get with not pushing this through would have been huge. We spent a lot of time trying to convince our friends of that fact.

Remarkably, this response was incredibly similar to another partisan-lean moderate legislative director:

LD: We spent a lot of time on this bill, but we had to defer to the leadership. Reid knew how to push this through, and we just weren't going to get everything we wanted.

Based on these responses, it is clear that these moderate senators did make a clear effort to push the legislation, but they seemed to only push the legislation to passage rather than play a role in writing the bill. That is to say, they did not play much of a role in shaping the bill but instead spent their time trying to pass the bill as is.

Much of the burden of this fell at the feet of the leadership and Reid, who again filled the amendment tree, preventing some Republicans and Democrats from offering amendments on the floor. While both swing state senators and safe state senators objected to the process—many LDs reported wasting a lot of time drafting amendments that were ultimately trashed by the leadership—most acknowledged that if the amendments were passed, the bill would have died on the floor.

End Results on the Bill

The bottom line in the legislative game is whether legislators win, or are ultimately "happy" with the final draft of the legislation. If indeed ideological moderates are powerful and pivotal in the lawmaking game, their end satisfaction ultimately trumps all. That is to say, if the bills ultimately match their ideological preferences, then the time they spend on the bill means less as leaders have already taken them into account in their final framing of the bill.

Figure 5.5 illustrates an interesting mix of results regarding overall satisfaction.

On the No Budget No Pay Act, the swing state and partisan-lean state senators were, on average, more satisfied than the safe state senators. Since this was a bill that played only a large rhetorical role for conservatives, it is hard to imagine a situation in which the partisan warrior would be satisfied with the bill but the swing state and cross-pressured senators unsatisfied. That is to say, partisan-lean state senators have little incentive to battle for a resolution that benefits them, as the polarized environment would only cause them greater problems.

Considering that partisan-lean state Democrats had to deal with the looming threat of a Tea Party challenge, participating on the bill or playing a highly visible or pivotal role would have likely galvanized the opposition. As one moderate Democrat put it, "Politics back home was divisive every time this issue came up. We were happy that our primary objective was fulfilled—passing this bill." Another moderate Democrat emphasized that the issue was a "Big Deal. Being in a red state makes voting on these types of

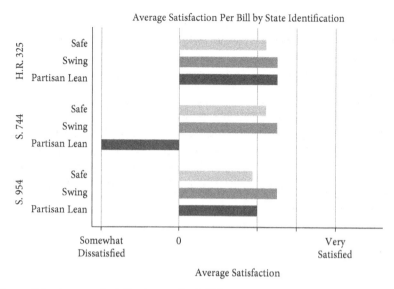

Figure 5.5. Average Satisfaction on Each Bill

issues incredibly difficult." On the other hand, the Republican rank-and-file senators were upset with the overall outcome. Since many wanted spending cuts attached to a debt limit increase, the clean extension proved to be less than optimal. Every Republican reported dissatisfaction, as they had to deal with an increasingly angst filled base.

Meanwhile, Democrats mainly viewed the bill as "gimmicky" and something that needed to be done. Since the Democratic rank-and-file senators came from states in which the politics on the issue were relatively consensual, few were worried about a backlash from voters or an uprising from the Tea Party. Most simply seemed begrudgingly satisfied at the bill.

Within the Democratic Party leadership, there was little report of any fanfare on the issue, as most were relieved that the bill would pass. Indeed, one member of the leadership argued that the issue "could have provided some fodder back home, but constituents were mostly tired of the debate." The Republican leadership was also somewhat torn on the issue, as they wanted more concessions from Democrats but realized that they needed to pass the bill.

On the immigration bill, Figure 5.5 demonstrates that partisan-lean state senators were not only less satisfied with the bill, but they were, on average, dissatisfied with the bill. The "Gang of Eight" bill was a bill that was

touted as a bipartisan solution to finding a compromise on immigration re-
form. While there are senators here that are from swing states (Bennet and
Rubio), neither run to the middle as they both run to their respective bases.
Also noteworthy is the participation of the two members of the Democratic
leadership, Richard Durbin, the Democrats' second ranking member, and
Charles Schumer, the third ranking member.

While the bill was viewed as a bipartisan compromise and adding four
Republicans ensured bill passage even with moderate defections, the concern obviously would be defending against the filibuster where sixty votes
would be needed to move the bill past debate and to a final vote. The question remains, What votes should be sought after? Again, if the most pivotal
members are the moderates, it should be natural to begin and end the search
for votes with members who sit in the middle of the chamber. Instead, the
Democratic leadership decided on allowing the Corker-Hoeven Border
Enforcement Amendment to be put up for a vote to bring along more
Republican votes. Indeed, Chapter 4 demonstrates that this should not be
surprising, as moderates view this issue, regardless of content, as especially
problematic.

The amendment itself was a clear effort to reach out to conservatives
who were more concerned about border enforcement. The amendment
called for an increase of nearly 40,000 border patrol agents at the cost of
approximately $30 billion. It also called for aerial monitoring and 700
miles of new fencing.[13] The amendment passed with sixty-nine votes, a
signal that there might be enough votes to prevent a filibuster on the actual bill.

Interestingly, though, the ones who felt left out of the process were the
moderates. When asked about the process overall and overall satisfaction,
one moderate legislative director responded:

LD: We wanted more amendments, but the leadership just would not
allow the processing of a lot of amendments. It felt like other senators were
holding the system hostage.

Another Democratic moderate argued:

LD: [The Corker-Hoeven Amendment] just went too far. But, since we're
not a border state, we felt we could be more pragmatic than other senators.

Even on the other side of the aisle, Republican moderates viewed the process as too polarized and void of moderation. One Republican moderate also said:

> LD: Ideologically the bill lined up with the party's goals. We thought it went a bit far, but we knew we didn't have any influence, so we just stayed out of the process.

Meanwhile, the partisan warriors were more or less pleased with the bill except a few ideological Republicans. Among the Democrats I was able to speak with, most expressed satisfaction with the bill and an understanding that a compromise had to be made to achieve "big" legislation. Other Democrats noted that their vote was never in doubt, so they neither participated nor had any desire to get involved in the debate. Republicans who were opposed to the deal complained about Harry Reid's practice of filling the amendment tree. One member of the Republican leadership argued that had the Cornyn Amendment been adopted, his senator would have voted yes. Others complained that the Corker-Hoeven Amendment ended up being the moderate alternative to the more conservative options that were lined up by other members of the Republican caucus, despite the overall conservative nature of the amendment.

Based on these interviews, it seems to be that the biggest losers on the bill may have been the moderates who were all but resigned to their limited roles assigned to them by the party leadership. All of the senators who sat in the middle ultimately voted in favor of the bill, despite having major reservations. Meanwhile, many of the Republicans I was able to speak to described how they were upset with the process and ultimately used that to justify their "nay" vote.

Of course, it could be argued that a lower-salience bill like the agriculture bill may yield an arena in which moderates are not the ones who are proverbially steamrolled, but the pivotal power players. Indeed, swing state senators and partisan-lean state senators reported greater satisfaction with this bill as compared to the safe state senators. However, much of the satisfaction seems to be from the fact that many of these senators were reliant on agricultural subsidies for their states. Indeed, one swing state senator's legislative director with an agricultural sub-constituency said:

LD: Overall we were pretty satisfied—the bill passed and we got the subsidies, but it felt like we didn't have much of a say in how the bill looked. We just could not propose any amendments.

Another partisan-lean state moderate senator said:

LD: We were satisfied, but it really could have been a better bill for [my state]. Still, we were able to get one amendment in, which was better than the majority of our peers.

Meanwhile, rank-and-file senators from both parties reported nearly no opinion on the bill. Most were satisfied not because of the content, but because it was one of a handful of bills that were passed with relative ease and little consequence to their electoral circumstances. As a result, it could then be argued that moderates did play a pivotal role in this legislation, but not nearly the powerful role that conventional wisdom makes it out to be. Indeed, it seems that the power they exercised was power to push the legislation (which may have already been consensual enough for senators to vote in favor of) rather than shaping the actual legislation.

Conclusion

To conclude our meeting, one legislative director for a partisan lean-state moderate senator said:

LD: The caucus takes care of its own. We [speaking of their senator] win a lot because we reach across the aisle and work with Republicans and Democrats, but we most often look to our leadership.

This seems to be the case when looking at individual senator behavior in the modern era. While moderates viewed bills as high priorities and even spent a great deal of time on legislation, they reported being dissatisfied with two of the three bills and were only satisfied with the last bill because they needed the key provision of agriculture subsidies. Indeed, as a legislative director for one member of the leadership put it:

LD: We spend most of our time thinking about how we're going to protect moderates, not so much listening to them. Right now, we're looking to protect Mark Pryor [a Democrat from Arkansas who went on to lose reelection], but we can't talk to him, and he won't talk to us.

This line of Mark Pryor may sum up senatorial behavior for moderates—work hard, but do not be pivotal. Even then, you may go on to lose your reelection battle.

6

Behind the Scenes

Measuring Influence on Legislation

In the previous chapters, we have seen that moderate senators do not participate in bills, either through amendments or defending them through speeches, and frequently choose the most opportune path in terms of their vote choices on legislation. Even when it is against their stated preferences, and despite spending time and resources and prioritizing legislation, they are rarely fully satisfied with the legislative outcome. Still, this all focuses on how the individual legislator behaves. That is to say, it focuses on how moderates behave but falls short in that it fails to register how other senators view their moderate counterparts. For example, do leaders and bill supporters have to continually lobby and cajole their centrist colleagues to vote for their bill? How often are they contacted vis-à-vis their counterparts? Furthermore, thus far, we have yet to gain an accurate gauge of how much leverage moderates have regarding building coalitions and lobbying their colleagues to vote with them.

Indeed, during the 2009 negotiations to pass President Obama's stimulus bill, then chief of staff Rahm Emanuel met with five centrists (really four plus Joe Lieberman, an independent who caucused with the Democrats and was viewed as socially conservative and a war hawk) about passing the bill— Susan Collins (R-ME), Olympia Snowe (R-ME), Arlen Specter (at the time, R-PA, but who later switched parties), and Ben Nelson (D-NE). Emanuel emphasized the need to act quickly to pass the legislation, and Collins, Snowe, Lieberman, and Specter promptly agreed. Nelson, however, astutely realized his increased leverage and demanded policy concessions before he could decide to vote in favor of the bill. Instead of negotiating, however, Emanuel pulled Nelson aside and promised vague, future concessions[1] in exchange for his vote now, to which Nelson agreed.[2] Is this the norm? Do party leaders view pivotal moderates as just that? Or instead, do party leaders view moderates as thorns in their sides that have to be "dealt with," as Emmanuel had to deal with Nelson? Furthermore, aside from how party leaders view

Life in the Middle. Neilan S. Chaturvedi, Oxford University Press. © Oxford University Press 2021.
DOI: 10.1093/oso/9780197599723.003.0006

moderates, are moderates able to build coalitions themselves using their influence?

Perhaps such lobbying and bargaining as Ben Nelson's example are just anomalies, and party leaders frame legislation in such a way that it appeals to centrists without actually having formal negotiations. Indeed, it may be that party leaders or the framers of legislation have already shaped legislation to meet the needs of moderates, but they are simply dissatisfied because it does not perfectly align with their preferences. For example, to protect moderate senators from casting controversial votes, Harry Reid limited amendments and the number of bills voted on—a move that backfired and angered many partisan-lean state Democrats who were looking to find a way to distinguish themselves from other Democrats (see, for example, Chaturvedi 2017a).

In any case, the data analysis presented thus far has been relatively one-sided in that we have not yet considered how others respond to these senators. In this chapter, I again turn to the interview data from eighteen legislative directors of senators from the 113th Congress. Specifically, I asked the legislative directors to measure how often members of the leadership, moderates, and rank-and-file senators lobbied them for their vote on a piece of legislation. I also asked them to rate their colleagues on the level of influence they had on the same three bills discussed in Chapter 5. Specifically, I asked them whether the senator in question had a direct or indirect influence on the content of the legislation. Table 6.1 lays out the expectations for these questions.

If moderates can play a powerful or important role, we should see those members lobbying others and pushing for their vote and rated as directly influential on the legislation. Still, as I mentioned earlier, we must also consider the possibility moderates are so powerful that they need not even lobby— other legislators will already take their preferences into account, as they are indirectly influential on the content of the legislation.

If, however, moderates are not powerful, we should not see them lobby other legislators because not only would it be ineffective, but doing so would suggest that they wanted to play a pivotal role that could put them in the limelight. Similarly, moderates should have no outstanding or noteworthy direct influence, as compared to their rank-and-file counterparts, for the same reasons. Indeed, their impact should genuinely be less if they are trying to protect the traceability of their actions. Finally, moderates should have little indirect influence as well, as their votes are not truly pivotal—partisans from the other side who may find the legislation palatable, even if their

Table 6.1. Expectations for Lobbying and Influence

	Powerful Senators	Marginalized Senators
Lobbying	Unclear—Moderates may contact others to gain support, or may force others to their position given their leverage.	Moderates simply do not have the power to lobby others and will not do so.
Direct Influence	Moderates can have a direct influence on the bill by forcing leaders to move legislation to their ideal point.	Moderates are only as powerful as their counterparts and have no special powers of direct influence.
Indirect Influence	Moderates can have indirect influence if leaders anticipate their policy preferences and move legislation to their ideal point.	Moderate votes are not needed, as coalitions are typically built in a bipartisan fashion, eliminating the need for the leadership to anticipate their needs.

ideological identity runs counter to that can easily replace them. In the following sections, I will examine these points in more depth.

Lobbying for Support

Coalition building is an important, though fairly underrated, task in the US Senate. While many laud the efforts of bipartisan coalitions like the immigration bill's "Gang of Eight," or the "Gang of Fourteen" that temporarily stopped the dreaded "nuclear option" that would have ended the use of filibusters on judicial nominees (only to have the option exercised in 2017), as well as the efforts or broad coalition builders like Ted Kennedy, it often goes unnoticed that broad coalitions need coalition builders. Indeed, in an era in which party leaders have become increasingly polarized, the presumption would be that others, including rank-and-file Democrats and Republicans, or, moderates, would play this role. This conclusion is, of course, the message that moderates in the Senate want their constituents to believe of themselves, but as Grimmer (2013) notes, the message that voters get is not often the one that accurately reflects the record in Congress. For example, in her 2014 Senate reelection race, Susan Collins emphasized an identity of being a coalition builder who works with Democrats and Republicans.[3] While it is true that Collins did vote with Democrats many times in her career (see, for example, Chapter 4), is it accurate to characterize her as a coalition builder? That is to say, while the media, social science scholarship, and indeed moderates themselves often tell a story in which moderate legislators are the "grown-ups" in the room that are above partisan rancor, are they truly just marginal actors in a partisan game?

To gain traction on this question, I asked the legislative directors to rate how often members of the Democratic and Republican leadership contacted their office on the piece of legislation in question. I also asked about committee leaders, the White House, and a randomly selected group of eight senators who sit close to either the median pivot or filibuster pivot positions mixed with twelve rank-and-file Democrats and Republicans. From among the same group from Chapter 5, the legislative directors were asked, "Think back to the bill in question. Looking at the names on the list, approximately how often did the following individuals attempt to influence your senator's decision on how to vote on the bill?" The LDs were then asked to check under "occasionally" and "frequently" or leave the boxes blank if not contacted at all for each senator and the White House. Again, the form is available in Appendix C.

Except John Cornyn, the Republican whip, the leadership dominated the lobbying process when compared to pivotal moderates and rank-and-file Democrats and Republicans. Harry Reid had contact with nearly every legislative director's office through either occasional or frequent lobbying, while Durbin had contact with fewer offices but was much more frequent in his lobbying. Mitch McConnell had fewer points of contact with the group of legislative directors I spoke to here but was much more frequent in his contacts. Among the moderates, Joe Manchin and Mark Warner were the most active in their lobbying efforts, with Joe Manchin having six instances of occasional lobbying and one instance of frequent lobbying, while Warner had six instances of frequently lobbying an office. Perhaps even more telling, when I asked what the content of the Manchin's six instances of occasional lobbying was, the LD responded:

> LD: I'm not sure if you would classify this as lobbying, but most of the nature of the talk with Manchin's folks would be about what our type of senators [referring to the senator's region] should do on this legislation. It was almost like a courtesy that we were doing each other.

While this is a form of coalition building, in that Manchin's office seems to be looking for a regional consensus, this goes to suggest that even the lobbying efforts by moderates were rather weak. These lobbying effects are also clearly dwarfed when compared to the party leaders, and even some rank-and-file Democrats and Republicans. Among the rank-and-file Democrats and Republicans, John McCain and Bob Corker were both active in their lobbying efforts.

What is more glaring, however, is the lack of lobbying from other members of the moderates group. Donnelly, Kirk, McCaskill, and Udall all had fewer than four lobbying interactions with the offices I spoke to. Mark Pryor's lack of interactions is particularly glaring. As a vulnerable incumbent seeking reelection, Pryor could be seen as the theoretically most powerful moderate. Indeed, losing his seat would prove to be detrimental to the Democratic leadership, and as such, they should be willing to negotiate at every turn to give Pryor more to talk about with his reelection. Yet even Pryor, with quite a bit of negotiating leverage and capital, was limited in his lobbying interactions. I examine each bill more in depth in the following sections.

Lobbying on HR 325, No Budget No Pay

As we observed in Chapter 5, the No Budget No Pay, H.R. 325 bill was driven mostly by the House of Representatives. Nevertheless, the leadership in the Senate had to muster enough votes to gain support to pass the controversial House bill.

The leadership did much of the lobbying work. Interestingly, each member of the pivotal moderates, as well as the rank-and-file groups, was reported to have made some lobbying contact with the offices interviewed. Still, one legislative director described inter-office lobbying in a different context.

> NC: What was the nature of these lobbying efforts?
>
> LD: On these types of bills we like to talk to each other to see what everyone's thinking is—meaning, they talked to us and had a position, but were open to changing their position as long as we as a group could figure out what would be best for us, politically.

That is, these occasional contacts are less about lobbying to vote a certain way than they are about creating a consensus on a piece of legislation.

On the No Budget No Pay Act, moderates were not doing the bulk of the lobbying action. Perhaps a more important question then is, were they the senators who were most lobbied? Table 6.2 illustrates the lobbying patterns of

Table 6.2. Total Number of Mentions of Contact by Members of the Leadership for Each Type of Senator (by Group)

Leadership (Democratic)	Partisan-Lean State Respondents			Swing State Respondents			Safe State Respondents		
	Occasional	Frequent	Total	Occasional	Frequent	Total	Occasional	Frequent	Total
Reid	3	0	3/5 (60%)	0	1	1/4 (25%)	3	1	4/9 (44%)
Durbin	1	1	2/5 (40%)	0	1	1/4 (25%)	3	1	4/9 (44%)
(Republican)									
McConnell	0	1	1/5 (20%)	1	0	1/4 (25%)	0	2	2/9 (22%)
Cornyn	0	1	1/5 (20%)	0	0	0/4 (0%)	1	0	1/9 (22%)

the leadership and how often they lobbied the senators I interviewed to affect their votes.[4]

Looking at the number of mentions of contact with a senator (occasional or frequent) in total, safe state senators were lobbied the most, followed by partisan-lean state senators, and then swing state senators, who were rarely talked to at all. Indeed, three of the five partisan-lean state senators were contacted by Reid, though only occasionally, compared to three of the nine safe state respondents reporting occasional contact with Reid and one safe state respondent reporting frequent contact with Reid. Durbin, the majority whip, was less active, lobbying three safe state senators occasionally and one frequently, compared to one partisan-lean state senator occasionally and one frequently. Furthermore, swing state respondents reported little contact, with only one of the four respondents reporting frequent contact with Reid and Durbin. This is counterintuitive to what we would expect to see in a spatial model in which the senators in the middle should be lobbied the heaviest. Interestingly, only one partisan-lean state senator reported frequent lobbying from Mitch McConnell and John Cornyn, respectively, which seems like a missed opportunity of sorts for the Republican leadership since the partisan-lean state senators are the likeliest senators the leadership would be able to pick off from the majority to vote with their side. Indeed, only one swing state senator reported any contact (here, frequent) from either McConnell or Cornyn. Contrast this to two safe state senators reporting contact from McConnell and one safe state senator reporting contact from Cornyn. All this suggests that on this particular bill, the Republican leadership did not feel that partisan-lean state and swing state senators were worth lobbying.

Also, fellow moderates did not communicate with the partisan-lean group, as only one LD reported being contacted by a moderate occasionally. Table 6.3 lists the lobbying efforts by both moderates and the rank-and-file senators listed on the interview questionnaire.

Of the eight randomly selected moderates and the twelve randomly selected rank-and-file partisans, only one moderate, Joe Manchin, had occasional contact with a partisan-lean state senator. None of the four swing state senators interviewed reported contact from either the eight moderates or the twelve rank-and-file partisans. Contrastingly, of the nine safe state respondents, at least one reported occasional contact with every senator on the list. Of the moderates on the list, Joe Manchin and Mark Warner contacted two safe state respondents, while Isakson and Inhofe contacted two safe state respondents from the rank-and-file party of the list.

Table 6.3. Total Number of Mentions of Contact by Members of the Leadership for Each Type of Senator (by Group)

	Partisan-Lean State Respondents			Swing State Respondents			Safe State Respondents		
	Occasional	Frequent	Total	Occasional	Frequent	Total	Occasional	Frequent	Total
Moderates									
Joe Manchin	1	0	1/5 (20%)	0	0	0/4 (0%)	2	0	2/9 (22%)
Mark Begich	0	0	0/5 (0%)	0	0	0/4 (0%)	1	0	1/9 (11%)
Claire McCaskill	0	0	0/5 (0%)	0	0	0/4 (0%)	1	0	1/9 (11%)
Mark Pryor	0	0	0/5 (0%)	0	0	0/4 (0%)	1	0	1/9 (11%)
Joe Donnelly	0	0	0/5 (0%)	0	0	0/4 (0%)	1	0	1/9 (11%)
Mark Warner	0	0	0/5 (0%)	0	0	0/4 (0%)	2	0	2/9 (22%)
Mark Kirk	0	0	0/5 (0%)	0	0	0/4 (0%)	1	0	1/9 (11%)
Heidi Heitkamp	0	0	0/5 (0%)	0	0	0/4 (0%)	1	0	1/9 (11%)
Rank and File									
Chris Murphy	0	0	0/5 (0%)	0	0	0/4 (0%)	1	0	1/9 (11%)
Lisa Murkowski	0	0	0/5 (0%)	0	0	0/4 (0%)	1	0	1/9 (11%)
Johnny Isakson	0	0	0/5 (0%)	0	0	0/4 (0%)	2	0	2/9 (22%)
Jack Reed	0	0	0/5 (0%)	0	0	0/4 (0%)	1	0	1/9 (11%)
John McCain	0	0	0/5 (0%)	0	0	0/4 (0%)	1	0	1/9 (11%)
James Inhofe	0	0	0/5 (0%)	0	0	0/4 (0%)	2	0	2/9 (22%)
Deb Fischer	0	0	0/5 (0%)	0	0	0/4 (0%)	1	0	1/9 (11%)
John Barrasso	0	0	0/5 (0%)	0	0	0/4 (0%)	1	0	1/9 (11%)
Pat Roberts	0	0	0/5 (0%)	0	0	0/4 (0%)	1	0	1/9 (11%)
Bob Corker	0	0	0/5 (0%)	0	0	0/4 (0%)	1	0	1/9 (11%)
Mark Udall	0	0	0/5 (0%)	0	0	0/4 (0%)	1	0	1/9 (11%)
Mike Johanns	0	0	0/5 (0%)	0	0	0/4 (0%)	1	0	1/9 (11%)

Still, it is difficult to draw major conclusions from this particular bill. As mentioned in Chapter 5, the No Budget No Pay Act was viewed by most of the legislative directors as a gimmicky bill that was passed out of necessity for liberals and Democrats and was a sort of "red meat" for the conservatives and their base. Indeed, the lobbying efforts toward the rank and file may be a result of this partisan battle in that conservative Republicans required significant whipping from the leadership and rank-and-file members. The immigration reform bill provides a more precise example of how negotiations are done behind closed doors on salient and highly publicized legislation.

Lobbying on S.744, Immigration Reform

Again, as we noted in Chapter 5, the immigration reform bill debated in the 113th Congress is an interesting case study to examine the question at hand. It is a highly salient bill that was debated heavily in Congress with a lot of media attention. It had a bipartisan "Gang of Eight" senators, who again were not moderate senators but rather partisans and party leaders who negotiated the overall substance of the bill. Finally, it holds an interesting dynamic in which border states are much more incentivized to take the lead in ensuring passage of the bill than other senators.

As a result, this case study should shed more light on the overall power of moderates in the Senate. If, after all, moderates are powerful, they will either lobby for a renegotiation of the agreed-upon deal written by the Gang of Eight, or the Gang of Eight will have incorporated the moderates' preferences into the bill. Furthermore, since all of the partisan-lean state senators come from non-border states, they could theoretically ask for more concessions in exchange for their vote.

As mentioned in the previous chapter, the Senate exclusively drove this particular bill, unlike the No Budget No Pay Act. Still, there are similarities in the lobbying patterns between the two bills. As with the No Budget No Pay Act, most of the lobbying was done by the Senate leadership. Part of this is likely because of the power dynamics already discussed, but Dick Durbin, the Senate Democratic whip, was also a member of the Gang of Eight and most certainly played a role as one of the bill's framers as well. Among the rank and file, the two members doing the most lobbying were John McCain and Bob Corker. Again, this is to be expected, as McCain, like Durbin, was a member of the Gang of Eight. Similarly, while Corker was not a member of the Gang of Eight, he was instrumental in the passage of the bill as he and John Hoeven (R-ND) proposed an amendment aimed at appeasing conservatives who thought the bill was too soft on border enforcement.[5]

Different from the No Budget No Pay Act, however, is that few rank-and-file members outside of McCain and Corker did any lobbying. Indeed, while Jack Reed and Johnny Isakson did lobby one other senator respectively, the other rank-and-file members were quiet. The moderates, by comparison, were much more active. For example, of the offices I interviewed, Mark Pryor lobbied two offices frequently and one office occasionally. Another senator in the election cycle, Joe Manchin, lobbied one office frequently and two offices occasionally. Furthermore, Joe Donnelly (D-ID) spoke with two offices frequently, and Mark Warner (D-VA) spoke with two offices occasionally. While this is not exactly a picture of power, this does suggest that there are lobbying efforts from potentially pivotal players. Furthermore, it could also suggest that they are engaging in selectively strategic lobbying, trying to lobby only the offices where they may have a greater impact.

Still, the legislative directors tapered this idea, as the conversations were, again, not lobbying in the traditional sense of the word. One legislative director described their conversation with Manchin as:

> LD: Manchin would talk to us about the Corker amendment to gauge where we were on it. I think his goal was to push us on board, but his office never outright made a play for us in that direction. It almost felt as if he would vote for it if he could get enough people with him, but if not, he'd just sit this debate out.

This is hardly a play of power. If anything, the "lobbying" efforts demonstrate an effort to be anything but pivotal. It seems that Manchin is more concerned with avoiding being pivotal and thus avoiding traceability on the issue. In assuring that a large consensus is built on the amendment, Manchin guarantees that the culpability of the amendment will not fall on him.

Undeniably, the number of contacts and their frequency are higher for moderates than they are the rank and file, but they pale in comparison to the leadership and the bill's actual framers. Furthermore, if these pivotal moderates truly were influential in their lobbying efforts, they would probably focus their efforts on more of the chamber, rather than one or two senators, though again, it could be a strategic focusing on senators whose votes they can sway.

Looking again specifically at whom the leadership contacted, we see a similar pattern to what we saw with the No Budget No Pay Act. This is presented in Table 6.4.

Table 6.4. Total Number of Mentions of Contact by Members of the Leadership for Each Type of Senator (by Group)

Leadership	Partisan-Lean State Respondents			Swing State Respondents			Safe State Respondents		
	Occasional	Frequent	Total	Occasional	Frequent	Total	Occasional	Frequent	Total
(Democratic)									
Reid	1	1	2/5 (40%)	0	1	1/4 (25%)	4	0	4/9 (44%)
Durbin	2	1	3/5 (60%)	0	2	2/4 (50%)	3	4	7/9 (78%)
(Republican)									
McConnell	1	0	1/5 (20%)	0	0	0/4 (0%)	0	0	0/9 (0%)
Cornyn	1	0	1/5 (20%)	0	0	0/4 (0%)	0	1	1/9 (22%)

Reid's lobbying efforts were proportionally split among the respondents between partisan-lean state respondents and safe state respondents. Of the partisan-lean state respondents, one reported occasional contact with Reid while another reported frequent contact. Still, four of the nine safe state senators reported occasional contact with Reid. What is perhaps more relevant is Durbin's participation on this bill as, again, he was one of the original members of the "Gang of Eight." Durbin lobbied two partisan-lean state senators occasionally and one frequently along with two swing state senators. Still, of the nine safe state respondents interviewed, seven reported either occasional or frequent contact. Proportionally, then, Durbin, a key player on this bill and a member of the leadership, lobbied safe state respondents more than partisan-lean state and swing state senators.

The Republican leadership was less active on this bill across the three respondent categories, as McConnell and Cornyn each lobbied one partisan-lean state senator occasionally. They lobbied none of the swing state respondents, and only Cornyn lobbied one of the safe state respondents occasionally. While less active, the Republican leadership treated all three groups relatively equally.

Table 6.5 examines the total number of mentions of contact with members of the rank and file and moderates by each type of group for the immigration bill.

Lobbying efforts by moderates were much more visible on the immigration bill than the debt bill. Joe Manchin, Claire McCaskill, Mark Pryor, and Mark Kirk all made occasional contact with one partisan-lean state respondent. Joe Manchin also had one mention of occasional contact and one mention of frequent contact from swing state respondents. This is in addition to one mention of frequent contact by Begich and one mention of frequent contact from Kirk among the swing state respondents. Among the safe state respondents, Begich had occasional contact with one office, Pryor had frequent contact with two offices, Donnelly had frequent contact with one office, Warner had frequent contact with two offices, and Heitkamp had frequent contact with one office. The patterns here are less clear—while moderates did have contact with partisan-lean state respondents, the contacts were occasional. The number of contacts with swing state respondents was even lower. Still, while the number of contacts with safe state respondents was higher, proportionally they were similar to that of the partisan lean state respondents. The key difference seems to be the frequency of contact, however. Note that there were six mentions of frequent contact between the list of moderates

Table 6.5. Total Number of Mentions of Contact by Members of the Rank and File and Moderates for Each Type of Senator (by Group)

	Partisan-Lean State Respondents			Swing State Respondents			Safe State Respondents		
	Occasional	Frequent	Total	Occasional	Frequent	Total	Occasional	Frequent	Total
Moderates									
Joe Manchin	1	0	1/5 (20%)	1	1	2/4 (50%)	0	0	0/9 (0%)
Mark Begich	0	0	0/5 (0%)	0	1	1/4 (25%)	1	0	1/9 (11%)
Claire McCaskill	1	0	1/5 (20%)	0	0	0/4 (0%)	0	0	0/9 (0%)
Mark Pryor	1	0	1/5 (20%)	0	0	0/4 (0%)	0	2	2/9 (22%)
Joe Donnelly	0	0	0/5 (0%)	0	0	0/4 (0%)	0	1	1/9 (11%)
Mark Warner	0	0	0/5 (0%)	0	0	0/4 (0%)	0	2	2/9 (22%)
Mark Kirk	1	0	1/5 (20%)	0	1	1/4 (25%)	0	0	0/9 (11%)
Heidi Heitkamp	0	0	0/5 (0%)	0	0	0/4 (0%)	0	1	1/9 (11%)
Rank and File									
Chris Murphy	0	0	0/5 (0%)	0	0	0/4 (0%)	0	0	0/9 (0%)
Lisa Murkowski	0	0	0/5 (0%)	0	0	0/4 (0%)	0	0	0/9 (0%)
Johnny Isakson	0	0	0/5 (0%)	0	0	0/4 (0%)	1	0	1/9 (22%)
Jack Reed	0	0	0/5 (0%)	0	0	0/4 (0%)	0	1	1/9 (22%)
John McCain	2	0	2/5 (40%)	0	1	1/4 (25%)	1	2	3/9 (33%)
James Inhofe	0	0	0/5 (0%)	0	0	0/4 (0%)	0	0	0/9 (0%)
Deb Fischer	0	0	0/5 (0%)	0	0	0/4 (0%)	0	0	0/9 (0%)
John Barrasso	0	0	0/5 (0%)	0	0	0/4 (0%)	0	0	0/9 (0%)
Pat Roberts	0	0	0/5 (0%)	0	0	0/4 (0%)	0	0	0/9 (0%)
Bob Corker	0	1	1/5 (20%)	2	0	2/4 (50%)	3	1	4/9 (44%)
Mark Udall	0	0	0/5 (0%)	0	0	0/4 (0%)	0	0	0/9 (0%)
Mike Johanns	0	0	0/5 (0%)	0	0	0/4 (0%)	0	0	0/9 (0%)

and the swing state respondents. Comparatively, there were no mentions of frequent contact between the list of moderates and the partisan-lean state respondents.

Turning to the list of rank-and-file senators, the most active senators were the ones who were principal to the legislation like McCain, who had two mentions of occasional contact with partisan-lean state senators, one mention of frequent contact with swing state senators, and three mentions (one occasional and two frequent) of contact with safe state senators. Similarly, Corker was active as well, with one mention of frequent contact with partisan-lean state senators, two mentions of occasional contact with swing state senators, and four mentions (three occasional and one frequent) with safe state senators. More important, proportionally, Corker lobbied more safe state respondents ,while McCain lobbied the same number of safe state respondents as partisan-lean state and swing state respondents but had more mentions of frequent contact among the safe state respondents. Again, this paints a different picture of whom senators viewed as the most important people to contact on a bill.

Lobbying on S.954, Agriculture Reform

While the other two bills examined in these two chapters have been highly salient, well-covered bills that many Americans were well versed on, S.954, the agriculture reform bill, was less so. The bill itself is an odd compromise: in exchange for continued farm subsidies (albeit smaller in size), conservatives pushed for cuts to the food stamp program. The legislation as written should put many legislators in a difficult position—those with farm interests need this bill to pass, but many are partisan-lean state Democrats who may also struggle with a reduction in the food stamp program. The collective choice logic should ring true here: potentially pivotal moderates should be able to push or pull the legislation to their desired spot. Without a strong media presence on the bill, legislators can repackage the rhetoric on the bill and its passage tailored to their constituencies.

Here again, the leadership is doing the bulk of the lobbying, even on a low-salience bill like this one. Much of this, as one legislative director said, was vote counting done by Durbin, and to a lesser extent, Reid. Overall, the total number of contacts and the frequency are fewer in number than the other two bills. Of course, this is not particularly surprising—the bill was not a high priority for many members of the Senate (see Chapter 5, for example). Moderates were more active in their lobbying efforts, but only a specific bunch were particularly active. Senators Pryor, Warner, and Heitkamp, representing Arkansas, Virginia, and North Dakota, respectively, were the most active in the efforts to influence their peers, presumably because agriculture is an essential part of their electoral coalition. However, their participation on the bill is not necessarily unique; rank-and-file Republicans Deb Fischer and Pat Roberts, representing Nebraska and Kansas, respectively, were just as active, if not more so. Table 6.6 demonstrates the patterns of who was lobbied by the leadership within my set of interviews.

The pattern for lobbying seems to be unremarkably different among the three groups. Reid's lobbying patterns proportionally are similar among the three groups. That is, he lobbied only one partisan-lean respondent but did lobby two swing-state respondents (one frequently), and two safe state respondents (one frequently). Durbin proportionally had more contact with partisan-lean state respondents, having two mentions of occasional contact and one mention of frequent contact compared to only two mentions of occasional contact with swing state respondents and two mentions of occasional contact with safe state respondents.

McConnell's lobbying patterns are relatively similar to his partisan counterparts in that proportionally, he lobbied the three groups almost equally. Only Cornyn was different in that he lobbied one partisan-lean state respondent frequently and no respondents from the swing state or safe state sample. This suggests that the leadership treats all three of these groups similarly regarding lobbying efforts, with the notable exception of the majority whip, who proportionally spent more time lobbying partisan-lean state and swing state senators. Indeed, this may be where potentially pivotal moderates can realize their potential—on low-salience bills with easily avoidable traceability.

Table 6.7 examines the total number of mentions of contact by members of the moderate group and the rank-and-file group for each type of senator.

Looking first at the behavior of the moderate's group, only one, Heitkamp, had any contact with any of the five partisan-lean state senators (and even then, it was with only one of the five). Only Pryor and Heitkamp had contact with swing state senators (one mention apiece, occasional and frequent, respectively). All but Mark Kirk had a mention of either occasional or frequent contact among the safe state senators. While this suggests that moderates did

Table 6.6. Total Number of Mentions of Contact by Members of the Leadership for Each Type of Senator (by Group)

Leadership	Partisan-Lean State Respondents			Swing State Respondents			Safe State Respondents		
(Democratic)	Occasional	Frequent	Total	Occasional	Frequent	Total	Occasional	Frequent	Total
Reid	1	0	1/5 (20%)	1	1	2/4 (25%)	1	1	2/9 (22%)
Durbin	2	1	3/5 (60%)	2	0	2/4 (50%)	2	0	2/9 (22%)
(Republican)									
McConnell	1	0	1/5 (20%)	1	0	1/4 (25%)	0	2	2/9 (22%)
Cornyn	0	1	1/5 (20%)	0	0	0/4 (0%)	0	0	0/9 (0%)

Table 6.7. Total Number of Mentions of Contact by Members of the Rank and File and Moderates for Each Type of Senator (by Group)

	Partisan-Lean State Respondents			Swing State Respondents			Safe State Respondents		
	Occasional	Frequent	Total	Occasional	Frequent	Total	Occasional	Frequent	Total
Moderates									
Joe Manchin	0	0	0/5 (0%)	0	0	0/4 (0%)	1	0	1/9 (11%)
Mark Begich	0	0	0/5 (0%)	0	0	0/4 (0%)	1	0	1/9 (11%)
Claire McCaskill	0	0	0/5 (0%)	0	0	0/4 (0%)	1	0	1/9 (11%)
Mark Pryor	0	0	0/5 (0%)	1	0	1/4 (25%)	1	0	1/9 (11%)
Joe Donnelly	0	0	0/5 (0%)	0	0	0/4 (0%)	1	0	1/9 (11%)
Mark Warner	0	0	0/5 (0%)	0	0	0/4 (0%)	0	2	2/9 (22%)
Mark Kirk	0	0	0/5 (0%)	0	0	0/4 (0%)	0	0	0/9 (0%)
Heidi Heitkamp	1	0	1/5 (20%)	0	1	1/4 (25%)	2	0	2/9 (22%)
Rank and File									
Chris Murphy	0	0	0/5 (0%)	0	0	0/4 (0%)	0	0	0/9 (0%)
Lisa Murkowski	0	0	0/5 (0%)	1	0	1/4 (25%)	0	0	0/9 (0%)
Johnny Isakson	0	0	0/5 (0%)	0	0	0/4 (0%)	0	0	0/9 (0%)
Jack Reed	0	0	0/5 (0%)	0	0	0/4 (0%)	0	0	0/9 (0%)
John McCain	0	0	0/5 (0%)	0	0	0/4 (0%)	0	2	2/9 (22%)
James Inhofe	0	0	0/5 (0%)	0	0	0/4 (0%)	1	0	1/9 (11%)
Deb Fischer	1	0	1/5 (20%)	0	0	0/4 (0%)	1	1	2/9 (22%)
John Barrasso	0	0	0/5 (0%)	0	0	0/4 (0%)	0	0	0/9 (0%)
Pat Roberts	0	1	1/5 (20%)	1	0	1/4 (25%)	1	0	1/9 (11%)
Bob Corker	0	0	0/5 (0%)	0	0	0/4 (0%)	0	0	0/9 (0%)
Mark Udall	0	0	0/5 (0%)	0	0	0/4 (0%)	1	0	1/9 (11%)
Mike Johanns	0	0	0/5 (0%)	0	0	0/4 (0%)	1	0	1/9 (11%)

less of the lobbying, the responses in the previous table suggest that they are still viewed as critical votes by the leadership.

Few of the rank and file engaged in lobbying activities on this bill, but among those who did, only Fischer and Roberts had mentions of contact with the partisan-lean group (one mention apiece). Only Roberts and Murkowski had any contact with swing state senators. Again, if there were mentions of contact, it was with the safe state senators.

These results suggest that even when traceability is low, the lobbying behavior of pivotal moderates are not particularly distinguishable from the rank-and-file Democrats and Republicans and are certainly not more active than party leaders. Still, the respondents who were lobbied on this particular bill did lean slightly toward the partisan-lean state respondents and swing state respondents, suggesting that they may be somewhat more pivotal on these types of issues than elsewhere.

Patterns of Lobbying

So why is it that pivotal moderates do not lobby their peers to move legislation to their preferred ideological location? As one legislative director bluntly put it, "The senators on this list are just not influential." Indeed, this simple summary suggests that the assessment of the power dynamics in the Senate are, at the very least, flawed. The legislative director went on to say, "Senators like Claire McCaskill simply do not have a presence in the chamber. Senators like Manchin who are in the media a lot, try, but they often fail to deliver."

Another senator's legislative director blamed the lack of lobbying on the leadership:

LD: Today, the individual senator lacks power. We have essentially empowered our leadership to do most of the work for us. The leadership has the power to decide amendments and negotiate, while the opposition will give their terms for the agreement, or more often, their refusal to negotiate.

Senators who lack the power to offer real policy outcomes through the age-old tradition of logrolling simply cannot lobby their peers.

Other legislative directors pointed to the power of personal connections. Senators who have been in the chamber for a longer period understand the rules and procedures and have built personal ties with other legislators to be able to negotiate and offer incentives to build broader coalitions. Of course, those senators who have served in the chamber for a longer period are often within the leadership structure as well and have the ability to promise incentives and policy compromise. Most moderates simply do not fit these conditions.

Take, for example, Charles Schumer, the senior senator from New York. Time and again, the name that resonated most with nearly every legislative director was Schumer (one legislative director even wrote in bold letters in all capitals with exclamation points, "SCHUMER!!!"). At the time of the interviews, Schumer had been in the Senate for sixteen years and had recently been elected the chair of the policy committee for the Democrats. Due to his ties with many if not all of the senators in the chamber (Republicans and Democrats), most legislative directors saw him as the person to go to or to expect a call from on most legislation. As one legislative director summed it up, "Chuck Schumer can get Joe Manchin on board, Joe Manchin cannot get Chuck Schumer on board."

Finally, another rank-and-file legislative director offered that the power to provide incentives, through future legislation, earmarks, or campaign support, reigns supreme in coalition building. They argued:

> LD: Young folks stay quiet, mostly because they don't have much to offer. They can talk, and we'll listen, but we probably won't be swayed by anything they say. If Reid, Schumer, or Bennet (the Democratic Senatorial Campaign Committee Chair) come calling, we know we might get something on the docket or some help with future legislation.

Indeed, this contributes to polarization as well. After all, if all that senators are looking for is payoffs, then the opposition party cannot offer much, nor should they want to. Naturally, the opposition party would prefer a member of their party who votes with them most of the time than a moderate who votes with them some of the time. This was confirmed in my interviews with some retired senators. For example, Norm Coleman described a very polarized setting that limited his ability to gain any traction with the Democratic leadership:

> NC: How would you describe your relationship with the minority party and their leadership?

Senator Coleman: The minority leadership never reached out. I was in the election cycle when I was in the minority so yeah, they could have probably negotiated with me, but I think they were more concerned with defeating me. Evan Bayh (a moderate Democrat from Indiana) worked with me, but he got grief from Harry Reid for it.

Another Republican senator (at the time he was serving as a senator), Lincoln Chaffee, also described a unique negotiation process.

NC: How would you describe your relationship with the minority party and their leadership?

LC: I worked with some red state Democrats; John Breaux and Ben Nelson particularly stand out. We had the commonality of being in the wrong party [for our states]. I did not have much contact with (then minority leader) Tom Daschle, though.

While this explanation does suggest that moderates hold little power regarding their ability to build coalitions, it does not completely shut the door on the possibility that they may still influence the chamber. Indeed, as the rank-and-file legislative director in the previous paragraph suggested, party leaders can negotiate with incentives—presumably, the case could then be made that those senators sitting at the pivotal spots of the chamber (or close to them) hold the proverbial keys to the legislative train. That is, leaders should seek to please those select senators through either their direct or indirect involvement.

Influence—Direct and Indirect

At the heart of the issue at hand of assessing the power of moderates in the Senate is the question about their influence on legislation and, by extension, the chamber as a whole. This study thus far has spent the bulk of its time focused on the individual behavior of pivotal moderates. We have seen a lack of power exercised in amendments and speeches, voting and building coalitions, and lobbying. The argument can still be made that pivotal players need not make these power plays to be truly powerful. As one legislative director put it, "The Democratic leadership, more so than the Republican leadership, seems to be much more keenly aware of what their moderates can get away with, and perhaps more importantly, what they cannot get away with."

Certainly, this makes sense. If party leaders and bill sponsors know they need sixty votes to pass a bill, then the savviest among the group would plan by writing the bill in a way that would make it palatable to those sitting around the sixtieth vote. Their preferences assumed, moderates would have no need then to propose amendments or lobby and build broad coalitions—the work would be done for them. There may be some expectation from pivotal moderates of this. In his book, Lincoln Chafee wrote about a 2001 meeting with the newly elected vice president, Dick Cheney, in which Cheney met with Chafee and handful of other moderates. With the Bush-Cheney ticket having just won one of the closest elections in American history, Chafee was under the impression that Cheney would arrive with a conciliatory message in which the administration would focus on the priorities of the moderates, especially considering their razor-thin majority in the Senate. Importantly for the argument of this book, however, Cheney showed no hint of a conciliatory message and instead asked Chafee and his fellow moderates to support President-elect Bush and his conservative agenda (Chafee, 14).

So what effect did moderates have in the 113th Congress? Who was viewed as influential? To measure this, I asked the legislative directors I interviewed to once again look at the list of senators. I asked, "Looking at the list now, how would you rate these senators on their influence, direct or indirect? If the individual had no impact, you may skip to the next person." I defined "direct influence" to mean that the senator in question directly impacted the content of the bill through her efforts. "Indirect influence" was defined so that the senator in question impacted the content of the bill but only because other senators, like leaders or the bill's sponsors, took their preferences into account. To have an indirect influence on a bill, the senator in question must not have made any direct efforts to change the bill. Figure 6.1 summarizes the responses to this question across all three bills.

As expected, the Democratic leadership was viewed as having the most direct influence on legislation, followed by Mitch McConnell, the Republican minority leader, and then a slew of rank-and-file Republicans. Notably, John McCain, Pat Roberts, and Bob Corker were viewed as having a direct influence on legislation at a rate that was considerably higher than their peers. Among the moderates, there were no senators who were particularly directly influential in the aggregate.

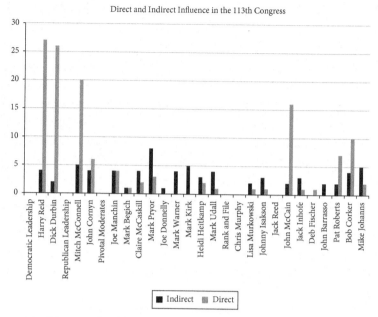

Figure 6.1. Direct and Indirect Influence in the 113th Congress

Switching gears to indirect influence, we get our first glimpse of power from pivotal moderates. Mark Pryor was rated among all his peers, including the Democratic and Republican leadership, as having the most indirect influence on legislation. Theoretically, Pryor should have the most potential to be pivotal as a moderate sitting in the middle of the chamber in a tough reelection race. Beyond Pryor, however, no other pivotal moderate was remarkable. Indeed, Mark Kirk had as many mentions of indirect influence as did backbencher Republican Mike Johanns. This may only be scant evidence of pivotal moderate power, though. As mentioned, among the moderates in this group that were randomly selected, Pryor was the only one who was facing reelection. Indeed, there seems to be no other unique feature distinguishing Pryor from his other partisan-lean state senators—Donnelly, McCaskill, Manchin, Begich, and Heitkamp—all of whom face similarly hostile constituencies back home. To get a greater sense of where Pryor's, and for that matter, any of the pivotal moderate's powers lie, let's turn our attention to the specific bills.

Influence on the Debt Ceiling

As has been noted repeatedly, this particular piece of legislation is unique in that it is almost universally recognized as a bill that was tailor-made for conservatives to appease their Tea Party base. It would, as a result, be quite a bit of a shock to see anyone other than party leaders or partisans as those who were the most influential on the bill. Figure 6.2 illustrates the responses of who was most influential, direct or indirect, on this bill.

As expected, hardly anyone outside of the Democratic and Republican leadership (aside from Cornyn) was viewed as directly influential. With the Republican Tea Party House members holding out support on this bill, the Senate was held more or less hostage as they had difficulty negotiating on this bill. Ultimately, the Senate passed the House version with few changes of their own. Regarding indirect influence, while there are mentions of Joe Manchin, Mark Begich, Mark Kirk, and Mark Warner (with two mentions of indirect influence), these seem more like anomalies rather than substantive views. This seems to be the case, as members like John McCain, James Inhofe, John Barrasso, and Mike Johanns also got mentions. It could be argued that these members (aside from McCain) are especially conservative and thus

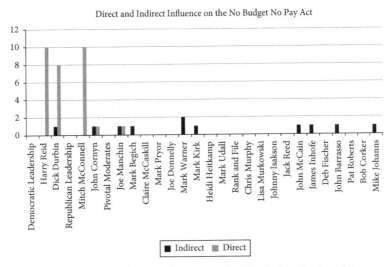

Figure 6.2. Direct and Indirect Influence on the No Budget No Pay Act

had some sway with Tea Party members, but this is likely just a flawed assessment by legislative directors who assumed ties between these senators and the Tea Party movement rather than any real indirect influence.

This suggests that pivotal moderates are not particularly powerful on legislation that is driven by partisan warriors, or here, party leaders and members of the Tea Party. It is safe to say that pivotal moderates were likely happy to see this bill disappear, rather than have any influence, direct or otherwise, at all.

Influence on the Immigration Bill

It is conceivable that pivotal moderates had more direct and indirect influence on the immigration bill. After all, there were more instances of contact, both occasional and frequent, among the group of moderates on the immigration bill than on the No Budget No Pay Act. Furthermore, since the bill itself was fairly polarizing, it is likely that a broad coalition would be needed to break a filibuster. Still, the bill was written by four fairly liberal Democrats and four fairly conservative Republicans. Their goal was less about building a moderate bill than it was about building a bill that would be palatable to each conference. Figure 6.3 shows the distribution of responses on who had direct and indirect influence.

The most influential person on this particular bill should come as no surprise as being John McCain.[6] As one of the members of the Gang of Eight, McCain was rated by sixteen of the eighteen legislative directors as having a direct impact on the legislation. The second highest number of mentions for direct influence is Dick Durbin, another member of the Gang of Eight, followed by Harry Reid, and then Bob Corker, who again, was not an original member of the Gang of Eight but was instrumental in gaining the support of some conservative members of the chamber through his amendment. Again, none of the moderates was rated as having much direct influence.

In terms of indirect influence, we see that Mark Pryor had the highest number of mentions for indirect influence, followed by Mitch McConnell and Mark Udall, who had three mentions apiece. Pryor seems to be an outlier here. While Udall has three mentions of indirect influence, Pryor is the only one who registers higher than any other member that was asked about. As one legislative director put it:

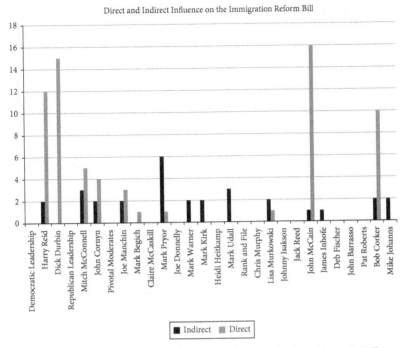

Figure 6.3. Direct and Indirect Influence on the Immigration Reform Bill

The Gang of Eight influenced the bill, but they had to be concerned about McConnell and the conference as a whole. If McConnell didn't like it, I can't see many of us supporting the bill.

Again, it seems that Pryor's position as a potentially pivotal moderate who was in a tough reelection cycle put him in a position to be more pivotal, at least indirectly. That is to say, his colleagues did not seem to think that Pryor himself was exerting pivotal power, but instead, the framers of the bill and party leaders were considering his precarious position while writing the bill.

Influence on Agriculture Reform

Finally, let's turn now to our last bill, the agriculture reform bill. It is also possible that here, pivotal moderates had some influence. Unlike the previous bills, the regional incentives that go into this bill may force the bill's sponsors to take at least some of the pivotal moderates seriously. Still, this says less about their position in the legislature and more about regional politics. Figure 6.4 illustrates the responses to the influence question for the agriculture reform bill.

Regarding direct influence, Pat Roberts, a senator from Kansas and a member of the Agriculture Committee, held the most influence among the group of senators here.[7] Again we see both Reid and McConnell being rated as having a direct influence on the bill, despite not being completely involved in the lobbying process of the bill. What is notable, however, is the senators who were rated as having an indirect influence on the content of the bill.

Here, Claire McCaskill stands out among the group. Heitkamp, Kirk, and Pryor also had multiple mentions of having an indirect influence on the bill as well. Still, among this group, only McCaskill's influence stands out, as Isakson had just as much influence as Heitkamp, and Johanns and Corker were also rated as having an indirect influence at the same rate as Kirk and Pryor. As a result, this likely has less to do with pivotal politics and more to do with regional issues.

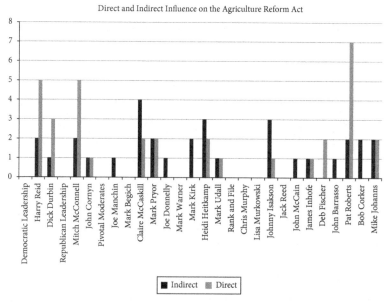

Figure 6.4. Direct and Indirect Influence on the Agriculture Reform Act

Possible Explanations

Who was most influential? It seems, for the most part, that Mark Pryor held some influence within the chamber, if only through indirect influence. As one member of the leadership told me, "You have to protect Pryor, he's up for reelection, and he's marked for a loss." Perhaps, then, the case can be made that pivotal moderates are indeed powerful when they are up for reelection and it is clear that they need help in their race. Still, this power is indirect in that the senator and his office are not engaging in the legislative process, but rather bill framers and party leaders are considering their pressures when writing and pushing legislation. Indeed, this legislative director continued:

> The logic is to release team players to vote how they want to. Pryor has been a team player, and so we need to look out for him.

Another legislative director said:

> The leadership takes election year strategy very seriously. They do take into consideration moderates who are in difficult positions. That being said, they won't jettison bills just to protect them.

The senators interviewed as well echoed this sentiment. For example, Lincoln Chafee described a particularly vulnerable time in which the party leadership came to his support:

> LC: I thought of switching [parties] the day after the 2004 election because Rhode Island didn't like Bush and Cheney—but McConnell called me and said he knew what I was thinking about [in terms of switching parties and] reelection but said that if I stay he will help me on highway and base realignment and it was true. He stuck to his word—I got everything I asked for—but it wasn't enough.

For Pryor, the story ended similarly as the level of protection did not translate into electoral success. Immediately after this session, Pryor went on to lose his reelection race by nearly 17 percent. Despite his efforts to distance himself from the Democratic leadership, his opponent, Tom Cotton, tied Pryor to Obama and the Democratic legislation, which led to his ultimate demise.

What about the other potentially pivotal moderates? McCaskill, contrary to the legislative director who assessed her power as nonexistent, was viewed as indirectly influential on the agriculture bill—but was this due to her politics? Other rank-and-file Democrats and Republicans were also listed as indirectly influential as well, mostly due to their regional concerns and ties to agriculture.

Finally, it is clear that potentially pivotal moderates have little to no direct influence on legislation. Even senators who consistently brag about being bipartisan coalition builders like Joe Manchin and Mark Warner were rated relatively low in this category. As one legislative director put it, "Manchin loves to strike deals. The problem is that his deals never go anywhere." Whether through fear of traceability or sheer inability, moderates simply have no distinguishable influence outside of election-year considerations.

All this points to some findings. The potential power that moderate senators have is not one that is exerted directly, if at all. Party leaders consider the preferences of these senators indirectly or through the lens of electoral pressures that may make voting on the bill difficult or damaging. Still, it seems that this is only true for moderates who are in an election cycle and particularly vulnerable.

7

Conclusion

Balancing Electoral Pressures and Finding Power

In his influential book on the US Senate entitled *Citadel*, William Whyte (1956) describes the body as "the world's most exclusive club," which was managed by a small inner circle. Often described as the seat with the most power, second only to the president, aspiring politicians seek the office of a senator to gain political power. Whyte may have been right, but for different reasons than he posited in his book. Indeed, the small inner circle of Senate leadership is the source of much political power. As this book has demonstrated, not all Senate seats are created equally. Indeed, every senator has the goals of achieving public policy victories, but not all senators have the ability to do so on all public policy platforms. R. Douglas Arnold (1990), in his book on congressional action, states:

> [M]embers of Congress care intensely about reelection. Although they are not single-minded seekers of reelection, reelection is their principal goal. This means simply that legislators will do nothing to advance their goals if such activities threaten their principal goal. If reelection is not at risk, they are free to pursue other goals, including enacting their visions of good public policy or achieving influence within Congress. (5)

If every member does indeed care intensely about reelection, then this statement proves to be even more consequential for centrists in the Senate. That is to say, sitting in the center is more about surviving than it is legislating.

In Chapter 2 I discussed how centrists in the Senate do not represent moderate constituencies but are elected by constituencies that force the senator to create an artificially moderate identity. In reality, the constituencies that elect moderates come from one of two types of states: (1) states that give the appearance of being ideologically moderate but are really internally polarized and moderate only in the aggregate as seen in the dual-peaked or swing

Life in the Middle. Neilan S. Chaturvedi, Oxford University Press. © Oxford University Press 2021.
DOI: 10.1093/oso/9780197599723.003.0007

states, or (2) those that are advantaged to the senator's opposition, thus forcing them to move to the ideological center, as seen in the partisan-lean states. In any case, the constituencies that centrists rely on for reelection are so volatile that their principal goal of reelection is never certain. That is to say, senators sitting in the middle are in constant electoral peril as their votes on key legislation are much more consequential for them than for their partisan counterparts. As a result, Arnold's assessment that legislators will only pursue their goals of enacting good public policy and achieving influence once their reelection is secure proves to be fatal regarding lawmaking for moderates. That is, centrists are rarely in a position of electoral certainty and so are rarely in a position to pursue their goals.

Chapter 3 demonstrated the effects of poor electoral circumstances on legislative behavior. Chapter 3 also examined some of the specifics of legislative behavior by looking at the Affordable Care Act and the Medicare Modernization Act. Admittedly, these are two very visible and highly salient bills. Yet, in this chapter, we saw how moderates avoided shaping policy. Indeed, a powerful senator would exert power on salient bills. Instead of taking the lead, as the lawmaking literature hypothesizes, moderates decided instead to shirk their lawmaking duties and took a back seat to other members of Congress. When it came time to debate the legislation, centrists removed themselves from the debate altogether, and even when senators did speak on the legislation, they avoided taking a clear position by making ambiguous statements or taking ambivalent positions. Chapter 3 also confirmed that this behavior was not merely isolated to these two bills, as senators sitting in the middle rarely attempted to impact key legislation through the amendment process.

When it came to the voting choice, Chapter 4 demonstrated that many moderates chose to vote against their preferred position in a move to bolster their party while sacrificing their own policy goals. Again, this is consistent with Arnold's theory on congressional action, as legislators are more likely to defer to their party if it improves their chances for reelection. Furthermore, party image matters as well, and as such, senators in the middle may vote against their interests to bolster their party's image. Still, these same senators must seek opportunities to vote against their party, but doing so only when they are not pivotal to the process. Though this is certainly not ideal, legislators are foremost concerned with reelection, and with centrists having precarious electoral circumstances, they must do whatever they can to maintain their voting blocs.

Chapter 4 also demonstrated that voting against one's preferences was not unique to those two bills examined as case studies in this book. On salient bills, centrists do indeed vote against their preferences to yield their power to the party as a whole. This presumably gives the party strength to enact policies that can bolster their reputation; again, a key that would help with reelection. Though it could be argued that legislators vote against their preferences because they receive payoffs, either through pork barrel spending or special considerations for their state, legislators do not get compensation for voting against themselves. Indeed, as discussed in previous chapters, Mary Landrieu's "compensation" for voting for the Affordable Care Act was, in actuality, an effort by Landrieu to fulfill her Republican governor's request for more Medicaid funding. When senators vote against their preferences and the preferences of their party, the goal is then to distinguish oneself from the party while simultaneously maintaining the core elements of that party's platform.

All of this, however, focused on data from the "outside." That is, while the evidence strongly suggests that centrists do not overtly use political power, they do have some power behind the scenes. In Chapters 5 and 6 we explored this dynamic and found very little evidence to support this hypothesis. Indeed, those centrists that were deemed powerful were only influential due to the regional aspects of the bill, or, in the case of Mark Pryor, due to their exceptionally precarious electoral positioning and impending electoral death. Even then, Pryor was unable to act truly pivotal. While his colleagues did view him as indirectly influential, the sentiments were not overwhelming nor were they universal. That is, Pryor was still influential only on certain bills, and even then, he was not so much exerting political power as the leadership was framing arguments to protect him.

Based on these results, we can conclude some things about lawmaking in the US Senate. First, not all lawmakers are created equal. While many legislators come from states that have homogenous positions on most issues, centrists come from states in which the optimal policy position is less than clear. This, of course, puts senators in the precarious position of having to balance a position in which they must adopt positions from either side. This situation lends itself to less-than-ideal policy goals for most centrists.

Second, moderates are about as pivotal as their colleagues. That is to say, moderates matter in the sense that fifty-one votes are required to pass legislation, and sixty votes are needed to invoke cloture, but the implied power in being the "fifty-first" or "sixtieth" vote is lackluster at best, at least for moderates. Simply put, moderates not only cannot influence legislation but, more important, they do not desire to impact legislation. On most bills, centrists would rather avoid any position taking at all. It could still however be the case that non-centrists are able to exert power by falling into the role eschewed by moderates.

Third, it can be concluded that parties do indeed matter in the Senate, an institution long known for its individuality and penchant for maverick behavior. Senators who sit in the ideological center provide the counter-example to this and rely on their party to cut the costs of voting on salient legislation. As a result, party leaders are the focal point while centrists are merely compromised players trying to stay alive. By relying on party leaders, centrists can cut the costs of pioneering new legislation and be seen as either the writer of unpopular legislation or the pivotal voter who passed unpopular legislation.

This is not to say, of course, that moderates are completely powerless and void of any influence or public policy goals. As mentioned in Chapter 2, when running for election and then reelection in the 1980s, Arlen Specter was able to champion many legislative victories on crime and public safety issues. Ben Nelson was able to advocate for some agriculture bills for farmers that gained him the endorsement of the numerous farmer groups (Walton 2006). However, on the so-called big-ticket items, Specter and Nelson both voted against themselves and yielded their votes and influence to party leaders.

Furthermore, moderates themselves see their positions as opportunities for legislation that otherwise would go unconsidered. For example, when asked about the difficulties of lawmaking as a moderate, Mary Landrieu explained that her position in the middle allowed her to pursue policy goals that others would not have:

> ML: [Being a moderate] allows you to be radically pragmatic and not hunkered down in the ideological corners. Most of us are willing to move across the aisle to get things done.

Mark Begich echoed this sentiment largely as well. Calling himself an "independent Democrat," Begich argued that the position allowed him to move on legislation that otherwise would not have been looked at:

> MB: I believe in Democratic issues, but I consider myself independent. This gives me a chance to represent Alaska. My position as an independent

Democrat allowed me to get oil companies into the Arctic. Most Democrats would have opposed this, but I talked to anti-war Democrats making the argument that it was a way to avoid Middle East oil.

Begich went on to clarify that he does believe in climate change and supports legislation to curb the effects of human pollution on the phenomenon, but his argument on his political power is interesting. Since Begich was elected from a red state, he had to compromise his position on climate change in favor of direct economic benefits from Arctic drilling. However, in doing so, he was able to gain the support of Democrats who would otherwise have been opposed to such action.

Still, these examples say less about power and more about policy pragmatism. That is, being in the middle allows senators to facilitate conversations with party members who would otherwise be unwilling to consider an issue. Even still, this is reliant on a regional incentive to participate on an issue or a need to demonstrate a willingness to work with the opposition party. Indeed, Landrieu went on to list Senators George Voinovich, John McCain, Susan Collins, and Olympia Snowe as colleagues who would be willing to work with her on legislation. Still, she did point out that another senator who attempted to compromise, Bob Bennett, tried to legislate from the middle and was "beat up by both the right and the left."

This has implications for both polarization as well as gridlock. While many would argue that polarization directly affects gridlock, I will examine each separately.

Polarization

As mentioned, polarization encompasses a large portion of the study of Congress and lawmaking in the United States. In Chapter 1, I outlined much of the polarization literature, which argues that while the US populace remains ideologically similar to previous generations, lawmakers and elites have become increasingly ideologically polarized. Still, even as ideological moderates become less of the norm and more of the exception, many have leaned heavily on the existence of moderates as a sign that polarization is limited.

Based on the findings in this book, however, it is clear that moderates are simply not who people believe them to be. If moderates are not ideologically moderate but are only balancing their ideology, then this suggests that party polarization is indeed a real threat. As parties become more and more homogeneous, the so-called moderates will become increasingly marginalized. Party leaders hold the most power as members of the Senate react to the costs of legislating as members of the House of Representatives do. Indeed, the body that was once called a "saucer to cool the hot tea that is the House of Representatives" is increasingly more like the tea than the saucer in this regard.

Indeed, as voters at the mass level continue to sort themselves more accurately into their partisan camps, elite politicians will continue to polarize as well. As such, swing state senators will be in an increasingly precarious position in which the ideological balancing game is less optimal to representing the base. Furthermore, savvy politicians from partisan-lean states could view the middle as more dangerous than switching parties. Even still, moderates from partisan-lean states could be few and far between as the number of moderate voters needed to elect such senators continues to dwindle.

Of course, if moderates who remain in the chamber use strategies that limit their involvement or influence on key legislation, the outlook on the legislative process as a deliberative process must necessarily be reevaluated. While proponents of the Pivotal Politics model claim that, "In the presence of a few moderates, supermajority procedures provide an additional guarantee that new policies will be moderate and old policies will stay moderate," clearly the implications of the previous chapters dictate otherwise (Krehbiel 2008, 100). That is, legislation is not moderate, but much more polarized, and the so-called moderates who are said to be regulating the process are incapable of doing so. Indeed, while it is possible that moderate senators can act as the "radically pragmatic" players in the legislative process, all too often we see them play this role on smaller, regional issues more than the larger policy debates that the chamber engages in. All of this is to suggest that the Senate has become much more like the Cox and McCubbins (1993; 2004) characterizations of the House in which the Senate has centralized power within the leadership.

Following Krehbiel's (2008) logic on lawmaking, let's imagine a hypothetical nine-member legislature to work as an analogy for today's Senate. In this situation, all nine members are organized on a liberal-to-conservative continuum in which liberal members are represented on the left and conservative members on the right. In this particular legislature, there are four ideologically homogeneous, liberal Democrats and three ideologically homogenous, conservative Republicans. The remaining two members are ideologically centrists.

The liberal Democrats have a slight majority over the conservative Republicans but need at least one moderate to vote with them to pass legislation under simple majority rules. Of course, the conservatives in this model could coax the moderates to vote with them, thus stopping the liberal group's agenda. Still, both moderates could side with the conservative Republicans or the liberal Democrats and pass their legislation. If we define "bad" policy as polarized policy that has little deliberation and "good" policy as a policy that is moderate and deliberate (Sinclair 2008), then previous theories of lawmaking would contend that the prospects for bad policy are slim as both sides require the assistance of moderates to pass legislation. Theoretically, this puts moderates in a position of power in which they can pass only what they want to pass, acting as a gatekeeper of sorts. Based on the findings in this book, we should expect that the ideological placement of the moderates means less to the situation while the party identification of the moderates means much more. If the moderates are both Republicans, that will put the conservatives in control, and as such, we would expect the Republicans to control the legislature and pass "bad" legislation. Similarly, if at least one of the moderates is a Democrat, we would expect that the Democrats would have control and also pass "bad" legislation since the moderates would likely be marginalized by their electoral status. So then, if moderates do not stand their ground, do not shape legislation, and frequently vote against their own beliefs, then in actuality, the prospects for good policy are slim.

As moderates yield their power to party leaders, it is the more ideological members of Congress who get their preferences met. Theoretically, this suggests that salient and partisan bills that are passed by razor-thin margins are polarized and not deliberative. In fact, for legislation to not be polarized, a member of the opposition would need to agree to the bill that is not a centrist to shape the bill. (Recall that this initially happened with the Medicare Reform Act, when Ted Kennedy, the liberal Democrat from Massachusetts, signed on as one of the authors of the bill, bringing the initially conservative proposal to the middle.[1] Had Kennedy stayed on, it likely would have provided the necessary cover to make the bill seem bipartisan, thus allowing vulnerable moderates to vote according to their policy preferences.) However, Chapter 4 demonstrates that this was not the outcome as many moderates voted against their stated preferences. On most salient legislation, this type of situation seems to be less than likely—though I will come back to this idea in more detail when examining the implications of this study on gridlock.

Even looking to the more contemporary case study, The Affordable Care Act, even years after its implementation, remained unpopular with most voters.[2] In a poll conducted by CNN/ORC International nearly three years after its enactment, 54 percent of voters oppose the healthcare law. While a small portion of those surveyed believe that it is not liberal enough (15 percent), the larger portion of voters believes it is too liberal. Even though calling the Affordable Care Act a "bad law" may be a stretch, the American people do not seem to approve of the bill, and largely it seems to be based on ideological reasons.

Concerning polarization, these results also imply a poor choice for voters. With turnout percentages in the United States remaining in the high 50s among registered voters, the American populace remains without a party that directly represents them. Without a party that can be truly pragmatic in a way that forgoes party loyalty, voter turnout will continue to be affected adversely. This may be why Congress as a whole has an approval rating that is lower than Genghis Khan, cockroaches, and Nickelback (Peckham 2013).

All of the implications of this study are not negative, however. Instead, they are simply a reframing and a change in understanding of how lawmaking works in the US Senate. To understand this, let's switch our attention from polarization to the prospects for gridlock.

Gridlock?

The prospects for gridlock are not necessarily greater as a result of this study, but the reliance on moderates to ease gridlock should be reexamined. Under previous models, as long as one moderate existed, gridlock could be overcome as moderates could act as dealmakers and powerbrokers to pass the necessary legislation. Of course, the findings in this book argue otherwise, and largely marginalize the role of moderates in this sense. Nevertheless, it is not gridlock that needs to be reexamined, but instead our concepts of ideology.

It is true that the findings here on first glance prescribe increased gridlock over time. This should not be the case only going forward, but the findings here should work to explain past instances of lawmaking as well. That is, if there will be gridlock in the future, there should have been gridlock in the past, as moderates should be weak in most time periods, as long as they are not representing moderate constituencies. So then, why do some laws get passed while others do not?

Moderates may not take the lead on legislation, but they still must balance their voting to appease their constituents. As a result, legislation may end up being shaped by party leaders, but moderates must still choose to vote for or against the legislation. Of course, their decision may be affected by which party they are from and which party is proposing the legislation, and what their vote may do for their constituents, but they may provide the pivotal vote—whether they like it or not.

Again, turning to one of the cases in Chapters 5 and 6, a "Gang of Eight" senators, comprising four Republicans (Marco Rubio, John McCain, Lindsay Graham, and Jeff Flake) and four Democrats (Richard Durbin, Robert Menendez, Charles Schumer, and Patrick Leahy) led the way on the immigration reform bill. Noticeably, none of these eight senators is considered to be "moderate." Even McCain and Graham, who often choose to take on the identity of being moderates or even "mavericks" who buck their party and vote pragmatically, do not hold up to empirical calculations of their alleged ideology. Even still, two of the four Democrats, Richard Durbin and Charles Schumer, are leaders within the party. Based on the findings in the previous chapters, however, this should not be unusual, as moderates follow and do not lead.

Many, including members of the coalition, have stated that passing legislation on immigration reform would be difficult, and achieving sixty votes would be an arduous task at best. Harry Reid, the Senate majority leader, proclaimed,

> I think we have sixty votes. Remember, we start out at 55 Democrats. I think the most I'll lose is two or three. Let's say I wind up with 52 Democrats— I only need eight Republicans, and I already have four, so that should be pretty easy. (Quoted in Lesniewski 2013)

This "back of the napkin" math suggests that Reid had at least some confidence that four votes existed to pass the legislation in the Senate. While he does not suggest where he will get the votes, it seems that on the immigration bill, there will be enough Republicans willing to "cross the aisle" and vote with the proposal. This also suggests that this may be the best formula for passing legislation. After all, even though Obama enjoyed a large, and temporarily, filibuster-proof majority, Bush did not and had to bring on Democrats to pass many of his key proposals (i.e., Medicare Reform Act, No Child Left Behind).

All of this is to say that the lack of activity by moderates does not necessarily cause gridlock, but it certainly contributes to it—but for different reasons than previously assumed. It is not that moderates need to be appeased to gain their vote, but simply that circumstances must fit to build a voting coalition behind legislators who are willing to either, take credit for the legislation, or are willing to allow their party to take credit for the legislation. It is the rarity of this circumstance that contributes most to gridlock.

Surviving the Middle: Are Moderates Bad Legislators? No!

Thus far in this book, we have seen evidence that largely suggests that moderates are ineffective legislators, yet in many cases, that is simply not the case. Using the Center for Effective Lawmaking's legislative effectiveness scores, we can see that in terms of overall effectiveness, moderate senators match up more or less the same, and sometimes better than, their colleagues. Table 7.1 describes this comparison.

Table 7.1. Average Effectiveness Scores for Members of the Senate, 108th–113th Congresses

Congress	Average Effectiveness Score (Moderates*)	Average Effectiveness Score (Entire Senate)
108th	1.8	1.9
109th	1.73	1.94
110th	2.13	1.97
111th	2.13	1.89
112th	1.87	1.88
113th	1.93	1.93

* Moderates are defined as the fifteen senators closest to the ideological center.

The effectiveness scores rate legislators based on a three-point scale where a 1 corresponds to a score of "below expectations," a 2 corresponds to a score of "meets expectations," and a 3 corresponds to a score of "exceeds expectations." These expectation scores are based on a legislative effectiveness score that is calculated using fifteen points of data that capture a legislator's ability to advance agenda items in the process. These range from the number of bills sponsored, received in action in committee, beyond committee, and floor action. These scores are then estimated as a benchmark score that takes the legislator's legislative effectiveness score and controls for the legislator's seniority, majority party status, and committee or subcommittee chair positions. Finally, these benchmark scores are then measured against three measures: if the benchmark score is greater than 1.5, the legislator is coded as "above expectations"; if the benchmark score is less than .5 she is coded as "below expectations"; and a score between .5 and 1.5 is coded as "meets expectations" (Volden and Wiseman 2013).

Table 7.1 suggests that moderates are no less effective, and in certain sessions, slightly more effective than their colleagues. So where are moderates effective? Grimmer (2013) argues that moderates focus on appropriations over firm position-taking on legislation and issues. Even still, in my interviews with retired senators, some senators alluded to creating a persona that stands above partisanship and ideology. For example, when asked how moderates could cultivate safe identities with their constituents, Mark Begich talked about creating an independent identity that stands outside of the two-party system. Byron Dorgan went even further. When asked to advise current senators on how they could survive the middle, Dorgan said:

BD: [Moderate senators] will always be targeted. But they have to carve out records of independence and create a kind of understanding with their constituencies. They know where they came from.

For senators from small states, he gave further advice:

BD: I had eleven statewide elections, and I did well. Most people didn't view me in a partisan way. They called me by my first name, and most were comfortable with me and trusted me. When I came to Congress, the others from my state did not hold town meetings. I did them, 5–7 a day, and got to know the state. The best shield against a negative attack is to make sure people know who you are.

Lincoln Chafee also agreed with this advice, saying:

> LC: Communication is key. A senator should constantly be updating his
> constituents on what he is doing for them, and importantly, why he is
> doing them.

Political science literature also suggests that senators strive to carve out
their own distinct reputations on the state and national levels. In her work
examining how senators from the same state and different party behave in
the legislative arena (e.g., David Vitter a Republican and Mary Landrieu a
Democrat, both representing Louisiana), Wendy Schiller finds that these
senators compete for strong constituent recognition and approval ratings,
which creates a dynamic of competition and cooperation (Schiller 2000;
Schiller and Cassidy 2011). In partisan-lean states, where we see moderate
Democrats alongside conservative Republicans or moderate Republicans
alongside liberal Democrats, we can assume that the moderates, for the most
part, are looking for ways to represent their core constituencies and not necessarily the entire state. Indeed, data from the last few election cycles demonstrate when these more localized political reputations have yielded positive
electoral returns.

Table 7.2 looks at the moderates who were up for reelection in the last
three election cycles.

Of the three moderates in 2016, only Portman survived reelection. Kirk
lost reelection by a large margin, while Ayotte lost her reelection race by a
very small margin (.1%). All three were targeted early and recruited strong
challengers. Kirk's opponent, Tammy Duckworth, is an Iraq War veteran,
former assistant secretary of Veteran's Affairs, and a former member of the
US House of Representatives.[3] Maggie Hassan was the popular incumbent
governor of New Hampshire when she decided to challenge Ayotte for the
Senate seat. Finally, Strickland was also a former governor of Ohio who was
initially predicted to give Portman a strong general election challenge.

So why did Portman win but the other two lose? Kirk started off his reelection race on poor fitting compared to the other two as he was elected from
a partisan-lean state. Because he was serving as a vote against much of the
Democratic agenda from a Democratic state, the argument could be made
that he failed to distinguish himself enough from the Republican brand.
Ayotte and Portman, however, were both from swing states—yet both had
starkly different reelection races. One distinguishing factor that set Portman

Table 7.2. Reelection Results for Moderate Senators from 2012 to 2016

Year	Incumbent	Opponent	State	Outcome	Margin
2016	Mark Kirk (R)	Tammy Duckworth (D)	IL	Incumbent loss	14%
2016	Kelly Ayotte (R)	Maggie Hassan (D)	NH	Incumbent loss	.1%
2016	Rob Portman (R)	Ted Strickland (D)	OH	Incumbent win	21.4%
2014	Mark Begich (D)	Dan Sullivan (R)	AK	Incumbent loss	3.2%
2014	Mark Pryor (D)	Tom Cotton (R)	AR	Incumbent loss	17%
2014	Mary Landrieu (D)	Bill Cassidy (R)	LA	Incumbent loss	15.8%
2014	Kay Hagan (D)	Thom Tillis (R)	NC	Incumbent loss	1.7%
2014	Mark Warner (D)	Ed Gillespie (R)	VA	Incumbent win	.8%
2014	Susan Collins (R)	Shenna Bellows (R)	ME	Incumbent win	37%
2012	Jon Tester (D)	Denny Rehberg (R)	MT	Incumbent win	3.9%
2012	Claire McCaskill (D)	Todd Aiken (R)	MO	Incumbent win	15.5%
2012	Joe Manchin (D)	John Raese (R)	WV	Incumbent win	24%
2012	Bill Nelson (D)	Connie Mack (R)	FL	Incumbent win	13%
2012	Scott Brown (R)	Elizabeth Warren (D)	MA	Incumbent loss	7.4%

aside was that he was able to gain the endorsement of Ohio's influential labor unions.[4] While labor unions are typically a core component of the Democratic coalition, Portman was able to make a convincing case that his voting record supported Ohio's unions and, as a result, gained their endorsement. Indeed, this identity, while counter to the Republican mainstream, led Portman to retain his seat.

Still, a localized persona is sometimes not enough to win reelection. The midterm elections of 2014 saw the defeats of some Democratic moderates, two of which were by large margins. First, Mark Begich lost his reelection race to Dan Sullivan by 3.4 percent. I was able to speak with Begich about his loss and what he thought influenced his race the most.

MB: We had some trouble with immigration, Ted Cruz came up and campaigned against me. Healthcare was also a huge issue; there were 27 percent rate increases just before the election. People were also getting notices about it, which ended up being like direct mail. Obama also had his lowest approval rating at this point [in Alaska].

Indeed, Begich claims that a few key votes were likely the most influential in shaping his campaign. Another senator that I interviewed, Mark Pryor, lost his reelection race to Tom Cotton by 17 percent. Naturally, much of what happened in Arkansas is likely a result of running in a state as a Democrat that is increasingly trending toward the Republican Party. As such, like Kirk in 2016, Pryor had a significant disadvantage. Still, Pryor credited his loss to outside forces:

> MP: The saying is that all politics is local. For my race, there were so many outside influences from SuperPACs and other outside groups that were twisting my record. They had so much money that it was hard to push back on all of it.

Mark Begich also pointed to outside influences as a reason for his loss as well:

> MB: The Koch Brothers [SuperPAC] came and lied and misrepresented my record as mayor, but we pushed back against that. The Sullivan PAC also spent a lot of money on ads.

With their position as the most vulnerable senators, moderate senators, then, seem to invite not only stiff competition from savvy politicians who time their electoral challenges well but also from outside interests who smell the proverbial "blood in the water." That is to say, SuperPACs from outside of the state will likely spend their resources on close, competitive races that will disproportionately impact moderate senators. While there is some question as to the effect of SuperPACs in elections, emerging literature on the topic suggests that they have a small but measurable influence on electoral outcomes (Chaturvedi 2017c).

Similarly, Mary Landrieu also lost her reelection by a large margin. When I asked her what she thought was the biggest contributor to her loss, she said, "Louisiana looks like a red state, but it is a pragmatic state. In 2014, people were angry, and they wanted change. It was always going to be a hard race."

So is there an optimal strategy? Based on the findings in the previous chapters, the optimal strategy seems to be avoiding problematic votes, or at the very least, attempting to lower the traceability to those votes. For example, every moderate Democrat on the list voted for the Affordable Care Act, but some of the moderates on this list were more visible than others. As demonstrated throughout this book, moderates should focus their attention on avoiding the political limelight on key issues.

Moderates should also attempt to co-opt and find areas of agreement with the opposition, especially in swing states. Susan Collins has been able to cultivate an image in Maine that is distinct from the Republican Party, so much so that Collins rarely gets strong general election challengers—even when she does, like in 2020, she is able to survive them. Indeed, like Portman, if moderates can create an image of a reasonable senator who takes positions from both sides, they may stave off any challenge from the opposition. Savvy politicians will recognize the importance of fighting off real challengers. Vulnerable incumbents like Jon Tester and Claire McCaskill were challenged by politicians who had too much political baggage to offer a real challenge. While certainly not the only reason he won his race, Tester's challenger, Denny Rehberg, while being the state's only representative in the US House, sued one of Montana's largest cities, Billings, and was criticized for the effect of the lawsuit.[5] McCaskill's challenger, also a member of the US House of Representatives, also had his political problems, stating at one point in the campaign that, "If it's a legitimate rape, the female body has ways to try to shut the whole thing down," in response to a question about his opposition to abortion even in cases of rape.[6] Still, even against faulty challengers, moderates need to remain cautious. If they are viewed as influential on policy, constituents are likely going to view them as problematic representatives. Indeed, a senator like Scott Brown served in the Senate as one of the most moderate senators in the modern era;[7] his record as being one of the senators who attempted to defeat Obamacare solidified his reputation as a loyal member of the Republican Party.

Finally, there are some cases in which no matter what the incumbent moderate does, they are marked by the opposition and will lose. As one legislative director put it in a previous chapter, it did not matter what the Democrats would do; Mark Pryor was going to lose his reelection race. Undoubtedly this describes much of what is happening in the middle of the Senate today.

To conclude, the political power and influence of centrists in the US Senate have been grossly overstated and overestimated. Mostly due to faulty assumptions, centrists have been characterized as the powerbrokers in Congress, but they are anything but. Instead, they are cautious and deliberate in their actions, always working to sustain their feeble electoral coalitions. While they may be able to enact specific policies, especially those that are regional or deal with policies that are often overlooked by other senators, their eyes are always on their constituents, even more so than other senators, with their influence largely marginalized.

Appendix A

Full Statistical Models

Statistical models for Chapter 3:

A.1: Negative Binomial Regression Predicting the Number of Amendments Filed on CQ Key Votes from 2003–2013		
	Coefficient	**Robust Standard Error**
Distance from the Middle	1.12***	.35
Republican	−.16.	.12
Leader	.09	.23
Committee Member	.75***	.19
108th Congress	.12	.15
109th Congress	−.01	.15
110th Congress	.42***	.14
111th Congress	−.73***	.18
Constant	−.29	.18
Log Likelihood	−2999.4957	
N=	2300	
Pseudo R-Squared	.012	

*P<.1, **P<.05, ***P<.01

To examine the number of amendments filed on *Congressional Quarterly* key votes from 2003 to 2013, I ran a negative binomial regression model predicting the number of amendments filed by senators in these Congresses. To measure ideological placement, I took the absolute value of each senator's first-dimensional DW-NOMINATE score to create a value that measures the distance the senator sits from the ideological center. I also included a dummy variable for the senator's party, here measured as Republicans and non-Republicans, a dummy variable for party leaders, and finally a dummy variable for relevant committee members. I also include dummy variables for each Congress from the 108th to the 111th (with the 112th Congress serving as the omitted Congress). Standard errors were clustered by each member of the Senate. Table 3.2 presents the results of this model. As expected, the distance from the middle variable is positive and statistically significant, meaning the further a senator sits from the middle, the more amendments they file. Similarly, committee members were also more likely to file amendments than their counterparts. This is, of course, most likely a result of their work on the bill or their specialization on the topic.

Appendix B

Bills Examined for Chapter 4

Congress	Bill Number
108	HJ Res. 2
108	HR 1308
108	HR 1904
108	HR 1997
108	HR 2660
108	HR 2989
108	HR 4
108	HR 4567
108	HR 6
108	S 1072
108	S 1637
108	S 1689
108	S 2061
108	S 2062
108	S 2400
108	S 3
108	S Con. Res. 23
108	S J. Res. 17
108	S J. Res. 40
108	S Con. Res. 23
109	HR 3199
109	HR 3199
109	HR 4297
109	HR 6
109	HR 8
109	HR 810
109	S 1932
109	S2611
109	S 3930
109	S 397
109	S 403
109	S 5
109	S J. Res. 12
110	HR 1424
110	HR 1495
110	HR 1585

Congress	Bill Number
110	HR 1585
110	HR 2
110	HR 2419
110	HR 3221
110	HR 5140
110	HR 6304
110	HR 6331
110	HR 7005
110	S 1257
110	S 1639
110	S 1927
110	S 3036
111	HJ Res 45
111	HR 1256
111	HR 1586
111	HR 2965
111	HR 4173
111	HR 5281
111	HR 627
111	S 1390
111	S 3628
111	S Con. Res. 13
111	S J. Res 26
112	HR 1
112	HR 1249
112	HR 3606
112	HR 8
112	S 1813
112	S 1813
112	S 223
112	S 3240
112	S 3254
112	S 3414
112	S 365
112	S 493
112	S 990
112	S J. Res. 36

Appendix C.1

Confidentiality Notice and Forms Used for Chapters 5 and 6

Re: Confidentiality Policy for All Interviews

Dear Respondent,

Thank you for agreeing to do this interview. This letter is to affirm in writing some of the policies I mentioned either over the phone or in person with you.

First off, this interview is for academic purposes only. Nothing that you and I discuss will be used in any popular media or journalistic outlets. The purpose of any information that you give me is for academic use only.

On a related note, anything you say is strictly "off the record." I will never use your name or identify you in any way. Furthermore, I will not associate your responses, remarks, or positions with your affiliation or identity in any way. I will not convey any portion of our conversation with any other people I might interview.

Third, this commitment of confidentiality extends to any collaborators, research assistants, or any other individuals who may work with me on parts of this project. Before granting anyone aside from myself access to any notes, recordings, or responses, the individual will sign a confidentiality agreement that I will keep on file. Their access will also be limited to academic use.

Finally, if you allow me to tape-record this interview, I will only use it for my own note-taking purposes. All recordings encrypted and are kept under lock and key and will not be released, distributed, or used by anyone that is not involved directly with this project.

If you have any questions or concerns, please do contact me at any time. Again, I thank you for your assistance on this project.

Sincerely,
Neilan S. Chaturvedi, Ph.D.

Appendix C.2

Methodology

1. Introduction, hand privacy/consent forms

Part 1: Self-reflection
Script: I'd like to ask you about three bills, two of them were talked about widely in the media, while the other one was only covered briefly, if at all, by the media. I'd like to first talk to you about bill H.R. 325, the bill that temporarily relieved the debt ceiling. What was your senator's position on the bill?

_____

Thinking back to the bill, did your senator view this as a low priority or high priority bill?

_____

Thinking back to the debate on [insert issue], how much of your office's time was spent on that issue compared to the other legislation you were working on. Was it far more, about the same, or far less time-consuming that other issues? [If they say "about the same" probe: Would you say it was above-average or below-average?]

_____

I now have a few questions about the period of time leading up to the bill. [Hand form 1.] Looking at the names on the list, approximately how often did the following individuals engage in face to face or over the phone interactions with your senator? If the individual did not speak with your senator you may skip to the next person.
Thank you. When your office was deciding on how to vote, how satisfied were you with the content of the bill?

_____

Looking at the politics of this back home in [insert state], was this a divisive issue or was it pretty consensual? Would you say this was typical of public opinion in [insert state]?

_____

Part 2: Reputation
Turning to the process more generally, I am hoping to get a better handle on how things work behind-the-scenes. Indeed, while I have read press accounts of what is going on, I know press reports often overstate some people's key role while overlooking others.

[HAND FORM 2]

Here is a sample of senators, some of which were prominently discussed in the press and others who were not. Again using [insert issue] as an example, from what you know, which of these senators had the greatest impact on the final bill's actual language, recognizing their influence could be DIRECT—that is, they personally got their specific preferences in the final bill—or INDIRECT—that is, colleagues got their specific preferences into the final bill?

Note, my focus is not on who was most active or visible, but whose influence can be seen in the legislative language.

Form 1

Think back to the bill in question. Looking at the names on the list, approximately how often did the following individuals attempt to influence your senator's decision on how to vote on the bill? If the individual did not speak with your senator you may skip to the next person.

	HR 325 (Debt Ceiling)		S 744 (Immigration)		S. 954 (Agriculture Reform)	
The Democratic Leadership	**Occasionally**	**Frequently**	**Occasionally**	**Frequently**	**Occasionally**	**Frequently**
Harry Reid	____	____	____	____	____	____
Richard Durbin	____	____	____	____	____	____
The Republican Leadership						
Mitch McConnell	____	____	____	____	____	____
John Cornyn	____	____	____	____	____	____
Committee Leaders						
Max Baucus	____	____	__X__	__X__	__X__	__X__
Orrin Hatch	____	____	__X__	__X__	__X__	__X__
Patrick Leahy	__X__	__X__	____	____	__X__	__X__
Chuck Grassley	__X__	__X__	____	____	__X__	__X__
Tom Carper	__X__	__X__	____	____	__X__	__X__
Tom Coburn	__X__	__X__	____	____	__X__	__X__
Debbie Stabenow	__X__	__X__	__X__	__X__	____	____
Thad Cochran	__X__	__X__	__X__	__X__	____	____
The White House	____	____	____	____	____	____
Senators						
Joe Manchin	____	____	____	____	____	____
Mark Begich	____	____	____	____	____	____
Chris Murphy	____	____	____	____	____	____
Lisa Murkowski	____	____	____	____	____	____
Johnny Isakson	____	____	____	____	____	____
Jack Reed	____	____	____	____	____	____
John McCain	____	____	____	____	____	____
James Inhofe	____	____	____	____	____	____
Claire McCaskill	____	____	____	____	____	____
Debra Fischer	____	____	____	____	____	____
Mark Pryor	____	____	____	____	____	____
Joseph Donnelly	____	____	____	____	____	____
John Barrasso	____	____	____	____	____	____
Mark Warner	____	____	____	____	____	____
Pat Roberts	____	____	____	____	____	____
Mark Kirk	____	____	____	____	____	____
Bob Corker	____	____	____	____	____	____
Mark Udall	____	____	____	____	____	____
Mike Johanns	____	____	____	____	____	____
Heidi Heitkamp	____	____	____	____	____	____

Form 2

Looking at the list now, how would you rate these senators on their influence, either direct or indirect? If the individual had no impact, you may skip to the next person.

The Democratic Leadership	HR 325 (Debt Ceiling)		S 744 (Immigration)		S. 954 (Agriculture Reform)	
	Direct	Indirect	Direct	Indirect	Direct	Indirect
Harry Reid	____	____	____	____	____	____
Richard Durbin	____	____	____	____	____	____
The Republican Leadership						
Mitch McConnell	____	____	____	____	____	____
John Cornyn	____	____	____	____	____	____
Committee Leaders						
Max Baucus	____	____	_x_	_x_	_x_	_x_
Orrin Hatch	____	____	_x_	_x_	_x_	_x_
Patrick Leahy	_x_	_x_	____	____	_x_	_x_
Chuck Grassley	_x_	_x_	____	____	_x_	_x_
Tom Carper	_x_	_x_	____	____	_x_	_x_
Tom Coburn	_x_	_x_	____	____	_x_	_x_
Debbie Stabenow	_x_	_x_	_x_	_x_	____	____
Thad Cochran	_x_	_x_	_x_	_x_	____	____
The White House	____	____	____	____	____	____
Senators						
Joe Manchin	____	____	____	____	____	____
Mark Begich	____	____	____	____	____	____
Chris Murphy	____	____	____	____	____	____
Lisa Murkowski	____	____	____	____	____	____
Johnny Isakson	____	____	____	____	____	____
Jack Reed	____	____	____	____	____	____
John McCain	____	____	____	____	____	____
James Inhofe	____	____	____	____	____	____
Claire McCaskill	____	____	____	____	____	____
Debra Fischer	____	____	____	____	____	____
Mark Pryor	____	____	____	____	____	____
Joseph Donnelly	____	____	____	____	____	____
John Barrasso	____	____	____	____	____	____
Mark Warner	____	____	____	____	____	____
Pat Roberts	____	____	____	____	____	____
Mark Kirk	____	____	____	____	____	____
Bob Corker	____	____	____	____	____	____
Mark Udall	____	____	____	____	____	____
Mike Johanns	____	____	____	____	____	____
Heidi Heitkamp	____	____	____	____	____	____

Notes

Chapter 1

1. Maite Jullian, "Maine Senators Seen as Major Players in the New Senate," *Bangor Daily News*, November 7, 2008.
2. Kimberly Amadeo, "What Was Obama's Stimulus Package?," *The Balance*, July 1, 2017.
3. Carl Hulse, "Maine Senators Break with Republican Party on Stimulus," *New York Times*, February 10, 2009.
4. Ibid.
5. Tim Collie, "Specter, Snowe, Collins, Anger GOP Base," *NewsMax*, February 8, 2009.
6. Hulse, "Maine Senators Break with Republican Party on Stimulus."
7. Jennifer Steinhauer, "Weighing the Effect of an Exit of Centrists," *New York Times*, October 8, 2012.
8. Michael Crowley, "Party of Lincoln," *The New Republic*, May 22, 2005.
9. It should be noted, however, that the argument that the American public is more polarized still under debate (see, i.e., DiMaggio et al. 1996; Fiorina 2006; McCarty et al. 2008).
10. Note: This pattern has not held up well in the era of Trump politics. In both 2016 and 2020, white voters lower on the socioeconomic scale voted overwhelmingly for the Republican Party. See exit polls, 2016; 2020.
11. Stein, Sam. 2010. "Bill Halter Running for Arkansas Senate: Progressive Democrat to Challenge Blanche Lincoln." *Huffington Post*, June 30.
12. The one exception here seems to be Lisa Murkowski (R-AK). Murkowski hails from a state that frequently votes for Republican candidates and is traditionally a right-leaning state. However, Murkowski remains very popular in the state. After losing a primary battle to a more conservative candidate, Murkowski won reelection by write-in vote. Murkowski has figured out a way to gain the favor of her voters beyond ideology.
13. While the number of Democrats varied throughout the Congress, the overall number through most of the session was fifty-eight.
14. There is also a rich literature on polarization in the House of Representatives (see, for example, Abramowitz et al. 2006; Adams et al. 2004; Arnold 1993; Burden 2004; Carson et al. 2003; 2007; Ferejohn 1977; Fiorina 1977; Holian et al. 1997; Jacobson 2000; Merrill and Grofman 1999). However, given that much of the literature on the House of Representatives focuses on aspects of the House that are unique to Congressional districts, I omit the discussion here.

Chapter 2

1. https://fivethirtyeight.com/features/swing-voters-and-elastic-states/.
2. Arkansas, by the definitions provided here, could be defined as a partisan-lean state, historically. While it has been a stronghold for Democrats at the statewide level in years past, in recent years, Arkansas has drifted firmly into the Republican Party's hands at the state and national levels.

Chapter 3

1. "Final Word," *National Journal*, Nationaljournal.com, June 5, 2012.
2. Mark Warren, "Help, We're in a Living Hell and Don't Know How to Get Out," *Esquire*, October 14, 2014, http://www.esquire.com/news-politics/news/a23553/congress-living-hell-1114/?src=nl&mag=esq&list=nl_enl_news&date=101514.
3. Under Senate procedural rules, any senator can propose an amendment, regardless of content (germane or non-germane), to almost any bill. However, the process requires structure, as only certain amendments can be pending simultaneously. For example, if there is an amendment to strike text from the bill and another proposal that amends the same text, then a proposal to amend the text to the bill should be considered before the amendment to strike the text is considered, as there needs to be text to amend for the other consideration (Beth et al. 2009; Chaturvedi 2017a; Smith 2014). To structure these considerations, the Senate parliamentarian places each amendment on a "tree" in which each "branch" represents an amendment. An amendment proposed to amend the content of the bill is listed as a first-degree amendment, or an amendment adjusting the actual bill on the agenda. Second-degree amendments are then amendments that either amend the first-degree amendment or replace or substitute it. On most bills, the total number of first and second-degree amendments is eleven (Mimms 2014). With the right of first recognition, the majority leader can fill every branch of the amendment tree with amendments that only minimally change the content of the bill. If the leader fills every branch, a senator wanting to propose another amendment would require unanimous consent or have one of the previous amendments disposed of (Beth et al. 2009).
4. Included in this data set is every key vote with at least a total number of five amendments proposed.
5. In May 2001, Republican senator Jim Jeffords of Vermont left the Republican Party and became an independent, caucusing with the Democrats. This party change broke the 50–50 tie in the Senate and handed complete control of the chamber to the Democrats. Still, the Democrats only controlled the Senate and not the House of Representatives or the presidency, and eventually lost the Senate again eighteen months later.
6. For ease of interpretation, I have included only the descriptive statistics and marginal effects from this statistical model. The full negative binomial regression along with a brief interpretation of the results can be found in Appendix A.

7. In his book, Senator Al Franken (D-MN) talks about the early efforts by the Democratic leadership to involve Republicans in forming the healthcare bill. Max Baucus, a Democrat from Montana and the powerful chair of the Senate, was tasked by Majority Leader Reid to write the bill. He initially formed a Gang of Six, three Democrats and three Republicans, to negotiate, but months into the discussions, Baucus acknowledged that the group would not be able to agree on a bill. Responding to Baucus's claim that the Republicans never had any intention of agreeing on a bill, Franken quotes former Republican Arlen Specter as saying, "Well, I could have told you that!" (Franken 2017, 251).

8. Indeed, in a 2017 vote to repeal the Affordable Care Act, three Republican senators voted against the repeal who had been present and voted against the Affordable Care Act in 2009. These senators were John McCain (R-AZ), Lisa Murkowski (R-AK), and Susan Collins (R-ME) (Pear and Kaplan 2017).

9. David M. Herszenhorn, "Shepherding a Bill with 564 Amendments," *New York Times*. September 21, 2009.

10. While technically cross-pressured by the definitions set out in Chapter 2, Jay Rockefeller and Bill Nelson were not listed as pivotal or potentially pivotal. Rockefeller was among the most liberal in their caucus and generally an outlier in terms of legislative behavior. As such, I exclude them from the analysis here as a moderate.

11. Proposing amendments to legislation that senators oppose in the aggregate is not unique. Former senator Jeff Sessions (R-AL) used the amendment process to offer fifteen amendments to the 2013 Bipartisan Immigration Bill, a bill that he vocally opposed. The amendments as written stripped the bill of most of its provisions and asked for greater security measures. Only one of his fifteen amendments was ultimately adopted (Fabian 2013).

12. Note that I limit the bounds to 0 and .6 because the confidence intervals were too large for the maximum value of 1 to be of substance.

13. Executive Committee Meeting to Consider Health Care Reform, September 22, 2009.

14. We should note here that Chafee eventually did change his partisanship. In September of 2007, Chafee left the Republican Party and identified himself as a political independent. In 2008, he endorsed Barack Obama for president. In 2012, he finally switched his affiliation to the Democratic Party (Sullivan 2013).

15. I also ran a negative binomial regression as a robustness check, but the results were not substantively or significantly different from the logistic regression results.

Chapter 4

1. The trustee model of representation is when the representative is elected to do what is best for the "common good." Edmund Burke summarizes the trustee model in his speech to the electors of Bristol by saying, "It is his duty to sacrifice his repose, his pleasures, his satisfactions, to theirs; and above all, ever, and in all cases, to prefer their interest to his own. But his unbiased opinion, his mature judgment, his enlightened

conscience, he ought not to sacrifice to you, to any man, or to any set of men living. These he does not derive from your pleasure; no, nor from the law and the constitution. They are a trust from Providence, for the abuse of which he is deeply answerable. Your representative owes you, not his industry only, but his judgment; and he betrays, instead of serving you, if he sacrifices it to your opinion" (Burke 1774).

2. Notably, in his political memoir, Al Franken also notes this vote as a turning point in the race. He writes, "by the next debate the course had changed dramatically. All summer long, the housing market had been in turmoil, and on September 29 the financial crisis reached a climax in the wake of Lehman Brothers going under. It took about a week for a $700 billion-plus bailout package to work its way through Congress. Coleman immediately came out for the bailout, telling voters in North Mankato that, 'the government could make 10 or 20 times what it pays on this, possibly.' . . . It's certainly possible that Norm's decision to support the bailout of Wall Street—and my decision to oppose it—was a factor in this swing" (Franken 2017, 154–155).

3. I look at fifteen here because we know on this particular bill that the pivotal vote was the sixtieth vote. As such, the fifteen senators examined are the fifteen senators closest to this position. I choose fifteen instead of ten to have the most conservative outlook on this positioning—for example, the further out we go ideologically, we should see more homogeneity in opinion regarding party polarization and ideology, but we see the opposite here.

4. In 2017, Collins voted against her party's efforts to pass a repeal of Obamacare, casting one of the deciding votes to kill the bill. Again, this seemingly contradictory vote, in which she voted to uphold a law that she voted against, demonstrates the difficulty behind voting decisions for moderates in the Senate.

5. I say "at least" once because of the limitations of the data set. It is certainly possible that Landrieu voted against herself multiple times.

6. Regional conflicts were coded by examining if the vote impacted a specific region of the country. If a region was specifically affected, it was coded as "1." All others were coded as "0."

7. https://www.vox.com/2018/10/5/17943276/susan-collins-speech-transcript-full-text-kavanaugh-vote.

Chapter 5

1. Initially, I attempted to select the senators randomly, but given the low response rate, I switched to the snowball method of conducting elite interviews. When I approached offices and legislative directors themselves (by email first, then in person), only a handful of legislative directors were amenable to contributing to the study. As mentioned in the text, many offices claimed that they had "been burned before," in which academics had approached them under the guise of conducting social science research, only to expose their answers publicly for political reasons. Others simply cited an office-wide rule that no academic studies would be allowed to be conducted. As

a result, I asked legislative directors I spoke with to refer me to others who might be willing to participate in the study. Most were willing to do so, and all but one legislative director allowed me to use their name when soliciting other interviews.

2. William Brangin, "Obama Reflects on Shellacking in Midterm Elections," *Washington Post*, November 3, 2010.

3. As noted, the Democrats did at one point have a supermajority of sixty seats in the Senate but lost it permanently when Scott Brown, a moderate Republican, was elected in a special election in Massachusetts to replace the late Ted Kennedy. As a result, the number dropped to fifty-three rather than fifty-four.

4. Karoun Demirjian, "Dean Heller Amendment: No Budget, No Pay for Lawmakers," *Las Vegas Sun*, July 12, 2013.

5. John Parkinson, "House Passes 'No Budget No Pay,' Extends Debt Limit." *ABC News*, January 23, 2013.

6. Ramsey Cox, "Senate Approves Debt Ceiling Bill in 64–34 Vote," *The Hill*, January 31, 2013.

7. Ibid.

8. This refers to the iteration of Lindsey Graham that existed before the Trump presidency.

9. Lauren Fox, " 'Gang of Eight Pleased' Obama Is Laying Low on Immigration Reform," *US News and World Report*, June 12, 2013.

10. Jonathan Topaz, "Ayotte Endorses Immigration Bill," *Politico*, June 9, 2013.

11. Ron Nixon, "Senate Passes Farm Bill; House Vote Is Less Sure," *New York Times*, June 10, 2013.

12. As discussed in Chapter 2, Harry Reid's use of the amendment tree was unprecedented. Indeed, one LD described Reid's use of the amendment tree as "majority party obstruction" in which the majority leader refused to allow any participation from the minority party. Naturally, this severely limits the participation of the minority party (and for that matter, the majority party as well) but as discussed in Chapter 3, it does not necessarily decrease the workload. For more see Chaturvedi (2017a).

13. Elsie Foley, "Immigration Border Reform Deal Reached," *Huffington Post*, June 20, 2013.

Chapter 6

1. It is interesting to note (and convenient to the argument in this book) that Nelson never received any such concessions. While some DC insiders argue that Emanuel repaid his debt to Nelson during the Affordable Care Act debate with the so-called Corn Husker Kickback, Chapter 3 and 4 discussed how Nelson and Nebraska never actually received that pork legislation because it was removed in committee after much criticism.

2. Ryan Lizza, "Ben Nelson and the Politics of Pork and Polarization," *New Yorker*, December 28, 2011.

3. Jennifer Van Allen, "Susan Collins Wins Reelection to the Senate," *Portland Press Herald*, November 5, 2014.

4. Note that given the confidentiality agreement that was agreed upon with the legislative directors, I am unable to reveal for whom the legislative directors worked. As a result, I examine them based on the type of state they represent. If they are on the staff of a senator from a state where the opposing party is in the majority, they are filed under "Partisan-Lean State," those working senators from states in which their party is in the majority are filed under "safe state," and the final category are swing state senators.

5. Curtis Houck, "Corker: If Bill Says 'Immigration Reform,' Some Senators Won't Support It," *CNS News*, June 24, 2013.

6. I should note that some legislative directors were frustrated with their choices here. Many of them wanted to emphasize just how instrumental Schumer was in the framing and pushing of this bill. More so than either Reid or Durbin, or even McCain, Schumer had contacted nearly every office that I spoke with. At the time of this writing, Schumer is now the in the Democratic leadership position after Reid retired, and his role on this bill, as well as others, is likely the reason why.

7. Aside from Roberts, the two senators who had the most influence were the committee leaders, Debbie Stabenow and Thad Cochran. I did ask senators to rate the influence of committee members as well, but in the interest of saving space, I have omitted those results here.

Chapter 7

1. This was, however, temporary as he soon dropped out of the bill when Republicans grew weary of conceding too much ground to Kennedy. For more information, see Chapter 3.

2. It should be noted that after efforts by Republicans to repeal and replace the Affordable Care Act with less popular replacements, the legislation gained the approval of many voters and is now more popular than unpopular.

3. https://www.duckworth.senate.gov/content/about-tammy.

4. http://thehill.com/policy/finance/290242-portman-secures-fourth-union-endorsement.

5. http://www.bozemandailychronicle.com/news/rehberg-again-defends-lawsuit-over-billings-fire/article_c5b5d222-8f74-11df-9400-001cc4c03286.html.

6. http://www.nytimes.com/2012/08/21/us/politics/rep-todd-akin-legitimate-rape-statement-and-reaction.html.

7. Brown's distance from the ideological center is smaller than any senator in the modern era. He is the closest a senator has gotten to be on the ideologically opposite side of the spectrum than any other senator.

References

Abramowitz, Alan. 1984. "National Issues, Strategic Politicians, and Voting Behavior in the 1980 and 1982 Congressional Elections." *American Journal of Political Science* 28: 710–721.

Abramowitz, Alan. 1985. "Economic Conditions, Presidential Popularity, and Voting Behavior in Midterm Congressional Elections." *Journal of Politics* 47(1): 31–43.

Abramowitz, Alan, Brad Alexander, and Matthew Gunning. 2006. "Incumbency, Redistricting, and the Decline of Competition in the U.S. House Elections." *Journal of Politics* 68: 75–88.

Abramowitz, Alan, and Jeffrey Allan Segal. 1992. *Senate Elections.* Ann Arbor: University of Michigan Press.

Achen, Christopher. 1978. "Measuring Representation." *American Journal of Political Science* 22(3): 475–510.

Adams, James, Benjamin Bishin, and Jay Dow. 2004. "Representation in Congressional Campaigns: Evidence for Discounting Directional Voting in U.S. Senate Elections." *Journal of Politics* 66(2): 326–347.

Ainsworth, Scott, and Marcus Flathman. 1995. "Unanimous Consent Agreements as Leadership Tools." *Legislative Studies Quarterly* 20: 177–195.

Aldrich, John H. 1995. *Why Parties?: The Origin and Transformation of Party Politics in America.* Chicago: University of Chicago Press.

Amadeo, Kimberly. 2017. "What Was Obama's Stimulus Package?" *The Balance,* July 1.

American Political Science Association. 1950. "Toward a More Responsible Two-Party System: A Report of the Committee on Political Parties." *American Political Science Review* 44(3): Part 2, supplement.

Ansolabehere, Stephen, James Snyder Jr., and Charles Stewart III. 2001. "The Effects of Party and Preferences on Congressional Roll-Call Voting." *Legislative Studies Quarterly* 26(4): 533–572.

Arnold, R. Douglas. 1990. *The Logic of Congressional Action.* New Haven: Yale University Press.

Arnold, R. Douglas. 1993. "Can Inattentive Citizens Control Their Elected Representatives?" In *Congress Reconsidered,* 5th ed., edited by Lawrence C. Dodd and Bruce Oppenheimer, 401–416. Washington, DC: Congressional Quarterly Press.

Baker, Ross K. 2011. "Touching the Bones: Interviewing and Direct Observational Studies of Congress." In *The Oxford Handbook of the American Congress,* edited by Eric Schickler and Frances E. Lee, 95–114. New York: Oxford University Press.

Bartels, Larry. 1991. "Constituency Opinion and Congressional Policymaking: The Reagan Defense Buildup." *American Political Science Review* 85(2): 457–474.

Beaussier, Anne-Laure. 2012. "The Patient Protection and Affordable Care Act: The Victory of Unorthodox Lawmaking." *Journal of Health Politics, Policy, and Law* 37(5): 741–778.

Beckmann, Matthew. 2009. *Pushing the Agenda: Presidential Leadership in U.S. Lawmaking 1953-2004*. New York: Cambridge University Press.

Beckmann, Matthew, Neilan S. Chaturvedi, and Jennifer Garcia. 2017. "Targeting the Treatment: The Strategy behind Lyndon Johnson's Lobbying." *Legislative Studies Quarterly* 42(2): 211-234.

Beckmann, Matthew, and Richard Hall. 2013. "Elite Interviewing in Washington: Political Science's Methods in a Practitioner's World." In *Interviewing in Political Science Research*, edited by Layna Mosley, 196-209. Ithaca, NY: Cornell University Press.

Bernstein, Robert. 1989. *Elections, Representation, and Congressional Voting Behavior: The Myth of Constituency Control*. Englewood Cliffs, NJ: Prentice Hall.

Berry, William, Evan Ringquist, Richard Fording, and Russell Hanson. 1998. "Measuring Citizen and Government Ideology in American States, 1960-93." *American Journal of Political Science* 42: 327-348.

Beth, R. S., Heitshusen, V., Heniff, B., Jr., and Rybicki, E. 2009, September 3-6. Leadership tools for managing the U.S. Senate. Paper presented at the Annual Meeting of the American Political Science Association, Toronto, Ontario, Canada.

Bianco, William T. 1994. *Trust: Representatives and Constituents*. Ann Arbor: University of Michigan Press.

Binder, Sarah. 2004. "The Limits of Senatorial Courtesy." *Legislative Studies Quarterly* 29(1): 5-22.

Binder, Sarah, and Steven Smith. 1997. *Politics or Principle?: Filibustering in the United States Senate*. Washington, DC: Brookings Institution.

Bishin, Benjamin. 2008. *Tyranny of the Minority: The Subconstituency Politics Theory of Representation*. Philadelphia: Temple University.

Bishop, Bill. 2004. "A Steady Slide toward a More Partisan Union." *Austin American-Statesman*, May 30.

Black, Duncan. 1958. *The Theory of Committees and Elections*. Cambridge, UK: Cambridge University Press.

Blumenthal, David, and James Morone. 2010. *The Heart of Power: Health and Politics in the Oval Office*. Berkeley: University of California Press.

Boehmke, Frederick, and Richard Witmer. 2004. "Disentangling Diffusion: The Effects of Social Learning and Economic Competition on State Policy Innovation and Expansion." *Political Research Quarterly* 57: 39-51.

Bond, Jon. 1983. "The Influence of Constituency Diversity on Electoral Competition in Voting for Congress, 1974-1978." *Legislative Studies Quarterly* 8(2): 201-217.

Bond, Jon, and Richard Fleisher. 1990. "Assessing Presidential Support in the House II: Lessons from George Bush." Presented at the Annual Meeting of the American Political Science Association.

Bond, Jon, Richard Fleisher, and Jeffrey Stonecash. 2009. "The Rise and Decline of Moderates in the U.S. House and Senate from 1900-2006." Paper Presented at the 67th Annual National Meeting of the Midwest Political Science Association Chicago, April 2-5.

Brace, Paul, Kellie Sims Butler, Kevin Arceneaux, and Martin Johnson. 2002. "Public Opinion in the American States: New Perspectives Using National Survey Data." *American Journal of Political Science* 46: 173-189.

Brady, David, and Edward P. Schwartz. 1995. "Ideology and Interests in Congressional Voting: The Politics of Abortion in the US Senate." *Public Choice* 84(1): 25-48.

Brady, David W., and Craig Volden. 1998. *Revolving Gridlock: Politics and Policy from Carter to Clinton*. Boulder, CO: Westview Press.

Brangin, William. 2010. "Obama Reflects on Shellacking in Midterm Elections." *Washington Post*, November 3.

Burden, Barry. 2004. "Candidate Positioning in U.S. Congressional Elections." *British Journal of Political Science* 34(2): 211–227.

Burden, Barry, Gregory Caldeira, and Timothy Groseclose. 2000. "Measuring the Ideologies of Legislators Accurately." *Legislative Studies Quarterly* 25: 237–258.

Burke, Edmund. 1774. "Speech to the Electors in Bristol, 3 November, 1774." In *The Works of the Right Honourable Edmund Burke*. Chicago: University of Chicago Press.

Campbell, James, and Joe Sumners. 1990. "Presidential Coattails in Senate Elections." *American Political Science Review* 84(2): 513–524.

Cannan, John. 2013. "A Legislative History of the Affordable Care Act: How Legislative Procedure Shapes Legislative History." *Law Libr. J.* 105(131): 2013–2017.

Carson, Jamie L., Michael H. Crespin, Charles J. Finocchiaro, and David Rohde. 2003. "Linking Congressional Districts across Time: Redistricting and Party Polarization in Congress." Paper presented at the Midwest Political Science Association Conference, Chicago, April 3.

Carson, Jamie L., Michael H. Crespin, Charles J. Finocchiaro, and David Rohde. 2007. "Redistricting and Party Polarization in the U.S. House of Representatives." *American Politics Research* 35(6): 878–904.

Chafee, Lincoln. 2008. *Against the Tide*. New York: St. Martin's Press.

Chaturvedi, Neilan S. 2017a. "Filling the Amendment Tree: Majority Party Control, Procedures, and Polarization in the United States Senate." *American Politics Research* 46(4): 724–747.

Chaturvedi, Neilan S. 2017b. "Kings of the Hill?: An Examination of Centrist Behavior in the US Senate." *Social Science Quarterly* 98(5): 1250–1263.

Chaturvedi, Neilan S. 2017c. "Postdiluvian?: The Effects of Outside Spending on Senate Elections after *Citizens United* and *Speechnow.org v. FEC*." *The Forum* 15(2): 251–267.

Cohen, Jeffrey. 2006. "Conclusions: Where We Have Been, Where We Should Go." In *Public Opinion in State Politics*, edited by Jeffrey Cohen, 254–269. Stanford, CA: Stanford University Press.

Cohen, Linda, and Roger Knoll. 1991. "How to Vote, Whether to Vote: Strategies for Voting and Abstaining on Congressional Roll Calls." *Political Behavior* 13(2): 97–127.

Collie, Tim. 2009. "Specter, Snowe, Collins Anger GOP Base." *NewsMax*, Feb. 8.

Congressional Quarterly Almanac. 1970. Washington, DC: Congressional Quarterly (various issues).

Cover, Albert D. 1986. "Presidential Evaluations and Voting for Congress." *American Journal of Political Science* 30: 786–801.

Cox, Gary W., and Matthew D. McCubbins. 1993. *Legislative Leviathan: Party Government in the House*. Berkeley: University of California Press.

Cox, Gary W., and Matthew D. McCubbins. 2005. *Setting the Agenda: Responsible Party Government in the U.S. House of Representatives*. New York: Cambridge University Press.

Cox, Ramsey. 2013. "Senate Approves Debt Ceiling Bill in 64–34 Vote." *The Hill*, January 31.

Curry, James. 2015. *Legislating in the Dark: Information and Power in the House of Representatives*. Chicago: University of Chicago Press.

Dahl, Robert. 2001. *How Democratic Is the American Constitution?* New Haven: Yale University Press.

Dahlberg, Lincoln. 2001. "The Internet and Democratic Discourse: Exploring the Prospects of Online Deliberative Forums Extending the Public Sphere." *Information, Communication and Society* 4(4): 615–633.

Daschle, Tom, and Charles Robbins. 2013. *The U.S. Senate: Fundamentals of American Government.* New York: Thomas Dunne Books.

Davidson, Roger H., Walter Oleszek, Frances Lee, and Eric Schickler. 2017. *Congress and Its Members.* Los Angeles: Sage, CQ Press.

Demirjian, Karoun. 2013. "Dean Heller Amendment: No Budget, No Pay for Lawmakers." *Las Vegas Sun*, July 12.

Dickerson, John, and Douglas Waller. 2001. "Inside the Battle over the Patients' Bill of Rights." *Time*, June 18.

Dimaggio, Paul, John Evans, and Bethany Bryson. 1996. "Have Americans' Social Attitudes Become More Polarized?" *American Journal of Sociology* 102: 690–755.

Downs, Anthony. 1957. *An Economic Theory of Democracy.* New York: Harper and Row.

Erikson, Robert S. 1978. "Constituency Opinion and Congressional Behavior: A Reexamination of the Miller-Stokes Representation Data." *American Journal of Political Science* 22(3): 511–535.

Erikson, Robert, Gerald Wright, and John McIver. 1993. *Statehouse Democracy: Public Opinion and Policy in the American States.* Cambridge, UK: Cambridge University Press.

Esterburg, Kristin G. 2002. *Qualitative Methods in Social Research.* Boston: McGraw-Hill.

Eulau, Heinz, and Paul Karps. 1977. "The Puzzle of Representation: Specifying Components of Responsiveness." *Legislative Studies Quarterly* 2(3): 233–254.

Fabian, Jordan. 2013. "Jeff Sessions Wants to Single-Handedly Crush Immigration Reform." *ABC News*, June 3. http://abcnews.go.com/ABC_Univision/Politics/jeff-sessions-kill-immigration-reform-bill-thing/story?id=19311727.

Fenno, Richard. 1978. *Homestyle: Representation in Their Districts.* Boston: Little Brown.

Fenno, Richard. 1991. *Learning to Legislate: The Senate Education of Arlen Specter.* Washington, DC: CQ Press.

Ferejohn, John. 1977. "On the Decline of Competition in Congressional Elections." *American Political Science Review* 71: 166–176.

Fiorina, Morris. 1974. *Representatives, Roll Calls, and Constituencies.* Lexington, MA: Lexington Books.

Fiorina, Morris. 1977. "The Case of the Vanishing Marginals: The Bureaucracy Did It." *American Political Science Review* 71: 177–181.

Fiorina, Morris. 1983. "Who Is Responsible?: Further Evidence on the Hibbing-Alford Thesis." *American Journal of Political Science* 27(1): 158–164.

Fiorina, Morris. 2006. *Culture War?: The Myth of a Polarized America.* 2nd ed. New York: Pearson Longman.

Foley, Elsie. 2013. "Immigration Border Reform Deal Reached." *Huffington Post*, June 20.

Fox, Lauren. 2013. "'Gang of Eight Pleased' Obama Is Laying Low on Immigration Reform." *US News and World Report*, June 12.

Franken, Al. 2017. *Al Franken: Giant of the Senate.* New York: Hachette Book Group.

Gelman, Andrew, and Thomas Little. 1997. "Poststratification into Many Categories Using Hierarchical Logistic Regression." *Survey Methodology* 23: 127–135.

Gimpel, James, and Jason Schuknecht. 2003. *Patchwork Nation: Sectionalism and Political Change in American Politics.* Ann Arbor: University of Michigan Press.

Godbout, Jean Francois, and Bei Yu. 2009. "Speeches and Legislative Extremism in the U.S. Senate." In *Do They Walk Like They Talk? Speech and Action in Policy Processes*, edited by Louis Imbeau, 279–290. New York: Springer.

Good, Chris. 2012. "Mourdock Defeats Lugar in GOP Indiana Senate Primary." *ABC World News*, May 8.

Grimmer, Justin. 2013. *Representational Style in Congress: What Legislators Say and Why It Matters*. New York: Cambridge University Press.

Groseclose, Timothy, and James Snyder. 1996. "Buying Supermajorities." *American Political Science Review* 90: 303–315.

Grossmann, Matthew, and David A. Hopkins. 2016. *Asymmetric Politics: Ideological Republicans and Group Interest Democrats*. New York: Oxford University Press.

Hall, Richard. 1996. *Participation in Congress*. New Haven: Yale University Press.

Heckman, James, and Snyder, James. 1997. "The Impact of Federal Spending on House Election Outcomes." *Journal of Political Economy* 105(1): 30–53.

Hero, Rodney, and Caroline Tolbert. 1995. "Latinos and Substantive Representation in the U.S. House of Representatives: Direct, Indirect, or Nonexistent?" *American Journal of Political Science* 39(3): 640–652.

Herrera, Richard, and Karen Shafer. 2004. "The Influence of Party on the Legislative Process: Constituents Are Key." Paper presented at the Annual Meeting of the American Political Science Association.

Hibbing, John R., and John R. Alford. 1981. "The Electoral Impact of Economic Conditions: Who Is Held Responsible?" *American Journal of Political Science* 25(3): 423–439.

Hill, Kim Quaile, and Patricia Hurley. 1999. "Dyadic Representation Reappraised." *American Journal of Political Science* 7(1): 109–137.

Hofferbert, Richard. 1966. "The Relation between Public Policy and Some Structural and Environmental Variables in the American States." *American Political Science Review* 60: 73–82.

Holian, David, Timothy Krebs, and Michael Walsh. 1997. "Constituency Opinion, Ross Perot, and Roll-Call Behavior in the U.S. House: The Case of the NAFTA." *Legislative Studies Quarterly* 22(3): 369–392.

Houck, Curtis. 2013. "Corker: If Bill Says 'Immigration Reform,' Some Senators Won't Support It." *CNS News*, June 24.

Hulse, Carl. 2009. "Maine Senators Break with Republican Party on Stimulus." *New York Times*, Feb. 10.

Jackson, John, and David King. 1989. "Public Goods, Private Interests, and Representation." *American Political Science Review* 83(4): 1143–1164.

Jacobson, Gary C. 1997. "Reversal of Fortune: The Transformation of US House Elections in the 1990s." *Legislative Studies Quarterly* 22(4): 586–596.

Jacobson, Gary C. 2000. "Party Polarization in National Politics: The Electoral Connection." In *Polarized Politics: The President and the Congress in a Partisan Era*, edited by Jon Bond and Richard Fleischer, 9–30. Washington, DC: Congressional Quarterly Press.

Jacobson, Gary C. 2004. *The Politics of Congressional Elections*. New York: Longman.

Jeong, Gyung-Ho, Gary J. Miller, Camilla Schofield, and Itai Sened. 2011. "Cracks in the Opposition: Immigration as a Wedge Issue for the Reagan Coalition." *American Journal of Political Science* 55(3): 511–525.

Jullian, Maite. 2008. "Snowe, Collins, Key Players across Aisle." *Bangor Daily News*, November 8.

Kau, Joseph, and Paul Rubin. 1979. "Self-interest, Ideology, and Logrolling in Congressional Voting." *Journal of Law and Economics* 22: 365–384.

Kernell, Samuel. 1977. "Presidential Popularity and Negative Wording." *American Political Science Review* 71: 44–66.

Kingdon, John. 1977. Models of legislative voting. *The Journal of Politics*, 39(3): 563–595.

Kingdon, John. 1989. *Congressmen's Voting Decisions*. Ann Arbor: University of Michigan Press.

Koch, Jeffrey W. 2002. "Gender Stereotypes and Citizens' Impressions of House Candidates' Ideological Orientations." *American Journal of Political Science* 46(2): 453–462.

Koger, Gregory. 2010. *Filibustering: A political history of obstruction in the House and Senate*. University of Chicago Press.

Krehbiel, Keith. 1996. "Institutional and Partisan Sources of Gridlock: A Theory of Divided and Unified Government." *Journal of Theoretical Politics* 8: 7–40.

Krehbiel, Keith. 1998. *Pivotal Politics: A Theory of U.S. Lawmaking*. Chicago: University of Chicago Press.

Krehbiel, Keith. 2008. "The Fragility of the Party Polarization Hypothesis" (comment on Sinclair). In *Red and Blue Nation?*, edited by David Brady and Pietro Nivola, 93–106. Vol. 2. Washington, DC: Brookings Institution Press.

Lax, Jeffrey, and Justin Phillips. 2009. "How Should We Estimate Public Opinion in the States?" *American Journal of Political Science* 53: 107–121.

Layman, Geoffrey, and Thomas Carsey. 2002. "Party Polarization and 'Conflict Extension' in the American Electorate." *American Journal of Political Science* 46: 786–802.

Lee, Frances. 2009. *Beyond Ideology: Politics, Principles, and Partisanship in the U.S. Senate*. Chicago: University of Chicago Press.

Lee, Frances E. 2011. "Making laws and making points: Senate governance in an era of uncertain majorities." *The Forum* 9(4).

Lesniewski, Niels. 2013. "Democrats Go 'Nuclear,' Eliminate Filibuster on Most Nominees." *Roll Call*, November 21.

Lizza, Ryan. 2011. "Ben Nelson and the Politics of Pork and Polarization." *New Yorker*, December 28.

Lupia, Arthur, and Tasha S. Philpot. 2005. "Views from Inside the Net: How Websites Affect Young Adults' Political Interest." *Journal of Politics* 67(4): 1122–1142.

Maite, Jullian. 2008. "Maine Senators Seen as Major Players in the New Senate." *Bangor Daily News*, November 7.

Marra, Robin, and Charles W. Ostrom Jr. 1989. "Explaining Seat Change in the U.S. House of Representatives, 1950–86." *American Journal of Political Science* 33(3): 541–569.

Matthews, Donald. 1960. *U.S. Senators and Their World*. Chapel Hill: University of North Carolina Press.

Mayhew, David. 1974. *Congress: The Electoral Connection*. New Haven: Yale University Press.

Mayhew, David. 1991. *Divided We Govern: Party Control, Lawmaking, and Investigations*. New Haven: Yale University Press.

Mayhew, David. 2005. *Divided We Govern: Party Control, Lawmaking, and Investigations 1946–2002*. New Haven: Yale University Press.

McCarty, Nolan, Keith Poole, and Howard Rosenthal. 1997. *Income Redistribution and the Realignment of American Politics*. Washington, DC: American Enterprise Institute.

McCarty, Nolan, Keith Poole, and Howard Rosenthal. 2003. "Political Polarization and Income Inequality." Working Paper.

McCarty, Nolan, Keith Poole, and Howard Rosenthal. 2006. *Polarized America: The Dance of Ideology and Unequal Riches*. Cambridge, MA: MIT Press.

McDonald, Michael, and Bernard Grofman. 1999. "Redistricting and the Polarization of the House of Representatives." Paper presented at the Annual Meeting of the Midwest Political Science Association Conference, Chicago, April 15–16.

Merrill, Samuel, and Bernard Grofman. 1999. *A Unified Theory of Voting: Directional and Proximity Models*. Cambridge, UK: Cambridge University Press.

Miler, Kristina C. 2010. *Constituency Representation in Congress: The View from Capitol Hill*. New York: Cambridge University Press.

Mimms, Sarah. 2014. "How Democrats Play the Obstruction Game." *The Atlantic*, April 7.

Moon, Marilyn. 2006. "Medicare, a Policy Primer." New York: Urban Institute.

Mooney, Christopher, and Mei-Hsien Lee. 1995. "Legislative Morality in the American States: The Case of Pre-*Roe* Abortion Regulation Reform." *American Journal of Political Science* 39: 599–627.

Muskal. Michael. 2010. "Rep. John Boozeman Ousts Sen. Blanche Lincoln in Arkansas." *Los Angeles Times*, November 2.

Nixon, Ron. 2013. "Senate Passes Farm Bill; House Vote Is Less Sure." *New York Times*, June 10.

Noah, Timothy. 2001. "Did the Democrats Sucker Jim Jeffords?" *Slate*, December 12.

Nokken, Timothy. 2000. "Confirmation Dynamics: A Model of Presidential Appointments to Independent Agencies." *Journal of Theoretical* Politics 12: 91–112.

Oberlander, Jonathan. 2007. "Learning from Failure in Health Care Reform." *New England Journal of Medicine* 357: 1677–1679.

Oppenheimer, Bruce Ian. 1974. *Oil and the Congressional Process*. Lexington, MA: Lexington Books.

Oppenheimer, Bruce. 2005. "Deep Red and Blue Congressional Districts." In *Congress Reconsidered*, edited by Lawrence C. Dodd and Bruce I. Oppenheimer, 135–158. 8th ed. Washington, DC: CQ Press.

Pacheco, Julianna. 2011. "Using National Surveys to Measure Dynamic U.S. State Public Opinion: A Guideline for Scholars and an Application." *State Politics and Policy Quarterly* 11: 415–439.

Page, Benjamin, Robert Shapiro, Paul Gronke, and Robert M. Rosenberg. 1984. "Constituency, Party and Representation in Congress." *Public Opinion Quarterly* 48(4): 741–756.

Park, David, Andrew Gellman, and Joseph Bafumi. 2004. "Bayesian Multilevel Estimation with Poststratification: State Level Estimates from National Polls." *Political Analysis* 12: 375–385.

Parkinson, John. 2013. "House Passes 'No Budget No Pay,' Extends Debt Limit." *ABC News*, January 23.

Pear, Robert. 2002. "GOP Drug Plan for Elderly Nears Passage in House." *New York Times*, June 22.

Pear, Robert, and Thomas Kaplan. 2017. "Senate Rejects Slimmed-Down Obamacare Repeal as McCain Votes No." *New York Times*, July 27.

Peckham, Matt. 2013. "Congress Now Less Popular than Head Lice, Cockroaches, and the Donald." *Time*, January 8.

Peress, Michael. 2011. "Securing the Base: Electoral Competition under Variable Turnout." *Public Choice* 148(1): 87–104.

Poole, Keith, and Howard Rosenthal. 1997. *Congress: A Political History of Roll Call Voting.* New York: Oxford University Press.

Reid, Harry. 2008. *The Good Fight: Hard Lessons from Searchlight to Washington.* New York: Berkley Trade Press.

Rogowski, J. C. 2014. "Electoral Choice, Ideological Conflict, and Political Participation." *American Journal of Political Science* 58(2): 479–494.

Rohde, David W. 1991. *Parties and Leaders in the Post-Reform House.* Chicago: University of Chicago Press.

Schattschneider, E. E. 1942. *Party Government.* New York: Farrar and Reinhart.

Schickler, Eric, and Frances Lee, eds. 2011. *The Oxford Handbook of the American Congress.* New York: Oxford University Press.

Schiller, Wendy. 2000. "Building Reputations and Shaping Careers: The Strategies of Individual Agenda Setting in the U.S. Senate." In *Congress at Work, Congress on Display*, edited by William Bianco, 47–68. Ann Arbor: University of Michigan Press.

Schiller, Wendy J., and Jennifer C. Cassidy. 2011. "Senate delegation dynamics in an age of party polarization." *The Forum* 9(4). De Gruyter.

Silver, Nate. 2012. "Swing Voters and Elastic States." *FiveThirtyEight*, https://fivethirtyeight.com/features/swing-voters-and-elastic-states/.

Shepsle, Kenneth A., and Barry R. Weingast. 1987. "The Institutional Foundations of Committee Power." *The American Political Science Review* 85–104.

Sinclair, Barbara. 1982. *Congressional Realignment.* Austin: University of Texas Press.

Sinclair, Barbara. 1989. *The Transformation of the U.S. Senate.* Baltimore: Johns Hopkins University Press.

Sinclair, Barbara. 1995. *Legislators, Leaders, and Lawmaking.* Baltimore: Johns Hopkins University Press.

Sinclair, Barbara. 2006. *Party Wars: Polarization and the Politics of National Policy Making.* Norman: University of Oklahoma Press.

Sinclair, Barbara. 2007. *Unorthodox Lawmaking: New Legislative Processes in the U.S. Congress.* Washington DC: CQ Press.

Sinclair, Barbara. 2008. "Spoiling the Sausages?: How a Polarized Congress Deliberates and Legislates." In *Red and Blue Nation?*, edited by David Brady and Pietro Nivola, 55–87. Vol. 2. Washington, DC: Brookings Institution Press.

Sinclair, Barbara. 2017. "The New World of U.S. Senators." In *Congress Reconsidered*, edited by Lawrence Dodd and Bruce Oppenheimer, 1–28. 11th ed. Los Angeles: Sage, CQ Press.

Smith, Steven. 2007. *Party Influence in Congress.* New York: Cambridge University Press.

Smith, Steven. 2014. *The Senate Syndrome.* Washington, DC: Brookings Institution.

Smith, Steven S., and Marcus Flathman. 1989. "Managing the Senate Floor: Complex Unanimous Consent Agreements since the 1950s." *Legislative Studies Quarterly* 14(3): 349–374.

Snyder, James. 1991. "On Buying Legislators." *Economics and Politics* 3(2): 93–109.

Stein, Sam. 2010. "Bill Halter Running for Arkansas Senate: Progressive Democrat to Challenge Blanche Lincoln." *Huffington Post*, June 30.

Steinhauer, Jennifer. 2012. "Weighing the Effect of an Exit of Centrists." *New York Times*, October 8.

Stonecash, Jeffrey M., Mark D. Brewer, and Mack D. Mariani. 2003. *Diverging Parties: Social Change, Realignment, and Political Polarization*. Boulder, CO: Westview Press.

Sullivan, Sean. 2013. "A Brief History of Lincoln Chafee's Party Identity Crisis." *Washington Post*, May 30.

Theriault, Sean. 2003. "Public Pressure and Punishment in the Politics of Congressional Pay Raises." *American Politics Research* 32: 444–464.

Theriault, Sean. 2006. "Party Polarization in the U.S. Congress: Member Replacement and Member Adaptation." *Party Politics* 12(4): 483–503.

Theriault, Sean. 2008. *Party Polarization in Congress*. New York: Cambridge University Press.

Tomz, Michael, and Robert P. Van Houweling. 2008. "Candidate Positioning and Voter Choice." *American Political Science Review* 102(3): 303–318.

Topaz, Jonathan. 2013. "Ayotte Endorses Immigration Bill." *Politico*, June 9.

Tufte, Edward R. 1975. "Determinants of the Outcomes of Midterm Congressional Elections." *American Political Science Review* 69: 812–826.

Van Allen, Jennifer. 2014. "Susan Collins Wins Reelection to the Senate." *Portland Press Herald*, November 5.

Volden, Craig, and Alan E. Wiseman. 2014. *Legislative effectiveness in the United States congress: The lawmakers*. Cambridge University Press.

Wahlke, John C. 1971. "Policy Demands and the System Support: The Role of the Represented." *British Journal of Political Science* 1(3): 271–290.

Walton, Don. 2006. "Tension Marked Nelson Endorsement." *Lincoln Journal Star*, July 17.

Warren, Mark. 2014. "Help, We're in a Living Hell and Don't Know How to Get Out." *Esquire*, October 14. http://www.esquire.com/news-politics/news/a23553/congress-living-hell1114/?src=nl&mag=esq&list=nl_enl_news&date=101514.

Wawro, Gregory, and Eric Schikler. 2006. *Filibuster: Obstruction and Lawmaking in the U.S. Senate*. Princeton, NJ: Princeton University Press.

Weber, Ronald, Anne Hopkins, Michael Mezey, and Frank Munger. 1972. "Computer Simulation of State Electorates." *Public Opinion Quarterly* 36: 549–565.

Whyte, William. 1956. *Citadel: The Story of the U.S. Senate*. New York: Harper and Brothers.

Wilensky, Gail. 2009. "Reforming Medicare's Physician Payment System." *New England Journal of Medicine* 360: 653–655.

Wilson, Woodrow. 1885. *Congressional Government: A Study in American Politics*. Boston: Houghton, Mifflin.

Yoshinaka, Antoine, and Christian Grose. 2011. "Ideological Hedging in Uncertain Times: Inconsistent Legislative Representation and Voter Enfranchisement." *British Journal of Political Science* 41: 765–794.

Index

Tables and figures are indicated by *t* and *f* following the page number